Praise for

The Alchemy of the Enneagram in Transforming Addiction

"*The Alchemy of the Enneagram in Transforming Addiction* is inspiring, informative, deeply personal, and uplifting, offering objective hope without denying the heavy work and self-responsibility of recovery, and self-realization. Michael imparts the invaluable teachings of the Enneagram in a way that is personal, passionate, engages the mind, and touches the heart. This book speaks to our universal suffering, the obstacles, but equally to our potential. His wisdom arises from his own lived experience. I know that Michael Naylor's new book will become a staple in every addiction professional's repertoire. His unique perspective on the Enneagram to approach addiction treatment may very well change the course of how we serve those in treatment. His gift is his personal accounts and making the types so real. I think this book is not just good for addiction, it is really great for everybody because it brings in empathic immediacy."

—Leah Chyten. LICSW, Diamond Approach teacher,
author of Light, Radiance, Splendor

"Michael Naylor's new book contains deep insight, extensive knowledge of the Enneagram, and compelling real-life stories of those in addiction recovery. This book will become a staple for therapists, addiction counselors, recovery coaches, spiritual directors, and other who support those in recovery. His great Enneagram lens around addiction may well change how we approach serving those in treatment. A worthy addition to your resource library."

—Lou Kaucic, Professional Co-Active Coach
and CEO of the Coaches Collective

"This important book acknowledges that recovery is not a 'one size fits all' process. Michael, an internationally celebrated Enneagram teacher, articulates the 9 discreet psychic structures that operate as delusions and veils to our recovery. This insight to our diversity, together with a sound knowledge of addiction patterns, both honors the complexity of our humanness and the need for a sophisticated approach to recovery. This is the manual for freedom from addiction and living a more fulfilling conscious life."

—Jutka Freiman, Director of Graduate Hoffman
Quadrinity Program and Enneagram Teacher/Trainer

"Michael is one of the most natural and authentic leaders I have worked with. His gentle style, quick wit, natural inclination to nurture others, and his listening heart shine through in his new book. His innovative approach to addiction treatment combines his incredible command of the Enneagram with heart-centered counseling."
—Deb Taylor, Spiritual Director, Unity Church, Oregon

"Michael Naylor shares his years of wisdom and offers practical guidelines, suggestions, and specific techniques for practitioners who help those gripped by addiction. He describes nine distinct paths for recovery and the telltale signs that each Enneagram type must watch out for. I highly recommend this book to every addiction professional and coach."
—Kathleen Stinnett, MCC, Author of *The Extraordinary Coach*

"Michael writes with integrity, compassion, and grace. In his book, he combines his highly developed skills as an Enneagram coach and addiction counselor with deep insight into type-specific protection mechanisms, relapse patterns, and point-by-point suggestions to support each type through their journey to recovery. Every addiction professional will value this addition to their resource library."
—Pamela Parker, Director of the Conscious Center International

"Michael Naylor's book is a valuable contribution to the sparse reading for and about men. It provides incredible insight into the forces of today's society that shape men's lives. The Enneagram framework leads the reader to understanding and healing the core suffering of men. Michael has developed a heart-centered approach to seeing the beauty in men and healing the male heart. I worked closely with Michael for eight years co-facilitating men's transformation groups and can attest to the love and care he feels and brings to men. This is a must-read for men working to heal their addictions."
— Stephan Andrew, CCS, LADC, LCSW, International MINT trainer/leader, Author of *Love in Action*, co-author of *Game Plan: A Man's Guide to Achieving Emotional Fitness*

"Michael is one of those rare people who combine great insight with genuine kindness. His work as an Enneagram coach has been a never-ending wellspring on my own journey. Trying to quantify the impact of Michael's Enneagram coaching in my life is like trying to count the stars in a desert sky. Michael has been the first Enneagram coach who could really reach me. He showed me a tool to be a better man, and start using my gifts to make a better world."

—Nelson Marsh, Iconoclastic Artist, Poet, Philosopher

"Thanks to Michael's book, the Enneagram as a tailor-made recovery tool is being made available for the first time to those professionals who help people in recovery. The anecdotal stories from the perspectives of the different type-domains are particularly insightful. Do not pass up this opportunity to discover what this book has to offer for your work as a recovery professional."

—Maggie Simpson-Crabaugh, Enneagram
Institute Certified Enneagram Teacher

"If you enjoy writing that's casually profound, poignant, colloquial and engaging, then you'll enjoy Michael Naylor's writing. If you have an interest in the Enneagram, there's no one better than Michael at making it accessible and applicable in ways that will make its impact on you meaningful to the bone. If you ever have an opportunity to participate in one of his Enneagram workshops, jump at it!"

—Bruce Ditnes, Retired Editor and Provocateur

"As a person who has worked in the substance use disorder field for the past 20 years, this book highlights the marriage between the disease of addiction and the discovery of a deep understanding of self. It is a perfect recipe to help individuals understand their core as well as how that relates to problematic substance use. I think this book will resonate with and benefit countless professionals in the field of addiction recovery."

—Kathy Prenevost, LMSW

"Michael's depth of knowledge of the Enneagram is incomparable. In his book, he shares this deep wisdom with compassion, humor, and kindness. I'm confident it will touch many lives."

—Jillian Hostenske, MS, Business, Accountant

"Michael is a deep soul. A real, authentic, accessible, and empathetic soul. A soul that has been forged and deepened in the fires of real life, challenges, struggle and ultimately faith, hard work, humility, grace, starting over and one step at a time. The result is a soul who is fully present, connected, light, playful yet fully committed to being with the person in front of him in deep and helpful ways. He is a gift. And his book, a transmission of his gifts."
—George Fleming, MA, InsightAction Breakthrough Coaching, Center for Conscious Potential

"Michael has been one of the most influential Enneagram teachers in my life—he has guided, coached and mentored me in some of the darkest places on my life's journey…. Always calling me back to presence and aligning with my truest self. He has shown me how to love myself with kindness and compassionate grace in a way that has allowed my soul to be made whole."
— Bev Gorman, RN, Riso-Hudson Certified Enneagram Coach

"I've attended multiple Enneagram workshops led by Michael and worked with him as an Enneagram coach for nearly a year. Michael has an intuitive and graceful way of conveying the depth and value of using the Enneagram to foster personal growth. With his help, I was able to have a courageous conversation with my son and come to an understanding and greater intimacy with him."
—Stephanie Aldrich, Health Policy Analysis and Consulting

"Michael Naylor has written a heartfelt and compassionate book that plumbs the souls of the Enneagram types in recovery. His writing imparts a felt experience of the inner landscape, dialogue and psychodynamics of recovering individuals. Michael artfully describes mining the shadow for the gold of self-knowledge and conscious choice. He shows us that the very thoughts, feelings and behaviors that enslave us hold the key to our liberation."
— Ron Esposito, MA, Life Coach, Enneagram Teacher and Recovery Facilitator, Conscious Living Center, Cincinnati, Ohio

The Alchemy of the Enneagram in Transforming Addiction

**A Guide for
Professionals**
Helping Men
Recover Their Lives

The Alchemy of the Enneagram in Transforming Addiction

Michael Naylor M.ED, LADC, CCS, CPCC

Foreword by Russ Hudson

Published by Maine Enneagram Press

For more information, visit https://enneagrammaine.com

ISBN (paperback): 979-8-9869420-0-1
ISBN (ebook): 979-8-9869420-1-8

Editing by Jessica Vineyard, Red Letter Editing, www.redletterediting.com
Book design by Christy Day, Constellation Book Services
Figure illustrations by Vance McDaniel Design
Martha Bullen, Jedi Master of Book Production, Bullen Publishing Services

Printed in the United States of America

To the many helping professionals who have given their blood, sweat, tears, and love to help those suffering from addictions. Thank you for your courage, tenacity, inspiration, and your heroic efforts. You have bridged the gap between life and death for many, and suffered with the pain of losing some to their addiction.

Contents

Acknowledgments

I want to thank Russ Hudson and Don Riso, my teachers at the Enneagram Institute, who laid the foundation for my understanding of the Enneagram through my certification and faculty process. My first serendipitous encounter was in 2006 at a Part One Training at the Mercy Center in Burlingame, San Francisco, when, minutes after Russ had started in on one of his funny-as-hell teaching jogs through the Type Eight, a resounding *yes* echoed through my core. I felt this yes everywhere in my body. The duet of Russ and Don was a joy to my heart and implanted in me an understanding of body, heart, and mind that I rely on today. Russ, in particular, has been a force of support, compassion, inspiration, confidence, and healing for me. Training personally with Don and Russ for several years was an amazing opportunity.

Much thanks to Lynda Roberts and Gayle Scott, as they contributed greatly to my understanding and teaching of the Enneagram. Their commitment to growth and the highest and clearest transmission of the Enneagram has touched me deeply.

Deep thanks to all of the teachers and students in the Enneagram world who have inspired and supported me. Thank you to serendipity, the guidance from the Unseen, when I was greeted with a deep and profound *yes* in my interior when I attended my first AA meeting forty years ago. Thank you to the vast array of recovering and attempting-to-recover men and women in Alcoholics Anonymous and in other modalities. You have been such a gift to me.

Most notable is my dear friend Eric S., a beautiful recovering Type Seven, brimming with abundant joy, compassion, creativity energy, and humanity. Thank you, Eric.

Thank you to a dear Diamond Heart teacher and friend Leah Chyten, who kept prodding me, sometimes kindly, sometimes fiercely, to finish this book. She said, "If you are deeply depressed, you must continue and finish the book. Only death can stop you. Get it?" which did get my attention. Thank you to Maggie Simpson and Linda Walters, whose encouragement to continue and publish was a great and loving service to me.

Thank you to my coach, Lou Kaucic, an unnaturally optimistic Type Seven, for his continual reminder of my strengths, for pushing me to let go of perfectionism on the journey to completion of the book, for paving the way for the completion of my Professional Coaching Certification with Co-Active Training Institute, and for inspiring me to apply the Enneagram to my coaching practice.

Thank you to Stephen Aronson, who, in 1996 during a therapy session, suggested that I read Don Riso's *Personality Types* and said, "Michael, pay attention to the Type Four." Upon reading that chapter, I was unmasked, seeing for the first time the vivid and powerful dynamics of my personality type. He also handed me *In Search of the Miraculous* by P. D. Ouspensky—a remarkable story about G. I. Gurdjieff—in which more humility lessons torched my self-image. Steve continues to be a light of guidance, assisting me in seeing more precisely (and with a sense of humor) the wild and tricky patterns of my Enneagram type, and guiding me to a more practical understanding of Gurdjieff, whose core teachings inform much of the work I do with the Enneagram.

Thank you to Stephen Andrew, for the many years together co-facilitating men's transformation and recovery groups, and for always reminding me of the potency of compassion for men.

Thank you to my loving, creative, courageous, and deeply supportive wife, Donna Lynn, whom I met twenty-six years ago when I was exiled to the Christmas pack-line at LL Bean by the walloping hand of fate. I was gripped by an incessant voice speaking through me: *I love you, Donna! I love you, Donna!* It was love at first sight. Thank you, Donna, for the many hours you have spent reading my words, critiquing, always reminding me of what is best and finest within me, and for loving me generously and steadily.

To my dear friend Richard Huston, my personal Samwise Gamgee, who has traveled with me through the Mines of Mordor, there and back again as Mr. Frodo would say, walking with me while I faced the Great Balrog of fate that had arisen unexpectedly as I was busy making other plans.

Thank you to other folks who inspired me: my Type Six dad and Type Two mom; my loyal and beloved Type Two sister, Kathy; my irrepressible and kind-hearted Type Nine daughter, Chloe; my oh-so-kind and quirky Type Five son, Christian; God in all forms (most notably, the periodic table); Pema Chödrön for her magnificent and continued teaching on unconditional friendliness and how to make peace with the dynamics of our personality patterns (most notably found in her books *The Wisdom of No Escape, Start Where You Are, Welcoming the Unwelcome,* and *When Things Fall Apart,* all ageless and timeless works on transforming our acquired patterns); Desmond Tutu; John Lennon (surely a Type Four); Eckhart Tolle; Leonard Cohen; J. G. Bennett; and all of the participants who have joined me in Enneagram workshops and inspired me with their authentic search for truth. You have been the food for my heart and soul.

Lastly, thank you to my awesome editor, Jessica Vineyard, a beloved Type Three (well, maybe an Eight), who has so skillfully organized my writing and translated it into a more clear and understandable work.

Also, I'd like to thank Christy Day for her beautiful book design artistry, and Martha Bullen for her guidance, project management, and book production expertise.

Foreword

BY RUSS HUDSON

The popular Enneagram has become familiar to millions of people, and it is no longer a surprise to learn that a new friend or acquaintance knows his or her Enneagram type. Many are reading online threads and watching podcasts to learn their "number." But even as the popularity of the Enneagram expands, the understanding of its true purpose and intent often becomes diluted and vague. The question of what we can learn from our type, and how we can use this knowledge for our development and healing, is not always present. The origins of the system come from spiritual, contemplative traditions, and the whole point of learning one's type was not to make a definitive statement about a person's identity but to reveal to them a central pattern or distortion that drove most of their problematic behaviors. To understand the Enneagram on this level takes years of learning and practice and is not something acquired through short term study. Of course, we all have to start somewhere, and learning our core Enneagram type can be a marvelous launch into a journey of self-knowledge and maturation. But we would be wise to realize that such a journey is measured in years, not weeks, and it requires lifelong dedication to a transformation of our lifestyle.

The same could be said for the process of recovery from addiction. While the basic tenets of recovery and of Alcohol Anonymous's

Twelve Steps and Twelve Traditions seem straightforward enough, knowing how to navigate the many traps and potential pitfalls along the way requires a great deal of experience and wisdom derived from that experience. Breaking the grip of an addiction is not merely the act of refraining from the addictive substance or behavior. There is a process of understanding and healing the underlying emotional issues that drove the person toward addictive behaviors in the first place. Knowing how to be with one's underlying suffering, and later, how to help others navigate their early traumas and challenges, is no small feat and goes well beyond comforting cliches and sayings. I cannot guide you somewhere I have not been.

This is where Michael Naylor's work comes in. You are holding in your hand what is, to my knowledge, the first significant book on using the Enneagram in the treatment of addiction. While it might be surprising that no such book has appeared before this, it is good to consider that this work is the result of two major fields of understanding: the Enneagram itself and the various methods of treating and healing addictions. As we have seen, both fields of endeavor *appear* to be basic and fairly straightforward; that is, "addicts just need to toughen up and stop taking their drug of choice," and "the Enneagram is just a description of nine types of people. Which one are you?" In fact, understanding either field is a vast undertaking that requires years of learning and experience. We are fortunate to have this book, as *The Alchemy of the Enneagram in Transforming Addiction* is born from Michael's long and profound apprenticeship in both fields.

I have known Michael for many years, and I can tell you that he has the needed learning and experience to tackle this huge subject. He has been studying the Enneagram for decades and has become a masterful teacher and guide for those seeking to understand this amazing tool in greater depth. He went through the entire training program that Don Richard Riso and I offered through the Enneagram Institute and familiarized himself with other Enneagram approaches as well. Both Don and I were struck by his passion for learning, his integrity, and his sincere wish to help others. So, when we were looking for some potential teachers to join us in the journey of bringing a more comprehensive and healing approach to the Enneagram to the world, we chose Michael as one of the people we felt could convey the essence of what this work was truly about. He taught with us and on our behalf for well over a decade and has subsequently become one of the most trusted and experienced teachers in the field. Never one to rest on his laurels, Michael has continued to learn about the system, to revisit assumptions, and to find better ways to communicate the core teachings of the work connected with the Enneagram.

There are few people on the planet who know the work that Don Riso and I did as well as Michael. He knows our teachings inside and out and is particularly skillful in conveying the meaning and purpose of Don's "Levels of Development," which are key to using the Enneagram for psychological healing and growth. This book presents these ideas with clarity and compassion, and as such, *The Alchemy of the Enneagram in Transforming Addiction* is an excellent primer on our work. Beyond this, Michael has customized the teachings, changing some of the language and emphasis, to use these tools more precisely for the work of recovery. I find his changes helpful, and they will no doubt make the work more accessible.

Make no mistake, this book is a hands-on, direct, and much-needed exploration of this topic. I am certain it will become a standard text for counselors of people in recovery as well as for those on their own journey to sobriety and freedom. While the focus here is a practical look at how the deeper inner work of the Enneagram can be of invaluable assistance to the process of recovery, the implications of this work pertain to everyone. We could say that the fixations of each of the nine Enneagram types represent core patterns of addiction, playing themselves out endlessly and in a variety of ways.

The Enneagram, in its original sense, was never about putting people into categories or boxes but rather was a teaching to facilitate the observation of the core of human suffering in each person that drives their more compulsive behaviors. Coming from spiritual and contemplative traditions, a central idea behind the Enneagram is that people are in a lot more suffering than they realize and that our ego is a product largely of the attempt to manage that suffering. It was originally a study of the ways in which we become caught up in habitual patterns of thinking, emotion, and behavior that are essentially defensive in nature—a way of numbing us from our core distress. It is not an enormous leap from that perspective to seeing the implications of this approach for the treatment of addictions.

Part of the great gift of this book is that Michael helps us see the relationship between various addictive behaviors and the underlying suffering that is driving them. He further shows us that not only do the nine Enneagram types offer insights and methods for addressing this core suffering but also that different types are helped by different methods. He methodically takes us through the nine types, offering tips for recovery, potential pitfalls, and scenarios that can lead to relapse, and showing that while there are some universal principles to the recovery process, there are also significant differences in what helps each type stay on track with their healing.

In this respect, Michael's long experience as an addiction counselor is evident and of great benefit. For each of the nine types he describes both inner and outer processes, illuminates some of the challenges in the early stages of recovery, describes some of the most likely causes of relapse, offers exercises and practices, and provides suggestions for counselors or loved ones to support a person of each particular type in recovery. Of particular value are his suggestions for each type in reframing ways of thinking and feeling that led to addictions and show another way forward. Further, he explains the nature of the "inner critic" patterns for each of the nine types and describes ways to counteract its negative and discouraging influence.

Part of the power of this book is that Michael Naylor knows this process from the inside out. He has been in recovery himself and explored a variety of methods and teachings to continue the process and to support his ongoing sobriety. In this respect, he comes across here as a wise older friend—someone who "knows the ropes" and is utterly free of judgment about any part of the journey. While some of the material might be seen as technical, he conveys it with lucidity and warmth, and the reader may well feel that they have a good traveling companion at their side. Nothing feels abstract because this work was born "in the trenches" and has been tested in real-life experiences.

On a personal note, I can share that when I was first involved in working with the Enneagram, I, too, was battling addictive tendencies and was engaged in twelve-step practices as part of my journey. When I met Don Riso, we drew great inspiration from the Steps and were surprised to learn that there are common roots between the Twelve Steps and the Twelve Traditions and the teachings behind the Enneagram. We shared our own journeys of healing with each other and educated ourselves about the work of recovery both in the twelve steps and in the broader psychotherapeutic community. All of this influenced our work with the Enneagram, and our early book *Enneagram Transformations* arose from our own grappling with the fourth step, often viewed as one of the most difficult parts of the twelve-step journey: "Made a searching and fearless moral inventory of ourselves." We realized that this was exactly what work with the Enneagram asked of us, and we explored the ways in which knowing our Enneagram type pattern might help fellow travelers in the work of recovery meet this challenging step.

In this sense, *The Alchemy of the Enneagram in Transforming Addiction* feels like the early work Don and I did coming full circle through Michael's brilliance and dedication. Much of what we did in those early days grew out of our own struggles and our wish to be truly free. We sensed then, and I still feel, that human beings are capable of so much more than we usually allow for ourselves. In the Enneagram tradition, we learn that beyond the painful patterns of personality lies our essential nature—the ground of our soul and spirit—and that we are in this world to grow and mature this deeper layer of our humanity. This is the source of our wisdom, compassion, courage, love, and many other qualities. We also learn that a person who has been through the fires of transformation is, in a sense, reborn as a person of virtues, a person capable of living spiritual values here in the world and contributing something healing and evolutionary to the human species.

For many of us, the idea of becoming an awakened person of kindness and virtue is of great appeal, but the journey begins with addressing our distress and the ways we have learned to numb ourselves to that pain. This is the heart of the recovery process, and it is also the heart of the Enneagram journey of transformation. It is all fundamentally the process of becoming what George Gurdjieff, the man who brought the Enneagram symbol to the attention of the modern world, referred to as *a human being without quotation marks.*

I know personally that Michael Naylor has been on that journey most of his life. He knows it well and has learned how to convey it to others. He has been through the fires of inner work and has guided many others through crucial elements of this process. At long last, he has put the wisdom and hope of that journey down in writing and is sharing it with the world, and with you. I trust this book will become a good friend to you and that you will come to appreciate Michael's wisdom and great heart as much as I do.

Many blessings on your journey of recovery, whatever its nature.

Russ Hudson
Copenhagen, Denmark
September 27, 2022

Introduction

By meeting people where they are at and treating them like human beings, and not trying to change them, actually opens up the possibility of transformation for them.

—GABOR MATE, *THE WISDOM OF TRAUMA*

Each of us has been deeply affected by addiction in our lives. It is rare that this is not the case. Many have experienced the heartrending descent of a loved one into the jaws of addiction; have watched as the loved one has lost jobs, relationships, health, and self-esteem; have observed as, time after time, the loved one has risen and sworn off his addiction only to slip back into the sea of sorrow. Nothing could be more heart-wrenching as we watch him die in slow motion, breath by breath.

Many have tirelessly tried to convince their loved one that he has a problem and is destroying his life, only to be told angrily, "I don't have a problem. What are you talking about? Leave me alone!" while the knife of addiction hangs from his heart and he, oblivious to his impending destruction. Shocked by his denial and powerless to change or save him, we are pierced by his blindness, resignation, willfulness, and hopelessness.

In like manner, those in Alcoholics Anonymous and Narcotics Anonymous have witnessed the many dear individuals who have gotten sober, begun to get healthy, begun to resurrect their shining souls, and then, five years clean and sober—ten, fifteen, twenty years—suddenly disappear like wind and are back into the hell of addiction. We later hear of a suicide or a heart attack or, all too often, nothing at all. Saddened, we face a grim fact: a great many who enter the road of recovery do not succeed. In time, one appreciates the AA and NA acknowledgment that addiction is a cunning and baffling disease of the soul. It can take the best of the best. It is a blinding force that, like a riptide, steals the ground from beneath a dear loved one in a heartbeat.

All of us in the addiction field, whether therapists, counselors, or those in recovery, make tremendous efforts to give men and women the eyes to see their addiction, to observe it and feel it before it strikes, to deepen their awareness so that when the more subtle and powerful aspects of their addiction arise, they can sense, smell, feel, taste, hear, and see it. We give people relapse-trigger lists to memorize, addiction education on the signs and symptoms of addiction and progression of the disease, and twelve-step programs to participate in, and still people relapse routinely.

What is the cause of this phenomenon? What inner wall of resistance has not been named and articulated that sends him flying back into the arms of his addictions to alcohol, drugs, food, sex, gambling, shopping, or other behaviors? The answers are unique and individual. In my case, serendipity intruded to help me gain sobriety. In 1996, with my heart breaking from the devastating feeling that I would never find myself or my purpose for existence, that there was something essential to my life that I was not grasping, I listened desperately as my therapist, Stephen, a sly, elfin grin on his face, said to me, "Why don't you read the book *Personality Types* by Don Riso?

It's about the nine Enneagram types. Take a look at Type Four."

Curious, and more than willing to do anything that would end the enduring suffering my fourteen years in recovery had not alleviated, I read about the Type Four. I was horrified at what I found. I discovered that the very characteristics I prided myself on were the exact ones that were causing relentless and repetitious suffering. Regardless of working a program of recovery, in spite of meditating and asking for help, I could not shake them. AA and NA were not designed to touch these features but had provided me a needed foundation of sobriety to confront them.

I learned that the unconscious features of my Type Four personality type—the psychic structure that I had inherited and been hardwired with at birth—were still running the show, unbeknownst to me. I was unable to access my true authenticity, where real love, self-worth, meaning, intimacy with others, and clarity about my purpose on earth resided. As I studied the Type Four, a previously unseen door to the treasures of my soul, along with the devils I could not see, was flung open. I was shocked at what had been hidden and shrouded in my type's delusion. (I am a unique and misunderstood outsider, more sensitive, emotionally deep, and creative than others, yet not properly seen or understood.) I would soon discover that each type was stuck in a type-specific delusion that causes the type's deeper suffering and eventual relapse.

As a result of the Enneagram and the inner eyes it gave me, this precious journey deepens and expands daily, weekly, yearly, my heart grateful for the real freedom I have been invited to. Instead of relapsing like so many of my compatriots—or rusting and hardening in my recovery positions about life—I began moving into a deeper alignment with my heart's desire and a deeper capacity to perceive and own, without self-hatred, those areas of my consciousness that still functioned automatically, painfully, and swiftly.

As Riso-Hudson write, "Effective growth approaches must take into account the fact that there are different kinds of people—different personality types. This diversity explains why what is good advice for one person can be disastrous for another. Telling some types that they need to focus more on feelings is like throwing water on a drowning man. Telling other types that they need to assert themselves more is as foolish as putting an anorexic person on a diet."[1]

In my addiction work with recovering folks utilizing the Enneagram, it has become clear to me that the Enneagram is not only pivotal for the maturation and development of an individual's recovery and capacity to mature but is also necessary for enabling individuals to navigate the incredibly difficult growth transitions necessary to fully actualize oneself and live fully. The Enneagram identifies the nine types of personality and how each type habitually forgets what is important to their growth and transformation in addiction recovery. Unless an individual begins to understand the type-specific way he falls asleep (a process that gets more subtle and more powerful the longer one is clean and sober) and how he forgets what is imminently important to his transformation, sooner or later, relapse will occur. Unwittingly he will pick up the substance behavior of his choice or rust in the grips of a dry drunk, chewing on resentment, meaninglessness, or soul emptiness after years of recovery, seemingly struck blind at a new door of recovery, be it year five, ten, fifteen, twenty, or thirty.

The Enneagram teaches that each personality type is endowed with specific core psychological and emotional weaknesses as well as strengths that can be matured and celebrated. That is, each type inhabits a different psychological and emotional world with type-specific challenges that he will predictably encounter at deeper levels throughout recovery.

---

1. Riso-Hudson, *Wisdom of the Enneagram*.

Put simply, each type has different psychological, physical, and emotional needs with different psychological, physical, and emotional blind spots and uniquely different paths of recovery. What is similar to all of them is the individual's need to become present to these type-specific habits, which are developed at a very early age and block his ability to experience and inhabit himself and reside in the here and now—the only place joy, happiness, and peace can be experienced.

We see this all the time: a man who is five, ten, fifteen years sober and still unable to be present to this precious moment, who is caught in the machinations of a distracting mind and inhibiting emotional personality habits. Robotically rattling off recovery slogans, judging self and others with recovery opinions, he is unable to reside in his spacious heart. Unable to savor kindness, compassion, or joy in the here and now, he is the antithesis of being happy, joyous, and free.

Every addicted individual has a type-specific blind spot, a psychological prison consisting of a core fear that drives his suffering, a deep wish to return to what is authentic and true within himself, and a fundamental commandment of who he must be to be loved. He has an emotional habit (called a passion, his type-specific emotional reaction to the heartbreaking loss of connection with his true self) and a mental habit (a fixation, his type-specific mental habit that obscures his ability to perceive objective reality), which create the psychological world he lives in. He also has an inner critic who reminds him what he must do to be lovable. These type-specific psychic structures, developed initially to protect an individual from the suffering and confusion of childhood, now inhibit his ability to comprehend reality, transform his addiction, and engage reality in a way that supports his positive growth and unfoldment.

In addition, each individual has a type-specific self-image, an idealized self-concept—who he believes he is whether his actions reflect this or not—that, when under the sway of his addiction or at various stages of his recovery, hypnotizes him. He imagines himself as being his ideal self, but his actions are the antithesis of this. He cannot objectively see how he shows up in the world nor accurately understand what he honestly experiences. It is the combination of these unconscious, often hard-to-see personality habits that keep him trapped at an impenetrable door of emotional and psychological stuckness, which, in turn, set him up for tragic relapse.

Until we address these type-specific differences, our treatment approaches and heartfelt attempts to help the addicted individual will enable only a small fraction of people to get clean and sober and thrive in their recovery. We will continue to have our hearts broken after we have given our very best to our beloved clients and the friends we so wish to serve. The Enneagram is an amazing tool that delivers the individual treatment and recovery plan that we have been seeking.

In recovery circles, we say that addiction is a three-fold disease: physical, mental, and emotional. To the extent that the individual heals these three factors within himself is the extent to which his spiritual life thrives and he feels a sense of unity, capability, and confidence. The Enneagram precisely addresses these three factors in each of the nine types, with the explicit goal of bringing unity, awareness, and happiness to the individual.

It is my hope and belief that the number of individuals who relapse while struggling with the cunning dynamics of addiction will decrease significantly as a result of the therapist or sponsor who skillfully uses the Enneagram. Those who do find the solid ground of recovery will have a tool at their disposal that allows them to continue to further expand and access the joy, courage, strength, peace, clarity, vision, creativity, and the love their souls yearn for. This is the ultimate goal of addiction recovery: the realization and celebration of the precious gifts spirit has endowed us with.

CHAPTER 1

The Basics of the Enneagram

The innocent mistake that keeps us caught in our own particular style of ignorance, unkindness, and shut-downness is that we are never encouraged to see clearly what is, with gentleness.

—PEMA CHÖDRÖN, *THE WISDOM OF NO ESCAPE*

The Enneagram is a system that describes the nine fundamental types of personality. "Ennea" means nine, and "gram" means model or type; hence, the nine types of personality.

The Enneagram symbol is that of nine points located around a circle, with a triangle and a six-sided figure called the hexad located inside the circle (see figure 1). The circle represents the One, God, Inner Unity, Conscious Awareness, the Absolute, Great Spirit, or the Unity of everything. The triangle represents the three centers of intelligence in a human being: the instinctive center, the emotional center, and the thinking center.

The triangle inside the circle has been a cornerstone of the Alcoholics Anonymous symbol for fifty or more years. The AA symbol represents the three sides of recovery—recovery, unity, service—while the triangle within the Enneagram represents the three sides of the human being: the body (sensing), the heart (feelings), and the head (thinking).

The circle represents full consciousness. When an individual becomes conscious in all three centers of intelligence, he becomes a fully conscious human being, present, awake, healthy, internally and externally unified, and in harmony with himself and life. He is not pulled in dozens of directions but is in a state of unity within himself. He knows himself and is at ease within himself—the very goal of addiction recovery. He is happy, joyous, free, serene, and able to navigate life optimally.

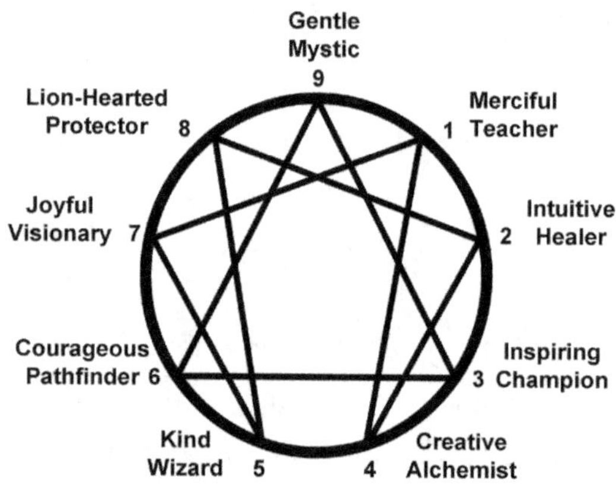

FIGURE 1. THE ENNEAGRAM

The hexad is the symbol for change. This is the six-sided figure that runs from 1 to 7 to 5 to 8 to 2 to 4 to 1 inside the circle. It symbolizes the reality that nothing is static, that everything is in a state of change, be it evolving or disintegrating. If a human being becomes conscious, he begins to evolve, expand, and experience reality on deeper and more satisfying levels. If he remains unconscious, then he moves in the direction of negativity and addiction. As is said in recovery circles, "You either grow or you go," meaning one is either evolving and expanding his awareness or inevitably preparing for a relapse back into unhappiness and addiction.

The Enneagram is a tool for assisting individuals to become conscious, aware, and joyfully engaged with themselves and their loved ones. It is a map out of the darkness of addiction and into the realm of freedom, well-being, and the capacity to create deep emotional bonds and generously share one's capacities with others.

THE ORIGINS OF THE ENNEAGRAM

The Enneagram symbol and its origins are unknown, but through a remarkable adventure, a man named George Ivanovitch Gurdjieff discovered the symbol at a monastery hidden in the hills of Afghanistan in the early 1900s. Through Gurdjieff, the symbol eventually made its way from Russia to America in 1915. (To get a glimpse of this remarkable journey, read *In Search of the Miraculous* by P. D. Ouspensky, or *Meetings with Remarkable Men* by Gurdjieff.) It was in the 1950s that Oscar Ichazo associated the nine points of the Enneagram symbol with nine different personality types, and then through the pioneering work of Don Riso (beginning in 1970) that the depth of the types was mapped out.

Riso, through intense research, created a model that mapped out nine levels of development (or "levels of presence") in each type, divided into three sections: healthy, average, and unhealthy. (Riso's treatise on this phenomenon is found in the book *Personality Types*. See Resources for more on the Enneagram and addiction.) These levels are critical for understanding addiction, the particular way it manifests in each type, and the specific challenges that each type faces in the journey to recovery and discovery of the true self.

Don Riso and Russ Hudson created a model of the psychic structure of the types, identifying the psychological paradigm that each type lives in and struggles with. The more unconscious an individual is as a result of trauma and addiction, the more he is imprisoned and blinded by the restrictive and compulsive defense mechanisms germane to his type. He has less freedom to objectively experience reality, to consciously choose his response, or to choose among possible alternatives. In addition, the more unconscious and constricted an individual is, the less likely he will respond with clarity and alertness or have the capacity to draw upon his innate gifts to navigate and celebrate life. His defensive reactions will limit his ability to engage with, enjoy, and trust people or to navigate life with grace, dignity, and confidence.

The Enneagram is designed to open the doors to an individual's freedom such that one's genuine self can arise and no longer be shrouded in misery. Knowledge of the psychic structure of one's type is critical for making this heroic journey through addiction and for releasing the defensive structures one has acquired due to one's history.

THE PSYCHIC STRUCTURE OF THE PERSONALITY

The internal psychic structure of each type consists of the following:

> The essential, or healthy, qualities of the type represents the innate gifts and qualities of authentic being that an individual is born with. When an individual is forced to disengage and close down his true qualities due to an environment that cannot support him, a basic fear arises in response to this soul shock. This basic fear represents the tremendous terror that ensues when contact with one's genuine qualities and real self is lost. The small child goes into a freak-out that Riso-Hudson call the "primal catastrophe." The more one is disconnected from his true essence and innate gifts, the more he experiences this fear, and the more rigid, defensive, and contracted he becomes in response to the loss.

In response to the basic fear, a basic desire, a deep wish, arises that reflects an individual's wish to manifest and reconnect to the inherent gifts of his type, to the innate gifts that he loves deeply and wishes to be in contact with.

The *passion*, or *emotional habit*, of the type reflects the emotional reaction and constriction one experiences when losing contact with one's true nature. When an individual's heart shuts down, be it from life trauma, addiction, inattention, or cultural constraints, then the particular emotional habit of the type is activated in service of self-protection from a broken heart.

The *fixation*, or *mental habit*, of the type works in concert with the passion to support the individual's disengagement from reality, thus inhibiting his capacity to know and sense what is real. Depending on how strongly the individual is under the power of his type-specific fixation and passion, he will be more or less unconscious and unable to clearly observe himself and the suffering he is causing himself and others. Addiction and substance abuse intensify the emotional passion and mental fixation of the individual, sending him into more reactive, impulsive, and constricted behavior, thereby increasing his suffering and his tendency to be driven deeper into addiction.

The *inner critic* represents the type-specific messages that an individual has learned to criticize and abandon himself, shutting down his true feelings, thoughts, and aliveness in order to be safe and avoid attacks from the environment. The inner critic and its soul-inhibiting messages develop in a child in reaction to the many "shoulds," expectations, rules, and judgments communicated to him through his parents, friends, caregivers, culture, school, teachers, and other sources. These shape his inner critic messages, which play like an audiotape through his mind.

When a child learns that he cannot safely express anger, joy, fear, enthusiasm, love, tenderness, honesty, and other qualities, he develops a type-specific inner critic message that supports the inhibition of what is real and true within him. He learns to act in a certain manner, shapeshifting to please or adapt to his caregiver's or culture's demands. The inner critic messages support the automatic operation of the fixation and passion of his type and serve to discourage his expansion, optimization, and free-flowing creativity. Initially developed to endure and numb the suffering of childhood, the inner critic mechanism is a prime source of unhappiness and addiction in adulthood, and keeps the individual locked in his Enneagram patterns.

The *self-image* consists of each type's identification with his innate capacities. For instance, Type Four draws on his sensitivity and creativity to develop an identity. When healthy, the Four's self-image reflects who he truly is. The Four says, "I am sensitive, creative, passionate, emotionally real, intuitive, and attuned to the depth and beauty of reality." His actions reflect his self-image. As the Type Four (or any type) loses contact with what is real and true within him, he continues to *believe* he is manifesting the healthy qualities of his self-image while his behaviors begin to move in a less healthy directions. The more unhealthy he becomes, the more his actual behaviors reflect the opposite of his innate gifts. For example, the less healthy Type Four treats individuals with insensitivity but imagines himself as sensitive. This distortion magnifies when addiction sets in, further diminishing his self-awareness.

These are the fundamental psychic structure building blocks of the individual's personality type. They are described in great detail in each chapter on the types.

THE TYPES IN RECOVERY

Each of us has inherited a particular personality type, or temperament, with which we navigate life. This is the lens through which we interpret, receive, and experience reality. When healthy, we express the positive qualities of our type in our own unique manner, while the negative manifestations are only mildly problematic. Keep in mind that we all have all of the type patterns available to us because they represent what is universally human, but we each have one central type pattern that is dominant and takes our attention most frequently.

When we are not healthy, our negative manifestations hold sway and we are often run by our defensive emotional and mental habits, which operate automatically and beyond our conscious control and insight. We take actions without our permission (similar to the alcoholic who realizes that he drinks without his permission). We act without real choice or real awareness; that is, we *react* rather than act, as with drinking and drugging addictions. When we are less healthy, we can't observe ourselves clearly or accurately, don't have eyes to see what triggers us and moves us into action, can't consciously see when our buttons have been pushed, and can't perceive with accuracy how our behavior affects others or ourselves. And yet, we think we understand reality, think we are interpreting correctly.

The bottom line is that we become sincerely deluded such that it appears that our problems are generated by others in our lives (unless we are one of the types that habitually blame themselves for everything). If *they* would just get healthier, act kinder, be more compassionate, then *my life* would be good!

Our individual type indicates a spectrum of positive and negative qualities and attributes with which we are endowed. It describes how we can positively embrace reality or leave reality and abandon ourselves and our gifts through our type-specific, unconscious habits.

The Enneagram is an extremely useful tool with which to approach addiction treatment. It will help the therapist, counselor, and sponsor more specifically address the unique characteristics each individual type exhibits in addiction. It provides a map of hope, clarity, and understanding for compassionately guiding the recovering person.

CHAPTER 2

The Three Centers of Intelligence

[Mysticism] happens whenever, by some wondrous "coincidence," our heart space, our mind space, and our body awareness are all simultaneously open and nonresistant.

—RICHARD ROHR

We all experience reality through the impressions we receive from three sources of information: sensations in the body, emotions, and thoughts. Sense, feel, think; that is what we do. These three *centers of intelligence* are located in the gut (sensation), the heart (feelings), and the mind (thoughts).

Each Enneagram type seems to have one center to which they are gravitationally pulled to bring them into balance (see figure 2), but we must be careful with this idea. In fact, every type is challenged to bring healthy awareness and healing into each center of intelligence and to nurture it. It is not a simple or linear task.

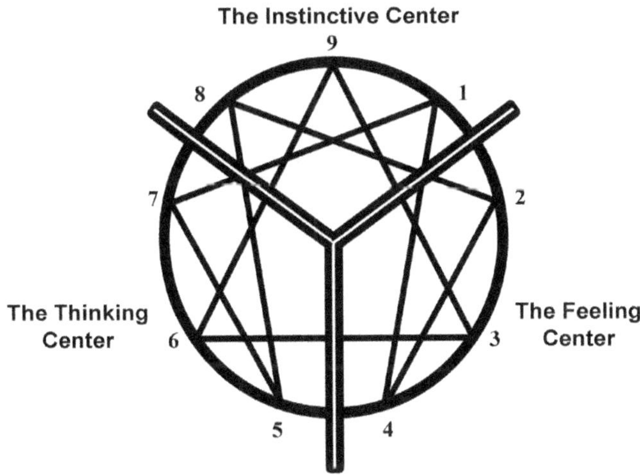

FIGURE 2. THE THREE CENTERS OF INTELLIGENCE

Many conversations in the Enneagram world revolve around waking up the body and making it more conscious. This is described as *embodying* the body, feeling the body's aliveness and energy course through us, embracing its intelligence and capacity for intuitive knowing. (Everyone knows what gut hunches are.) The body-oriented types are Eight, Nine, and One, but the following information is recommended for all types.

Many rehab clients discover that only some of the embodying capacity is available to them. If asked whether he can feel the life energy, the *chi*, within his body, many an individual will say that he can't. When asked whether he can sense his feet on the floor, often he can't, and this ability can take much time to learn and experience. Part of relaxing the habitual patterns of one's Enneagram type go hand in hand with waking up the body's center of intelligence. As a client begins to more deeply sense and relax his body, he will discover a clearer interior awareness of when his feeling patterns and reactivity are being triggered because feelings come through this door of sensation.

> Every person in rehab has the task to heal his emotional self, to digest and transform suffering so that his heart is still, calm, open, and able to experience the heights and depths of emotional experience.

My teacher would say that as a client learns to sense his body more skillfully, he builds an "interior observation station" in his body that enables him to *observe* and remain grounded when the ocean waves of emotional reactivity, the storms of the imagination, are at full tilt. Again, developing this skill is important for every type.

The heart types are the Two, Three, and Four, but the following information on the intelligence center of the heart applies to all types.

Every person in rehab has the task to heal his emotional self, to digest and transform suffering so that his heart is still, calm, open, and able to experience the heights and depths of emotional experience. Each type has inherited obscurations, blockages, hurts, rejections, and deep impressions of not being loved or wanted. These obstructions limit one's ability to feel love and trust love, to express love and compassion, and to know oneself. No one gets a free pass.

We have all buried our suffering to some extent in order to survive it. For instance, when we were kids, we had no tools to process our suffering unless we were gifted with parents who knew how to help with this. As adults, we utilize our personality patterns, our type patterns, to protect us from further suffering. We unknowingly inherit these predispositions as little children, and as adults, we are tasked with relaxing the patterns that once saved us from annihilation.

People in rehab have a particularly challenging time ahead. Since these patterns saved them from devastation or overwhelming suffering in childhood, it makes no sense at first to even consider relaxing them and invite a deep heart vulnerability to arise. This is why most people in rehab do not begin to do this work until they realize that the patterns themselves are the great sources of their suffering. Weirdly, what allowed them to survive in childhood now causes them the suffering they sought to avoid as kids. It is humbling to realize that so many must be thrown onto the road of recovery and that few volunteer. Everyone has heart-emotional healing work to do. Your job is to discover what that work looks like for your clients in rehab.

Then, the thinking center. The head-center types are the Five, Six, and Seven, but the following information on the head center and its healing apply to all of the types.

Each of us drinks in the impressions of our parents' beliefs, our culture's beliefs, our television-programmed beliefs. This impression stream is likely to inhabit the head center and show up as opinions, judgments, and beliefs. We all get mercilessly programmed and often do not notice the thought streams that move through us with the greatest of ease and that, if we are not meditation trained, meld into us as reality. This includes the self-image that we developed through all the sources we were exposed to: parents, childhood friends, grade school and high school, and our chaotic and ever-weirder culture.

Because of all this programming, every type is encouraged to develop a quiet mind, the capacity to still the ever raging thought stream, the inner movie that plays 24/7 on the movie screen of the mind. As an individual develops the capacity to calm his inner tsunami of thoughts and images, to relax and quiet his thought stream, he often also develops the ability to more objectivity take in reality without his learned judgments and opinions obscuring and distorting his capacity to be objective. In addition, as he gets better at quieting his mind, he acquires the ability to observe his Enneagram patterns more accurately. Then the whole universe cheers because he has an actual chance to transform, or at least to begin to sense the reality right in front of him. Herein his type patterns become more vivid, and he learns the gentle and humbling art of saying *I'm sorry*. As a dear friend often says in AA meetings, "If you haven't apologized this week, you're just not paying attention." When I bemoaned to my AA sponsor that I seemed to be apologizing more and more, he held his laughter at bay and said, "Not to worry. This gets much worse!" He was correct.

As you come to understand the types, you will see that there are identifiable, type-specific emotional and thinking habits that your clients have inherited that, while protecting them from overwhelming hurt, fear, or shame, also obscure their ability to interpret reality accurately when under stress. Your job is to help them observe these habits with unconditional friendliness toward themselves, which will begin to unhinge them from their entrancement.

When you know and understand these three centers of intelligence—the body, the heart, and the head—and develop the skill to apply them to your work with rehab clients, you will possess valuable tools to use as you help your clients navigate the wild terrain of their tumultuous inner world. Used skillfully and with compassion, this information has the power to deeply transform lives and allow recovering individuals to reside in a clearer and more peaceful interior.

CHAPTER 3

The Levels
of Health

If we observe ourselves truthfully and non-judgmentally,
seeing the mechanisms of our personality in action,
we can wake up, and our lives can be a miraculous
unfolding of beauty and joy.

—DON RISO AND RUSS HUDSON,
THE WISDOM OF THE ENNEAGRAM

Throughout the chapters on the Enneagram types, the levels of health are used to identify the various degrees of healthy and unhealthy states, or how awake and conscious an individual is, for each type.

There are nine levels of health: *healthy* at levels 1 through 3 (the individual is conscious and able to ascertain reality with accuracy), *average* at levels 4 through 6 (progressive loss of conscious awareness and relying on one's personality type patterns for self-defense), and *unhealthy* at levels 7 through 9 (descent into mental or emotional illness and destructive to self and others).[1] (See figure 3.)

---

1. The levels of health system and its structure comes directly from Don Riso and Russ Hudson's work found in *Personality Types*. There it is named as the levels of development. I prefer the terms "health" or "presence," but it all points to the same thing.

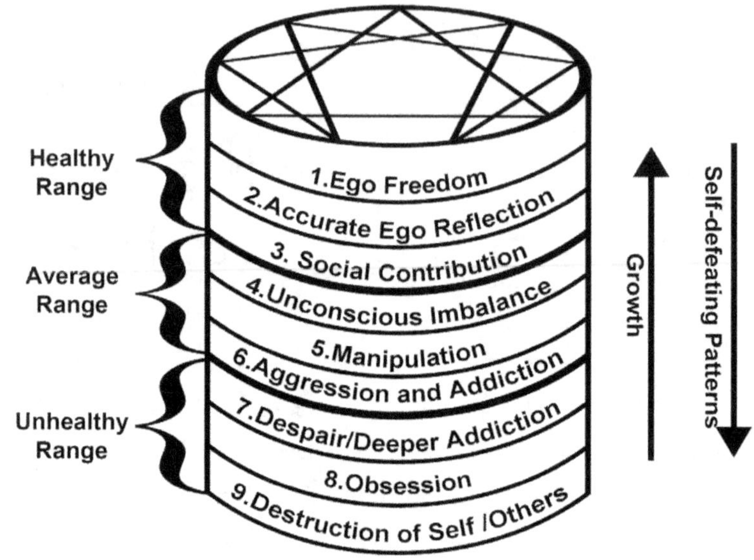

FIGURE 3. THE LEVELS OF HEALTH

HEALTHY BEHAVIOR

When an individual is functioning at a healthy level (1 through 3), he is flexible, spontaneous, joyful, open-minded, heartfelt, compassionate, and understanding of others. He objectively interprets reality, is courageous, balanced, creative, perceptive, and curious. He can endure difficulty with grace, flexibility, and intelligence. At home with himself, he is genuine, sincere, and unpretentious, and wears his personality (and its preferences) lightly and effectively. Aware of his reactive and emotional triggers and able to acknowledge them without acting them out, he avoids blaming others for his emotional reactions. He takes responsibility for himself and is empowered to make healthy changes when needed.

Similarly, he can see when others project their suffering onto him. He doesn't take it personally, doesn't take it into his soul, doesn't suffer from the attack but sees it for what it is: an errant projection. Because he is conscious, he can listen to his creative impulses and put them into action. He can utilize his intelligence and emotional nature in the service of self and others. Since he feels good, he naturally shares his well-being with those around them. He gives away the best of who he is.

With a quiet mind and open heart, the person at a healthy level sees the innate goodness in human beings and recognizes when that goodness has distorted into its opposite or is only partially embodied by an individual. In short, he has eyes to see what is real and true about human beings and himself. He is *conscious*. He is often delightful to be around because he gives others space to be themselves, is not compelled to judge or try to fix others, and can generously appreciate the beauty, value, and significance of others.

Trusting the innate capacity of his friends and loved ones to find out what is true for them, he listens to them with full attention without feeling he needs to advise or assume he knows what is best for them. He is teachable because he is not under the delusion of believing he knows everything. He is humble in this regard, which makes him more innately intelligent.

At the healthy levels, feeling good is an inside job and not dependent on external factors as the source of well-being.

WHEN CONSCIOUS AWARENESS DISAPPEARS

At the average levels of health (4 through 6), the individual mechanically blames and judges the external source for the suffering he experiences when an emotional trigger is touched by another or by a stressful circumstance. Feeling good and being happy depends on life matching his expectations, wants, and desires from the outside.

When an individual becomes addicted to a substance, he descends to level 6 or 7, where he is more constricted emotionally, mentally, and physically, and where his innate gifts and capacities constrict and disappear. He feels numb, depressed, lonely, ashamed, angry, and afraid, and uses substances to alter or numb his feelings. For example, in response to deep suffering and addiction, the Type Two's capacity for loving-kindness becomes shrouded in fear and manipulation; the One's capacity for fairness is distorted by strident judgment; the Seven's enthusiastic joy gets lost in impulsive hedonism; the Four's creative sensitivity is smothered by self-indulgence and entitlement.

Let's take a closer look at each of the levels of health.

LEVELS OF HEALTH

	LEVEL 1:	EGO FREEDOM
HEALTHY:	LEVEL 2:	ACCURATE EGO REFLECTION
	LEVEL 3:	SOCIAL CONTRIBUTION
	LEVEL 4:	UNCONSCIOUS IMBALANCE
AVERAGE:	LEVEL 5:	MANIPULATION
	LEVEL 6:	AGGRESSION AND ADDICTION
	LEVEL 7:	DESPAIR/DEEPER ADDICTION
UNHEALTHY:	LEVEL 8:	OBSESSION
	LEVEL 9:	DESTRUCTION OF SELF OR OTHERS

Healthy Levels

Level 1 to level 3: The individual is high functioning, in contact with his authenticity, and can manifest the gifts of his type. He is present; able to own his emotional triggers; and access a sense of joy, peace, and freedom internally. He is not dependent on external reality for happiness. He is open, able to savor and celebrate reality, and can shift and adapt to unexpected suffering or difficulty. He sees that everyone is doing their best and that no one is consciously trying to hurt him. He feels a deep connection with humanity, is right-sized and gracefully humble in the style of his type. He celebrates the best in others and cheers for their success. Radiant, kind, confident, he is a source of light to others. It doesn't get any better than this.

Average to Progressively Unhealthy Levels

Level 4: The individual strongly identifies with his personality and a particular social role that he tries to be and get others to identify with. His actions become an advertisement that says *this is who I am*. For instance, Type One takes on the role of the mentor/teacher and attempts to promote an image of "teacher" to those around him. His message to the world is, *I am the one who can improve the way you and I do things*. At level 4, his effort to be the teacher is not harsh or abrasive. Others find him to be likable, intelligent, and easy to be around. The social role becomes a mask that he uses to navigate reality.

At level 4, the mental fixation and emotional habit of each type make their entry. For Type One, the fixation of the judging mind and the emotional habit of resentment arise. The One begins to feel resentful over the fact that he does all the work, takes responsibility for everything, works harder than anyone else because of his feeling of obligation. He is becoming "the burdened one," carrying the responsibilities of others while judging their flaws. Since he sees what should be done, he must act on his perception. His personality, with its mechanical agenda, has taken over his objectivity.

Level 5: At level 5, all the tendencies of level 4—the emotional habit, fixation, social role, and so on—are exacerbated. The One, for example, goes from promoting his self-image to the world to trying to *manipulate* others to see him as the teacher. He becomes more critical about the errors of others and more obligated and insistent about improving others through his interventions. He is losing contact with what is good about other people and himself and is suffering more due to his disconnection with them. As a result of increased suffering, he reacts by applying his judgments and standards more harshly on others and himself. He has become unconscious of what drives his passion to criticize and improve others. All the types at level 5 become defensive in the style of their type.

All behavior from level 5 down is unconscious; that is, the individual doesn't have the eyes to see what he is doing nor the capacity to feel the damage he is causing. This is because the emotional center, the heart center, has shut down. His camera lens on reality has shrunk to a tiny pinhole, so he begins to miss everything, or at least misunderstand it. At this level an individual needs the support of healthy friends and guides to compassionately point out when he becomes mired in his type's patterns.

Level 6: From promoting a self-image at level 4 to manipulating others into seeing and approving his self-image at level 5, at level 6 the individual gets aggressive about forcing his personality agenda onto others and protecting his vulnerability. This correlates with a deepening but unconscious sense of despair within him. Type One, for example, gets aggressive about his principles and ideals, which correlates with reprimanding others, penalizing them when they don't follow his dictates, principles, or judgments. He is convinced that his standards are the correct ones for everyone else. Everything becomes black or white, right or wrong. He is furious when others don't share his standards.

At this level the individual begins to apply what is known as *The Leaden Rule* (from the work of Riso and Hudson): *Do unto others what you would least like having done to you.* He imposes on and punishes others with what he himself fears most. For example, the Eight, who fears being harmed and controlled, begins to threaten harm to others; the Three, who fears having no value, treats others as if they have no value; the Six, who fears having no support or guidance, makes others feel like they have no support or guidance.

At level 6, the individual acts in ways that are the opposite of his self-image but he perceives he is in accord with it. He is innocently deluded. Everyone but him sees this. The Four, who sees himself as deeply sensitive, rejects and humiliates those who don't have "good aesthetic taste." In fact, he despises them but can't see himself acting badly. His actions are done in the service of his being deeply sensitive and creative, and he is just trying to help them. Each type has its version of this, and all types at level 6 have their particular way of being aggressive, either passively or assertively. If one is acting badly but imagines he is acting healthily, he is not much fun to be around.

Severely Unhealthy Levels

The ailing soul at level 7, 8, or 9 must have outside help to stabilize himself if he is to return to health. Paradoxically, people at these levels often don't believe or perceive that they need help. *I'm not crazy. You are!*

Level 7: All the types at this level feel justified in being abusive and doing violence and harm to others, doing whatever it takes to devalue and ensure that others feel as bad as he does. Aggressiveness at level 6 turns into harming others physically, emotionally, and verbally at level 7. Mental illness begins here and deepens at levels 8 and 9.

Level 8: At level 8, the individual is gripped by compulsion and delusion. He becomes compulsively self-centered and deeply delusional in the style of his type.

Level 9: Suicide, murder, torture, abuse of all kinds, the darkest of the dark enter here, at level 9, be it toward the self or others.

MOVEMENT UP AND DOWN THE LEVELS

Everyone has a *center of gravity* located on the levels of health. That is, each of us has a customary level of awareness and sensitivity that moves up and down from this central position based on what is occurring within us during our day.

Recall that the levels measure the degree of one's presence or awareness. Let's say an individual's awareness is located at level 4. Here, the personality pattern is stable, and he does not create much mischief for himself or others. He has a social role that he utilizes to navigate reality. His negative manifestations are operating in a manageable fashion.

He goes to a retreat, where he becomes relaxed and undefended. He experiences the clarity of mind he really likes. He experiences deeper and more heartfelt connections with others around him. His *awareness* moves up to the higher levels (perhaps level 2 or 3) during the retreat, and he feels good, open, connected with himself and others. It is a mini-trip to inner heaven.

Shortly after he returns home, he notices that he has lost the positive traces of the retreat and is back to his normal experience of reality at level 4, where he is used to living and experiencing life. His retreat-induced openness and well-being constrict. He had the good grace of experiencing level 2 or 3, wherein his camera lens on reality revealed a more spacious and kind world and a more spacious and loving connection with himself. But his center of gravity, being gravitational, pulls him back to level 4.

A few days later, he has a terrible conflict with someone he loves. He gets angry and defensive, and feels brittle and restricted inside. His old patterns reassert. He tightens, hardens, or disassociates. Life grows dimmer. At the moment, he loses touch with what usually makes him happy or feel normal. He has dropped down to level 5 or 6. When he is out of the conflict and the tension releases, he returns to level 4, his default setting.

Each of us knows what it's like to be clear and aware or foggy, irritated, and confused on a given day. We notice that during the day we can go through a wide spectrum of experiences, from good to bad, and then back to our normal way of experiencing life. Real spiritual transformation is about moving the center of gravity up the levels, to the clearer and more present states of awareness, so that a deeper and more expanded state of awareness is stabilized within us; that is, it becomes our norm.

As an individual in recovery works on his spiritual transformation, he will notice over time that he has a much calmer daily experience than when he first arrived in treatment.

As an individual in recovery works on his spiritual transformation, he will notice over time that he has a much calmer daily experience than when he first arrived in treatment. He is less emotionally reactive. This represents a qualitative movement to a higher level of awareness or presence. He has moved his center of gravity up, perhaps from level 7 to level 5. Although he can swing back to level 7 temporarily, he no longer lives there. On good days he may experience level 4 or level 3.

When an addicted individual arrives in addiction recovery, his center of gravity is often located at level 6 or 7. Locked in a narrow type-specific personality prison, his range of choices for meeting his needs are small, repetitious, and rarely satisfying. His substance of choice has been the vehicle that has given him fleeting moments of joy, pleasure, and happiness, but by the time addiction is in full bloom, the positive benefits of his substance use have vanished. Now he uses substances to feel numb and less anxious. The worst of his personality type is fully in control.

Typical of living at level 6 and 7, he perceives life out of the fear-filled, deluded window of these levels. He becomes more certain that his delusions are a reality, often believing that he doesn't have a drinking or drugging problem, which is maddening and heartbreaking for loved ones. In addition, he is possessed by consuming selfishness regarding what he wants, needs, or deserves (level 6 and 7 manifestations = me, me, me!) even as he is being inundated with bone-cracking low self-esteem, as if he has returned to a raw state of early childhood and is solely concerned with his singular needs. In reality, he has shut down and can't sense the needs or feelings of others, let alone his own. In this deluded state, it appears that he doesn't care about his family, children, job, or health. The truth is, he is overwhelmed (which translates to a heart, mind, and soul that are closed like a fist) and unable to comprehend the truth of his situation; he is desperately trying to end or numb his suffering.

He has fallen down the rabbit hole of unawareness and can barely perceive any facet of reality with clarity or precision. This is the horrid nature of addiction. The further he falls down the levels of health, the more likely some kind of devastation will have to intercede to stop his descent, to inspire or guide him to get help. Individuals often get into recovery via the loss of everything they care about, but it is by no means the only way.

The addicted or substance-abusing individual is not easy to help. He is defensive and reactive, and blames others for his suffering.

This is the nature of being at level 6 or 7. As those who have attempted to get loved ones into addiction treatment will attest, the addicted individual is often tenaciously resistant to their attempts to help him, and for good reason. He is unable to embrace and see, sense, or feel what is real: that his life is in serious danger and he is destroying everything he cares about. However, if he gets clean and sober and lives in an environment of support and compassion, he will start to relax and get glimpses of reality. By not acting out his impulses to shame, blame, judge, or hurt others or himself, and staying sober, he will begin the process of truly seeing and healing his suffering. With continued inner work, he will begin to ascend to higher levels of health.

BEING CONSCIOUS

When an individual is at level 5 or below, he is living in a state of unconsciousness, although he may have times during his day when he is more conscious and present, meaning that he can objectively observe himself in action. If someone pushes an emotional button of vulnerability in him and he responds with quick anger or makes an aggressive attack to cover his feeling of vulnerability, in self-reflection he may say to himself, "Wow, I wasn't really under an attack by Thomas, but his tone of voice ignited fear inside me. Without thinking, I reacted as if he were bringing on a full-scale attack. I was scared for some reason. Instead of simply saying I was triggered by his tone of voice, I reacted with fear, anger, and attack, and put him on the defensive. It happened so quickly that I couldn't control it, and I completely lost track of the initial feeling of fear. None of this was planned. I need to apologize."

A conscious person can track these reactive, protective responses, and can quickly make amends in his communication. At the very least, he can quickly reflect and observe in the aftermath of the reactive explosion that yes, he was a little insane in his response, and in fact he wasn't there at all. What was there was his emotional *reaction* that got triggered before he could stop and think it through.

An unconscious person (level 5 and below) will accept his reactive response and feel that his overreaction was a necessary and correct interpretation of reality. At the healthy levels of expression (levels 1 to 3), the individual is less likely to misread the behavior of another as an attack or can notice in the moment that another's behavior is triggering something vulnerable or reactive in him. He will not impulsively retaliate with either withdrawal or counterattack (or whatever his type-reaction pattern is). This is precisely what happens at the average and unhealthy levels of health. An individual goes unconscious and doesn't know it. He is so hypnotized by his emotional reactions that he is unable to observe what he feels, how he reacts, and to what extent his response comes as a result of his internal sensitivity. His type-specific way of leaving reality takes charge. It feels right, nothing to question.

THE DYNAMICS OF THE UNCONSCIOUS

As an example of how a type's unconscious patterns can play out, let's look at a Type Eight. An Eight is inspired to be a leader and to take charge of his life. He has a basic fear of being violated and controlled. His triggers center around his perceived loss of control and his potential violation or betrayal by others. At the average levels of health and below, his gut response to perceived threats is unrestrained anger and assertion, forceful and quick. But when he is unaware of his triggers and is at a less healthy level of awareness, he is prone to attacking and confronting his environment, people, or groups when they aren't actually attacking or threatening him in the least.

If he remains unconscious to this internal response pattern, he will feel justified in attacking whenever he senses a threat, real or imagined (levels 5 to 7 dynamics). He will, in fact, inspire the betrayal that he fears. He will constantly monitor the environment for signs of betrayal or signs of someone trying to take his independence away or hurt him. He will snap into action whenever he intuits this is happening. In effect, he becomes an attack waiting to happen and experiences life through the tiny window of seeing life as a battle that he must defend himself against. The more unconscious he is (level 5 and below), the more he will be an attack dog waiting to be betrayed.

SELF-FULFILLING PROPHECY OF THE TYPE

When the Eight is charged for an attack, he has almost no freedom. This is the story of the levels; the lower down the levels an individual is, the less freedom he has to navigate life with flexibility. He begins to create the suffering he wishes to avoid. His ability to open up and experience loving connections with others, to feel the graceful flow of life, to trust life itself, and to inspire strength and courage in others will be greatly hindered.

Until he gets healthier, he will continually create and fulfill his prophecy that life is a battle and that he must defend himself against it or be harmed. His capacity to be at ease, vulnerable, and open to others will be minimal. He will have little range of movement to taste and experience the broad range of possibilities for joy, spontaneity, love, celebration, tenderness, and gentle reverie. Little real happiness will touch him, and his unhappiness will further support his belief that life is an unpleasant place where people will attack and harm him.

A SELF-FULFILLING PROPHECY

The addicted individual is in the grip of his self-fulfilling prophecy. As his heart, mind, and body close down, he unwittingly heads in the wrong direction. The Type Eight lives fearful of attack, and by his defensive and hardened nature, he paradoxically inspires individuals to attack him. The Nine lives fearful of conflict and separation; by disengaging from reality and avoiding conflict at all costs, he unwittingly creates the conflicts he wishes to avoid. The One lives fearful of being wrong and making errors, and yet his opinionated, harsh judgments lead him to make errors by inaccurately judging others. The Two lives fearful of having no love. Because of his unhealthy attempts to connect with and love others, his intrusive actions push them away. The Three lives fearful of failure, and while striving to promote an image of success at all costs, he offends those he wishes to please. The Four lives fearful of being insignificant, but through his desperate, envious, entitled behaviors, he creates insignificance in his life. The Five, afraid of not understanding life or having a place in the world, withdraws into his analyzing mind and loses contact with and his place in real life. The Six, filled with doubt and wanting security, creates more doubt and insecurity through his worrying, combative, anxious mind. The Seven, compulsively seeking true satisfaction and joy, creates unhappiness through his impulsive, scattered hedonism. At levels 6 and 7, the levels where addiction thrives, the individual's attempt to relieve his suffering invariably causes the precise suffering he seeks to avoid.

As an individual descends the levels of health, he moves from being calm and unfettered, without disguise or pretense, to being armored, constricted, machine-like, and robotic. His inner robot operates beyond his control, without his consent, and often without his awareness, coming fully online at level 5. He gets glimpses of his inner robot when someone in his life has the ability to touch something inside him that explodes like a bomb, and in a flash he is on fire with anger or drowning in shame or fear. Out of his mouth pours an insane stream of maniacal language that he has no control over, or he vanishes, all traces of himself morphed into something else. He has gone unconscious. Far in the back of his awareness a voice may be trying to reach him, saying, "Please, stop what you are doing. You are making a mess of things, and your perception is completely inaccurate. Stop now and you will lessen the number of apologies you will have to make and the shame that will follow."

Often in the aftermath of a fiery reaction, be it flight or fight, he will notice that he can hardly remember what he said or what was said to him. In the quiet moment of this observation, he will feel a flush of shame. Humiliation will grip him as he recognizes that he was completely unconscious amid the reaction, that he had no control or clarity. His inner robot was in charge.

The more conscious an individual becomes of his inner robot, his personality patterns, the less likely he will be caught up in the reactive patterns of his type, which blank out his awareness, and less likely to find himself suddenly picking up a drink or a drug.

The individual in recovery can learn to neutralize this inner robot by developing the ability to compassionately observe his patterns in action. Later we will investigate more opportunities for this.

CHAPTER 4

Type One—
The Merciful Teacher

The Enneagram is one marvelous spiritual tool that
names the nine most common strategies for survival or
"programs for happiness." It reveals we are all wounded
in our "feeling function."

—RICHARD ROHR, *BREATHING UNDER WATER*

The Type One, known as the perfectionist, reformer, and merciful teacher, is endowed with a great passion to do the right thing, to serve people selflessly, to live by a code of honesty and integrity. He walks his talk and is an inspiration to others. He is merciful, hard working, responsible and has the gift of being able to see the fundamental goodness in everyone and how hard they are trying to do the right thing.

THE INTERNAL PLAYING FIELD OF THE ONE

In addiction, the One is compelled and obligated to fix what he sees as wrong, and then becomes judgmental, self-righteous, critical, hateful, and harsh toward himself and others. His gift of service disappears. The following is a brief overview of the One's internal playing field.

Deep wound/relapse pattern: The deep wound of the One is his fear and belief that he is bad, defective, and unredeemable, that his instincts and feelings must be suppressed and controlled to avoid making mistakes.

Key commandment: The One's key commandment is to be error-free in any activity he engages such that no one will challenge his skillfulness. Errors signal that he is flawed and defective and thus not worthy, not good enough. He must be self-reliant and not in need of emotional support.

Deep wish: The One's deepest wish is to feel his innate goodness and what is fundamentally right and sacred about him and the world. He wants to be fair, reasonable, kind, and truthful, and to serve and improve the world for everyone.

How he sees himself: The One sees himself as someone who is reasonable, principled, impartial, fair, truthful, and inspired to improve himself and the world.

At level 4 and below: When the One is in an unhealthy state at level 4 or lower, he increasingly falls prey to his emotional habit of resentment. In this state, he is driven by his frustration with the imperfections he witnesses in himself and others and his heavy sense of responsibility to fix every flawed thing. Add to this his mental habit of judging himself, others, and reality as imperfect and his resentment intensifies.

Inner critic: The One's inner critic tells him he is good and lovable if he follows his ideals without error and doesn't make mistakes. Mistakes are not permitted, ever! When he does see something wrong, he is responsible for fixing it.

At his best: The One at his best is endowed with common sense, the capacity to see both sides of an issue, and the willingness to give up his personal needs for the service of the community. He tells the truth and lives by a standard of integrity that he expects himself to follow. He walks his talk and inspires others to do the same. He is merciful toward the flaws in others and sees that everyone is doing their best, including himself.

THE HEALTHY ONE

The healthy One exudes kindness, gentleness, patience, and a tender, earnest heart filled with real mercy for the suffering of others. He knows, feels, and sees how hard people struggle to be good, to do the right thing. Although he has an eye on what he could improve in others, he holds what he sees softly and gently.

The healthy One is lightly constricted by the hauntings of his inner critic. He has done the emotional work to heal many of the sufferings that caused him to heft his Type One shield in defense against the insults his inner critic is wired to deliver. This emotional healing has allowed him to relax in his body and heart and activate a quiet mind.

The healthy One is generously concerned about the well-being of others. At his best, he is called to find effective ways to serve others and improve their quality of life without criticism or self-righteousness. Honest, fair, and dedicated to a high standard of integrity, he can be counted on to take impeccable, responsible, skillful action.

Case Study: John

John is a healthy Type One. A shining light of truth, purpose, and hard work, he will deliver help with excellence and precision when needed. He is a connoisseur of rich and practical help, the go-to person for solid advice on how to do something well. In touch with his basic goodness, John has no need to improve or fix anyone else according to his standards. Slow and steady work has allowed his merciful and serene heart to come forward and occupy its rightful place. To the extent his heart has been healed and his defensive, judgment patterns are disarmed, he walks lighter in his own skin. He has excavated many layers of suffering and misunderstanding from his inherited core belief that he is evil and condemnable, especially the suffering he experienced from living with a dad who was emotionally violent and critical of him and a mom who disappeared when he was just a kid.

His journey in recovery has not been an easy one. Under stress, he notices that he loses contact with his graciousness and goes into work mode, trying to make himself and other people do things "right." Then he stiffens and becomes intrusive with his ideals, and others feel the pinch of his criticism.

This gets activated in particular when his sixteen-year-old Type Four son, Justin—who is deeply aware that he is not following anyone's expectations—rebels against his dad's Type One standards. In order to be true to himself, Justin violates his dad's code of right behavior. John then comes temporarily unhinged, his gut suddenly a fist, his anger and judgment-management plan of *don't react to my son* vanishing in the haze of his reaction.

Before he can blink, John is trying to right Justin by pointing out his disrespectful, lazy, irresponsible actions, trying to guilt him into being good. Of course, Justin simply smirks and lands a nonverbal hammer blow of *You are not the boss of me.* In eloquent Four style, Justin reminds his dad, "Lighten up. Why is everything so serious with you?" and walks off, untouched by his dad's passion, which fires John up even more. His inner critic then whispers, *You suck as a dad!* Guilt swallows him, followed by the wish to counterattack and try even harder to teach his son through intensified messages of *You are disrespectful.* Guilt becomes John's weapon of choice.

Although as a healthy One John's perfectionism is usually more quietly expressed today, internally he notices that he is often under the microscope of his tireless inner critic, who sees flaws everywhere and goads him to improve and make things better. The good news is that he is healthy enough to see his inner critic when it intrudes, and he isn't as easily hypnotized. The one exception is when his son presses his nuke button and implies that John is a failure as a dad. When he is healthy, John can laugh about this, and not become so strident that his body constricts and hardens into a vice grip.

An important wake-up call in John's recovery is noticing when he is gripping the steering wheel of what should be improved and feels the heavy weight of obligation driving him to fix everything and everyone that needs improvement, including himself. Now, because of his work to become present and aware, he can more often see when his personality habits begin to take over, and with the support of others, he can come back into a state of presence and awareness. He is then able to apologize when he has criticized and judged others, and amends come easier.

John has become less critical of himself and others; his capacity to relax and engage life with grace and humor has grown, and his belief that he is responsible for fixing everything has softened. He notices his level of health on a given day by his capacity to be in touch with his sense of humor, his internal calm, his grace in cutting himself and others slack, and his capacity to see what is good in the world. No one to improve today.

There is another important side to John, that of the warrior of truth. In the territory of ethics and right treatment of human beings, he can and does take a life-and-death stance. Dishonesty hits his viscera like a Mack truck, gripping him from the inside out. This was reflected when, as a leading clinician at the rehab where he worked, he discovered and witnessed the CEO of the organization fall prey to alcoholism accompanied by a whole host of harmful behaviors. Lost in the haze of his addiction, this man had episodes of aggressively bullying clients and staff. This put the facility and its mission of caring for the addicted vulnerable in jeopardy. The atmosphere of compassion was replaced by an atmosphere of fear and defensiveness.

The misalignment of the CEO's behaviors with the mission of the treatment center—to live by a code of honesty, transparency, compassion, fairness, and democracy—sent a deep shock into John's Type One core. He could not resist his call to duty and his reason for existence: telling the truth. He had to speak out; there was nothing to negotiate. In his heart of hearts, he felt that the CEO would want help, would want to see the trouble he was in, would never wish to express the negativity that was eating up the heart and soul of the counseling staff and the clients they served.

With profound and near-childlike earnestness and faith, and with the grounded humility and straight-up honesty of the One, John took healthy Type One action. He spoke his truth, plainly. He pointed out the elephant in the room. He spoke with kindness, conviction, mercy, love, and a profound sense of right. He took a risk that denial, even retribution, might be the comeback. He courageously said, "I can see your alcoholism has progressed. You are doing things that are hurting everyone and yourself. Please let me get you some help. There are resources to support you." However, John had failed to see the escape hatch that was created by his actions. Fearing the loss of their jobs, his fellow counselors who he thought were his allies, vacated the scene. As the healthy One does, he stood and fought alone.

He was fired. Click, bang, gone. He then faced a slew of punitive actions from his boss. Checks owed him were not forthcoming, his boss started rumors accusing John of theft and other dishonorable actions. John, in his allegiance to his values, could clearly see that the CEO had been blinded by his addiction. He felt the CEO's innocence while holding fiercely to the truth of the situation. This is the Type One at his best.

THE ONE IN ADDICTION

When he is at level 6 or 7, the addicted One expresses the opposite of his healthy qualities. He is aggressive and undermines individuals with his opinions and principles, either silently or openly, in the name of serving and improving them. Chewing on the heart-hardening substance of resentment and blinded by a narrow view of reality and how he and others should engage with it, he loses contact with his balanced wisdom and fairness. Driven to attack and criticize those who offend his standards (including himself), he has fallen far from being an exemplar of reasonable, patient, and well-thought-out principles.

Case Study: Billy

Billy is deeply affected by his father's alcoholism and has untreated adult-children-of-alcoholics wounding. That is, he grew up with a virulent, alcoholic dad, and in turn got addicted to substances and to his dad's rage. He always comes up with good reasons for indulging his constant anger and his drinking, both of which are driven by horrific, unowned emotional suffering. In essence, he inherited his father's patterns.

Billy's path as a Type One parent has been harrowing. Raging over the slightest error of execution by his children—leaving an unwashed cup in the sink or a shirt on the floor—he has gone nose to nose with them. Berating them nonstop in forty-five-minute tirades, barely taking a breath between sentences, pummeling them with reprimand, he has engraved in their souls the message that they are horrid children. He has infused them with gargantuan guilt over minuscule actions while passing on the emotional atmosphere he grew up in and was strangled in.

At his worst, Billy reverts to physical abuse, grabbing them by the arm and spanking them to their room. Adding alcohol to this behavior awakens a dragon whereby all the emotional abuse Billy received as a kid becomes a crazy, misguided, perfection that incinerates the souls of his children. He is breaking the will of the kids, undermining their self-confidence, and setting them up for homelessness and addiction. If he is lucky enough to achieve recovery, he may at some point understand that he has deeply wounded his children. This is not a certainty, however. Some are unable to do this because of the destruction of their memory. (The movie *Thanks for Sharing* captures this dynamic. The dad is a leader at AA but comes home and expects his son, who he has deeply hurt, to follow suit. Not until he finally begins to listen to his son does he realize the damage he has caused.)

In the grip of his suffering, Billy's Type One principles become weapons that discourage and dishearten the efforts of others. He rivets his children and wife with resentment-filled judgments. He is compelled to bring attention to what is wrong with people, places, and things. Overwhelmed by his sense of defectiveness and doing all he can to numb it, he delivers a message that others are evil, defective, and irredeemable, and his alcoholism exacerbates this.

Filled with self-hatred, Billy attempts to restore his well-being and integrity by trying to be good, trying to reform himself and his environment by making himself and others do things according to his ideals—and drinking to soothe his aching soul.

When he arrives in addiction recovery, Billy has violated the vast majority of his principles, has deeply harmed those he wishes to love, has often fallen sway to the chaotic impulses of his body and passion, and is riddled with shame and self-condemnation. His deepest fear has come true: he is defective, bad, and condemnable. He is the failure he feared he might be and seriously questions whether he is redeemable. His innate capacity to be a force of change, service, and reasonableness has vanished into the distortions of his addiction. Instead of being modest and balanced, he has fallen prey to self-indulgence and his impulsive feelings and desires, all the while asserting the rightness of his position. He is in hell. He is blind to his actions while everyone around him sees him with 20/20 vision. Quite a predicament.

If Billy's heart one day breaks open and he feels deep remorse for his past behavior, he will reach out to make amends, apologizing to his children from the core of his being. This will be the most difficult work because they will instinctively turn away from him, fearful of more hurt. Reconciliation will take time. It will be his necessary work.

THE FIRST TWELVE WEEKS IN TREATMENT

The newly sober and clean Type One arrives at a men's treatment facility filled with torturous and overbearing self-condemnation. His inner critic greets him with a ranting film clip of all his errors. Defensive, he begins casting aspersions on those who have failed him, including God, the liberals, the conservatives, the government, his spouse, humanity—you name it.

Addiction has forced his hand, stripped him of everything, and cornered him in a residential treatment facility. Horrified, he is realizing that his opinion-driven life has not worked and that he must turn to others to guide him from the darkness.

The newly sober One is in desperate need of forgiveness and the ability to see his flaws with a kind, merciful heart.

His innate gift to the groups he participates in is his bone-chilling honesty. On good days he will tell everyone exactly what he sees and is unconcerned about who sides with him. If he believes someone is not being honest or not living up to their commitment to recovery, he calls it as he sees it, direct and true. At his best, he can cut through his rationalizations and delusions and take an unsparing look at his failures with shuddering precision. (We could call this "withering honesty.") His downside is a tendency to see his errors with so much harshness and judgment that he nearly crushes his spirit or the spirits of those in group to dust.

The newly sober One is in desperate need of forgiveness and the ability to see his flaws with a kind, merciful heart. His deepest soul wish—to experience the fundamental goodness of self and others, and to serve others well—lives in a universe far, far away.

He can assess the weaknesses of others in vulnerable moments and strike with cold logic, yet doubt rails inside him: *Maybe I don't really know what I'm doing. Maybe I'm as lost as they are.* The truth is hard to swallow: he is one of these men whom he so harshly criticizes. He is just like them, imperfect, in trouble, humiliated, and addicted. Humility and mercy are the doors he must pass through. He, too, deserves and needs help and truckloads of mercy.

THE ONE'S PROTECTIVE MECHANISM IN EARLY RECOVERY

Afraid that his flaws will be seen, that he will be condemned as other than perfect, the One in early recovery constructs a tough boundary of protection fortified by his strident criticisms and right opinions. He arrives well defended and quick on the draw, compelled to assert his judgments and opinions as if protecting his very life. His inflexible opinions have become the replacement for losing touch with what is good within him and a buffer for avoiding the suffering his addiction has caused. Unconsciously the One says, "You will not get close enough to see my imperfections and failures. You will not have access to that part of me that feels I'm condemned and unforgivable. If I allow you to get close, you could touch my heartbreaking disappointment with myself. I cannot bear this!"

The newly sober One can barely sit still in groups. He is anxious to take concrete actions that can quickly clean up the external messes he sees in his life. He is a man of action; looking inward, into his heart, is uncharted territory. As he impatiently sits in treatment, memories of his errors flood him. In response, he is quick to notice who doesn't follow the rules and feels an overwhelming obligation to bring this to the attention of staff and the guilty clients. He points out the imperfections he sees in fellow clients and counselors with anger and condescension as his judging mind screams, *What is wrong with these guys? They have no commitment to working hard on their recovery.*

The One often becomes the renowned "cleaning police" at the treatment center. Never has the facility been so clean as it is under the scrutiny and passion of the One to rid the house of all dirt and disorder. Never mind that several weeks earlier he sat in his own apartment, dishes stacked to the ceiling, ants having formed a food line to and from the dishes to the left-open refrigerator door, his clothes unwashed and crumpled on the floor/bed/couch for weeks. Mired in blackout hell and an alcohol fog for years, with little ability to commit to anything but drinking or drugging, this reality faded into drunken amnesia.

I say to Paul, sober seven days, "Paul, are you aware of how passionate you are to bring order and chaos to the facility, to the clients, to myself and staff, when for the past years you've lived in crack-house-style disorder?" He looks back at me, a sudden alertness in his eyes, pauses, grins sheepishly, and says, "Yes, that's true. But that doesn't matter because *I'm back!*" We both laugh.

CORE RELAPSE PATTERN

The One habitually compares himself to an idealistic standard of right and wrong, good or bad, which he strives to achieve no matter how long he has been clean and sober. At the lower average levels of health (levels 5 through 7) he is saddled with an illusion that his standards should be followed by everyone, and he feels obligated to enforce them. He feels good when he meets his standards and bad when he doesn't.

When he enters addiction treatment, the standards he has established for himself and others have become stringent and harsh, with little room for error. Paradoxically, he has violated these very standards and fallen into rebellious, self-indulgent, addictive behaviors, which he has great difficulty recognizing and acknowledging. Since his errors are unacceptable, he often projects his flaws onto others. Wrapped in a psychological iron coat of self-control designed to avoid errant impulses, his heart and mind can barely breathe.

In addition, resentment is a core relapse trigger. It is based on the illusion that the One knows what is right and what he should be doing, thus self-condemning himself for not being perfect, while others appear clueless, lazy, unconcerned and disinterested in doing things right according to his standards. This sets up the One to be constantly resentful and angry at others, and while feeling he isn't working enough, sets him up to feel superior and righteous toward them. *The lazy fools.* Unwittingly, he develops an insidious habit of feeling resentful and frustrated, needing something to attach these feelings to.

I imagined that everyone was judging me the way I judged myself.

John, a healthy One, explains his struggle with feeling he is condemnable: "When I came into addiction treatment I mostly felt rage and self-hatred. How could I ever forgive myself for my errors? Everyone said I had to forgive myself. This would take me a long time to digest and understand. Sometimes they would be kind and merciful to me, and I'd reject them as being too soft, too lenient. I was initially drawn to men in recovery who were punitive and hard on me. I had to learn that I wasn't weak for accepting compassion."

About his self-judgment, John says, "I imagined that everyone was judging me the way I judged myself. I believed that the only thing that would fix me was punishment. It took me considerable time to notice when I was under the spell of 'I am a bad person' and my habit of totally hating on myself, punishing myself by screaming in my head, *You are a loser. You idiot. What's wrong with you!* No one wanted to spend time with me because I was so uptight. My kids would say, 'You are a downer! Lighten up, Dad!' I thought that receiving mercy would let me off the hook."

In early recovery John took pride in how hard he was on himself. A strange form of vanity developed, where he said to himself, *I am good because I do not let myself off the hook. I'm proud I treat myself harshly, that I can endure this and inflict this upon myself. Mercy is for irresponsible people.*

Terrence experienced his Oneness another way. "Throughout my whole drinking life I believed that everyone else was perfect and I was flawed. I was afraid to try anything new or challenging, afraid I'd fail or make a mistake. My escalating drinking fed into the fantasy that I had much to hide and that I was definitely flawed. I became intolerant of myself, relentlessly pushing myself to do more and more to meet a self-imposed bar of success. I thought that everything would be okay if I just avoided mistakes and worked harder to improve myself.

"I didn't realize until I'd sat in a lot of AA rooms that people are just as flawed and imperfect as I am, that parents, doctors, lawyers, and pilots are imperfect, that nobody plays by my strict and harsh rules and nobody cares much for them. I finally realized that I'd wasted the majority of my life tightly restricting my choices, options, and enjoyment of life. This has brought me tremendous humility and remorse and the desire to become healthier."

TRANSFORMATION IN RECOVERY

The One arrives in addiction recovery when the light of reality finally reaches him. Who he wanted to be, who he thought he was, he is not. Identified with the Type One self-image of *I am honest, fair, balanced, responsible, principled, accepting, and wise,* he experiences the wrenching awakening that he has lost contact with these qualities. He sees that his honesty has become a tool to punish others and himself. His passion to be fair has been turned to self-righteous superiority, and his principles of treating others with dignity has vanished in his condemnation of those who offend his ideals. Promoting the "truth," he lied to himself and denied what was real, dissociated from the moments in which he indulged himself and his instincts and blindly looked through his ever-shrinking, closed mind.

As the One becomes more self-aware, he will feel great remorse and sorrow as he realizes the harm he has caused. He must learn to receive mercy if he is to withstand the withering assaults by his inner critic. As my broadly smiling teacher would say, "Michael, if you punish yourself each time you discover a flaw, you reinforce the flaw so that it becomes more unconscious and powerful. I suggest you try mercy."

Helping the One

When working with the One as a therapist or sponsor, you must remember that to whatever extent the One criticizes you, other clients, the world, he also applies to himself, which can be hard to remember when you are being eviscerated. This behavior often keeps away those who can help him heal his sorrow, self-judgment, and disappointment. He is wired to be independent, self-reliant, and responsible for himself. He girds himself with a boundary of *I'm right and you aren't, so don't mess with me.* Held hostage by his opinions, he makes others feel unredeemable and condemnable. Squeezed into a knot of certainty by his standards, he experiences a false sense of independence and capacity.

What drives all of this is his rejection of his own imperfect humanness. Your doorway to helping the One is in embodying your own flaws with grace, kindness, grounded humility, and truth.

Demonstrate your self-acceptance of your humanness, that to be human is be flawed, and that embracing and observing one's flaws with a light and kind heart is what transforms the flaws.

> When working with the One as a therapist or sponsor, you must remember that to whatever extent the One criticizes you, other clients, the world, he also applies to himself, which can be hard to remember when you are being eviscerated.

The more you can reveal this healing process to the One with a gentle heart, and reveal to him that all human beings are filled with their fair share of flaws and mistakes made, that this is a continual slow but steady process, the more he will relax. When you spot his fierce judging process being revealed, with calm and kindness help him notice the trance he is in and his opportunity to soften what he is applying to self or other.

SUGGESTIONS FOR THE ONE

It will be incumbent upon you to provide supportive, helpful guidance to the One as he navigates his way to health. Share the following suggestions, perhaps just one a week so as not to overwhelm him.

Begin to mistrust the certainty of your opinions and judgments.

The recovering One easily believes that his perspective is the truth, whether it's about himself or others. He experiences this as a *fact* in the core of his body. He must learn to be aware when this phenomenon has put him in the trance of his being right and everyone else being very wrong. His task is to begin to mistrust or question the certainty of his opinion and to hold it with lightness (meaning, don't take yourself so darn seriously).

Try these suggestions to help him question his opinions and judgments:

- Encourage him to consciously put his judging on hold long enough to allow the words of others to touch him, to reach him.

- Instruct him in the following manner: "When you notice that you are entrenched by the state of rightness, first notice the sensations in your body, the tightness and tenseness in your viscera, trunk, hands, neck, and shoulders. This is a wake-up call that you've been taken by your Type One personality pattern. Breathe deeply, several breaths, and then, if you can, drop the story of being right and get curious about the opinion of others."

- Instruct him to imagine putting himself in the place of the other and finding what he agrees with or what he could agree with. Remind him that a key to his getting long-term sobriety is in becoming teachable, open, curious, and tolerant about the perspectives of others.

- Remind him often that in the arena of addiction, his addiction is way smarter than he is. It feeds on his ego and whispers, *You don't need help. You're smarter than these people. If people realize that you are in need of true help, they will give you the wrong advice. Don't trust any of them.*

- Help him to begin to see how clever his inner critic is and how it enters his thought stream through black-and-white judgments of others and self.

Begin to sense the suffering that your resentment and judging cause you.

The One's resentment of others, his judgment of others, causes him suffering that he may not be aware of.

Try these suggestions to help him sense his suffering:

- Remind him that if he slows down enough to sense his body, he will notice that underneath the heavy hand of his judgment and resentment is a terrible sadness, fear, and heartache. He will experience directly how much it hurts him to judge himself and others.
- Remind him that he must start to observe when he is hypnotized by this insidious type-specific pattern and is indicative of underlying feelings that he is avoiding.
- Instruct him in the following manner. "When you are caught in a state of judgment, sense deeply into your body and your heart. Notice what you discover. You may feel your heart is numb or flat or blocked, but see if you can feel behind the numbness."
- Instruct him that he might discover that the judgment he has been projecting onto others already sits in his own heart as a self-judgment; that is, his heart and his value are in a state of judgment, courtesy of his sneaky inner critic. Remind him that this practice will help him begin to neutralize his judging of others and allow him to open up to heartfelt connection with them.

You must begin to resist the urge to improve others.

The One impulsively and often unconsciously instructs others in how they can improve or be better or more "right" in his eyes.

Try these suggestions to help him resist the urge to improve others:

- Explain that by learning to quiet his mind through meditation, he will begin to spot his mind's ongoing judgment. He will begin to sense in his body—especially tightening of the jaw and gut—the feeling of obligation to improve, perfect, and take responsibility for the errors of others. Instruct him to stop and say an inner *no* to this habit when the urge to offer unsolicited advice arrives. Have him simply sit and observe this inner show of impulses, body sensations, and thoughts wrapped around improving someone else. Remind him that seeing what drives the machine is what destroys its hypnotic power.

- Encourage him to name it as a movie: *The End of Humanity—If Only They Would Listen to Me.* This will help him see the absurdity of it and that he is powerless to change others.

Begin to trust joy, celebration, and your inspiration.

The One often feels the compulsion to control another's experience of joy because they missed a detail the One considers important, or when their joyfulness irritates him. Something inside him scoffs at joy and resists it, tightens against it, is anti-joy, while he hides behind a cloak of, *I'm doing the right thing first. I'm being an adult.*

Try these suggestions to help him begin to trust his positive feelings and inspirations:

- Encourage him to name the inner killjoy as it arises: *Oh, there's Voldemort at it again, telling me that avoiding joy is being a good human being.*

- Instruct him that he must begin to disidentify from this

terminal adult entity and notice how the entity takes strange pride in denying him pleasure as a means of being "good."

- Help him make a "first aid kit" in the form of a small card he carries with him. He can pull out this card and look at the list of fun and adventurous things he can do right now, then choose one.

- Inform him that with a little effort, he will notice many miraculous things that occur each day. Suggest that he read the book *Joy on Demand* (see resources) and learn to nurture the art of joyful appreciation.

Journal daily.

Daily journaling will help the One become conscious of his judgmental mental habits.

Try these suggestions to help the One develop the habit for daily journaling:

- Author Natalie Goldberg describes a beautiful model for journaling in her book *Writing Down the Bones*. Share with him some of her tips:

- Encourage him to write ten minutes a day without editing, worrying about spelling or punctuation, worrying whether he is writing the worst stuff on planet earth (writing crap is part of the process). Let his thoughts just flow. He will quickly discover his swift-moving mechanism of perfectionism, judgment, and impossible standards of expectation, and with it, perhaps, a sense of humor. Even better, his intuitive creativity will show itself. With practice, he will see the humor in his madcap mind.

A MESSAGE FOR THE ONE

Share this message with the One in recovery:

> The real you doesn't need to be fixed or improved on. It patiently waits for presence to arise, to help you realize that what you have been seeking is already here, in this moment. You are not bad, irredeemable, or defective, not by a long shot, and sobriety will slowly but surely teach you this. In time, you will see the delightfulness of who you are, and as you relax, your sense of humor will arise. Your playful soul will have permission to be, and along with it, innate and balanced wisdom will gracefully and effortlessly inform you of the right time and right place it is needed.
>
> As you continue to unfold and embrace your deep goodness, awakening will further teach you that you are never, nor need be, able to judge anyone or anything objectively. You can drop this job and this habit by reminding yourself daily that you cannot control or change another human being, and breathe a huge sigh of relief. Then reality will reveal the rich sacredness and fundamental goodness that you are immersed in and a part of. Joy will become a friend to you.
>
> As a final recommendation, read Brené Brown's *The Gifts of Imperfection*. Brown is a self-identified Type One and offers wise words for the recovering One. Also read Desmond Tutu and the Dalai Lama's *Book of Joy*, perfect for your path forward. (See the resources for more information.)

CHAPTER 5

Type Two—
The Intuitive Healer

If your compassion does not include yourself,
it is incomplete.

—BUDDHA

The Type Two, known as the nurturer, mentor, and intuitive healer, is endowed with a generous and loving heart, sensitive to the nuances of other people's suffering, and naturally inclined to heal, help, or sometimes carry the sufferer until they can carry themselves. He is a loving, caring soul, a compassionate helper known for possessing and expressing unconditional love and kindness, for generously touching people with the sweetness of his heart. In addiction, however, he becomes certain he is not loved or valuable and becomes desperate to hold any connection with others regardless of the expense to himself. This pattern becomes the source of his relapse back to addiction.

THE INTERNAL PLAYING FIELD OF THE TWO

When the Two is in addiction, his internal playing field becomes unbalanced. He is driven by the horror of feeling that he is rejected, unwanted, disposable to anyone he cares for, and likely to be abandoned at any moment for the slightest infraction. The following is a brief overview of the Two's internal playing field.

Deep wound/relapse pattern: The deep wound of the Two is the feeling of being unlovable, unworthy of love, unwanted, and not needed. He feels he must make himself indispensable to others or else they will abandon him.

Key commandment: The Two's key commandment is to care for the needs of others to have a place in the world. He is only as valuable as the love he gives others. He must not need anything for himself.

Deep wish: The Two has a deep desire to love and be unconditionally loved, to be deeply connected with those whom he loves. He wants to truly help others in need, to be a force of love in their lives.

How he sees himself: The Two sees himself as always loving, kind, considerate, generous, and without any negative motivations toward others.

At level 4 and below: When the Two becomes unhealthy, he falls prey to the emotional habit of pride, in which he attends to everyone else's needs to the exclusion of his own. He perceives that he doesn't have needs. His mental habit of ingratiation keeps him continually thinking about others, worrying about them, and thinking of ways to make himself indispensable to them. He prides himself on believing he knows what others need.

Inner critic: The Two's inner critic tells him he is good only when he is connected to and considering others, when he is thinking and doing for others; otherwise, he is selfish. He cannot ask directly for what he needs.

At his best: When the Two is at his best he is generous and kind to others and himself. He doesn't need to save people from their suffering and is aware that he can't control, cure, or change another. He has good boundaries and loves with a clean heart, meaning no strings are attached. He loves abundantly and skillfully, knowing how to care for himself.

THE HEALTHY TWO

The healthy Type Two is a teacher and exemplar of loving-kindness, generosity, encouragement, and forgiveness. Open-hearted, he senses and feels the potential goodness and love in those he touches. He is passionate about connecting and being connected to people and is drawn to help them, to hear about them, to feel their hearts, to melt into the sweetness of others. And yet this is not a shallow, Hallmark-card loving-kindness. It's not a sappy nothingness that touches only the surface. It is strong, potent, and penetrating, and will change others at depth.

His loving gentleness will melt the hardened self-protective blockages in those he encounters; he will land like a nuclear explosion on their suppressed suffering and despair. True kindness penetrates. Tears will come. Suppressed rage and hurt will surface. Shame will arise from the bowels of his being. Love calls forth everything. Ultimately, connection with the healthy Two will give others what they have always wanted: a genuine connection with another human being and their own heart, a loving embrace for their suffering. This is the mission and the gift of the Two.

When the Two is healthy he knows the boundaries of his capacity to help, knows where empowering another and creating a dependency in the other begins and ends. The Two understands when help is needed and when he must stand away. He is aware when he starts to do the work of another and knows that this alone can deter an individual from discovering his personal will to grow. He knows the sacred boundaries that he must hold if the other person is to survive, learn to endure painful changes, and do his work; that he cannot control another. And yet he transmits a power that touches the heart of the other with a simple message: You can do this. I will walk beside you on this journey. You can do this.

If there is a flaw in the Two's beautiful soul radiance, it is wanting to help too much, to reach beyond his capacity. He has difficulty resting in the reality that full-blown generosity can be delivered in the silence of his being, that an action is not always required. He transmits loving help through his presence.

The healthy Two does not have to be the universal flow of love but a graceful thread of it. He knows that over-helping disempowers the other, weakens their resolve, and disconnects them from their real will and strength to grow and change.

Case Study: Thomas

Thomas, a beloved Two, came into addiction recovery twenty-four years ago, and it shows. Sitting at an AA meeting, his angular face and body embody stillness, grace, strength, and gentleness. The moment he speaks, a depth of compassion and kindness toward the men in the room struggling to be sober is apparent. He has been to the bottom, resurrected through insurmountable suffering and abuse, and has become a mountain of love. Behind him is a trail of desperate actions, attempts to find connection with others that would ease his hurting heart. He inadvertently rescued individuals who then drained him of every ounce of energy as he threw himself into them, whole hog. It is a situation akin to the dreaded relationships with vampires, who use their victims, drain them dry, and then leave them to die.

Compelled by an inexplicable desire to connect with anyone, somehow, somewhere, Thomas couldn't *not* do this. His twenty-four years of sobriety mark a steady effort to heal this path, to become aware of his type patterns that made him blind to reality, blind to the unhealthy individual he was pursuing, and soul-blind to his deep needs. But recovering men and women have taught him, helped him, and showed him the way.

Today his kind heart is magnetic and pulls men to him that otherwise would never approach him. Gnarled, toughened men sense him as a safe port. His demeanor is clear: it is safe to have a broken heart in his presence. You have nothing to hide. You will be held by love. There is room for you here, exactly as you are. He speaks simply and articulately, his wish being to encourage men with his faith, that if they work the steps of recovery, they will find their way. Moreover, when he has taken on another man to sponsor, he goes to any length to find out what will settle the man's aching, confused heart. His dedication to delivering kindness and caring knows no bounds, and his genius for finding the support a man needs is unbeatable. He feels the hearts of the men he works with, senses the little boy who has been abandoned, and is passionate about creating space for healing.

Those he sponsors know this and feel this. Enveloped in Thomas's kindness, compassion, and capacity to sense the sorrow of the wounded boy, the newly sober man feels the love of a good mother or nurturing father, perhaps for the first time. Being seen through Thomas's compassionate eyes, where forgiveness is available, where gentleness touches the sponsee, where one's deeper spirit is beheld, he reminds the sponsee on a visceral level that God, or the universe, or Thomas loves you and values you, that the sponsee is held by the gracious and powerful force of love. This is the holy healing power of the healthy Two.

THE TWO IN ADDICTION

When the Two becomes unhealthy, his addictions—alcohol, drugs, food, sugar, relationships, being overly nice, shopping, starving himself—are his supports. The addiction becomes his false heart and his false connection to himself. It fills the emptiness of his heart, the hole in the heart that so many in early recovery speak of.

When he is at level 6 or 7, the addicted Two arrives with a heart that is filled with painful emptiness, which begs to be filled with something, something that will sooth him, or distract him, or at least in the moment, change the feeling of being unlovable into something else. If he cannot feel his innate sweetness, lovableness, and preciousness, then what he faces is the horror of a five-year-old who has lost his mother or father. Something must be stuffed into this hole to soften the blow and make his existence tolerable.

Case Study: William

William arrived at a rehab treatment center after serving another five-year stint in prison. He is a sweet and kind-hearted Two, yet prison has driven his heart deep into the recesses of his soul. Buried deeply alongside his heart is the horrible loss of his mother when he was five, the loss of his dad at six, and the trail of rejections by foster parents. He was a wandering gypsy with no place to land or to call home.

In the presence of his Type Eight counselor, Dominic, the fierce force of truth bore down on William, reaching through his protective all-is-well shield until he suddenly broke into sobs of pain over his life losses. Gasping for breath, tears streaming down his cheeks, the eyes of an innocent boy stared back at Dominic. His deep moment of truth could only be felt in small measure. It is going to take many descents into this pain-well to digest and heal his suffering.

William did as many do in very early recovery. With an unhealed heart, he tried to find solace in the loving gaze of a woman. Margarette was a tall, lovely Type One, and was swept up by William's Type Two loving charisma at an AA meeting. Little did she know that she would be filling in for his heartbreaking loss of his mom when he was a little guy. This is the same loss and longing that had relentlessly driven his descent into addiction, into desperate acts of thievery to supply his habit, and long stays in federal prison. Nor was she aware that his intense, loving attention to her would quickly morph into an addiction to her, that if he could place himself in her pocket every day, he would.

Margarette temporarily became his lifeline away from the unquenchable pain in his broken heart. Smitten with her, he was quickly deaf, dumb, and blind to the dynamics of his addiction and the primary importance of putting his recovery first, foremost, center stage. The saying *Whatever you place in front of your recovery you will lose* became a faraway echo. He's heard it many times before. Yes, he knew the steps of recovery, he knew what to do (or, at least, his thinking center was jam-packed with years of recovery knowledge), but his aching heart was suddenly brain dead. His infatuation, just like his drugs of choice, was thinking for him. His acquired recovery wisdom went on mute.

In his buried current of sorrow for his mom was a survival instinct that screamed, *without Mom's love I can go no further; she is my oxygen.* When Margarette temporarily became his oxygen, her kindness fogged his reason and effortlessly overruled any access to his earned wisdom. His acquired wisdom developed through years of attempts to gain and keep sobriety vanished.

In the first week of group at the treatment center, before he was full-blown lost in his new infatuation, he reached out to others as the old-timer who knew the ropes, and with precise accuracy could outline the path to sustained recovery. His empathy and kindness were contagious. His kind eyes and generosity of spirit were a salve to suffering men. He looked and sounded as if he's *finally* in the game for real (his counselors pray), clearly embracing recovery first. But with lightning speed he found the love of his life—in fourteen short days.

Margarette now occupied most of his attention. William went through the mechanics of recovery, continued to recite recovery principles, but all of it was a front for his absorption into his woman. He instantly forgot his emergency, forgot that if he relapsed, he would go back to prison for another two years. The intoxication of his new love erased worry, practical consideration, and even the horror he had experienced relapsing back to prison on numerous occasions. This is what any good drug does; it wipes out the past, at least for the moment. As twelve-step folks put it, it's the forgetter's disease.

Starstruck, he wandered, drunk on the elixir of love, and once again, he was repeating his past. He was soul-starved for attention and affirmation, willing to sacrifice everything for any crumbs of love or kindness. And why wouldn't he?

Wearing himself out in his efforts to please Margarette, his real needs (i.e., the inner work of recovery) erased from awareness, he was driven by possessiveness and the fear that at any moment he would be abandoned by her—the bane of the unhealthy Two. He saw her through the lens of idealized love as his savior and redeemer. He would hold on to her for dear life, this *other* drug of choice—infatuation addiction—intoxicating (until it's not), numbing his sorrow and desperation. *What sorrow? I'm happy now, finally.*

As Margarette asked for more space, freedom from the clinging spiderweb of his neediness, his core fear of being abandoned was magnified. After a few fearful arguments regarding her needs, he relapsed. Several days later he found himself behind bars, a burglary charge trailing him like a hungry dog.

As a Two, driven by the sharp knife of *I'm not loved*, William will continue to get entangled with the next hopeful lovemate until he develops the will, strength, and resolve to resist this pattern. He will need the help of others to do so because, like his alcoholism, this is a pattern he is powerless over. It has a life of its own within his psyche. Thus, he must treat it as a primary addiction.

When he is at levels 6 and 7, his attempts to love and create loving relationships fail. As his sponsor has implored him, he must stay out of relationships for at *least a year*. He must face this Type Two addiction pattern: "I don't have relationships, I have hostages, and when I let go of someone, I'll always leave claw marks. I'll do just about anything to not be abandoned." His sponsor's or therapist's job is to help him see this pattern and point it out when he dissolves into it.

THE FIRST TWELVE WEEKS IN TREATMENT

When the Two arrives in treatment at a residential facility, he is already feeling a huge disconnect from his life. His primary source of identity—those whom he loves—is gone. He will be caught in the machinery of his thinking mind, wondering about his loved ones, wondering if he could have changed the outcomes he now faces if only he had only done this or that. Heartbroken, he is only temporarily slowed down from his usual mental pacing and will soon be on the go to reconnect and communicate with his loved ones, whether they are with him or not. He thinks about them and thinks about them, and it is difficult to bring his attention into the room, to himself and what he feels and needs.

As the Two attends AA meetings, he is often on the lookout for lost, wounded souls he can help and win over. *Who can I save?*

As the Two attends AA meetings, he is often on the lookout for lost, wounded souls he can help and win over. *Who can I save?* If he can find someone to love back to life, he will feel better, he will have a purpose. He won't have to sit in the suffering of disconnection from loved ones. In recovery groups he will talk about his girlfriend or his wife, how he worries about her, what she struggles with, how he would like to help her. It will often appear as though he has come to treatment to help her and other loved ones instead of dealing with his addiction issues. His habitual focus will be outside himself.

He is here to learn a fundamental lesson, which is alien territory for him: that he needs help, that he has an addiction. In the first days at the treatment center, he will be open to suggestions, but quick as a wink, as he feels better, his maneuvering mind will begin rescripting his priorities. Maybe his wife wasn't serious about leaving him. If he can only get her back, things will be fine. Maybe he doesn't really have an addiction problem.

His only problem, he thinks, is that he drank too much because he was so upset with how badly things were going in his relationship. He doesn't need addiction treatment. No, he just needs to get back home as fast as possible. He will be more careful with his drinking.

It will take him time to realize that his zealous efforts to create love and connection with his wife and family actually push them away or strangle them with his expectations.

THE TWO'S PROTECTIVE MECHANISM IN EARLY RECOVERY

The Two unconsciously learned to protect himself from rejection by not letting anyone know what he needs, or by simply disconnecting from his needs. His history has taught him that if he doesn't have needs, he can't be rejected—simple. A war wages within him: he wants to be connected and close to those he loves, but he invariably makes it impossible for others to genuinely love him because he can't reveal who he is, warts and all. He is terrified that his needs will deem him selfish in the eyes of his vicious inner critic. The rules are set: if he is to be loved, he must only have loving feelings toward others and only wish to do things for them. Ultimately, he protects himself by loving others, by putting his attention solely on their needs. How could they possibly reject him with the spotlight of his attention fully on them?

The Two has learned to reach in to help others before checking in with his own needs or giving himself permission to express and acknowledge all of his feelings. He has learned that this is selfish and makes him unlovable and worthy of being abandoned. The sponsor's or therapist's challenge is to help him notice when he has abandoned himself in the action of caring for another, or is avoiding his feelings of anger, sadness, and humiliation by reaching to support another. This is major recovery work for the Two at all stages of his sobriety

When I once asked a Two how he dealt with his needs and wants in early recovery, he replied, "What wants? What needs? I learned early that having wants meant I invited suffering and ridicule. So, that was the end of wants. I stopped wanting what I wanted. Who would want when it only brings suffering?" That is the key question for the Two: who would *want* if it only brings suffering? Thus, the heart-desires of the Two become masked, leaving him with a fake happy heart. This becomes the entrenched habit that makes his soul a feeding ground for addiction.

The Two faces questions such as, How do I get real? How do I begin to admit the human side of myself? How do I get honest with my anger? With my hurt? With my shame? How do I slow down enough to see, with compassion, that when I am suffering, I shift this hurt into helping others without being aware of whether my help is wanted? How do I see that this pattern sets me up for attracting emotional vampires who use my despair and good intentions to suck me dry? Why do I push away those healthy enough to be with me?

CORE RELAPSE PATTERN

The Two's core relapse pattern is in putting his attention on others to feel loved instead of turning inward to healing the source of his pattern, his rejection as a little one. This survival pattern, which truly allowed him to navigate difficult times, is instinctive and immediate, and will need the loving support and insights of others to begin to slow and ultimately derail the pattern. As is said in recovery, it will be four steps forward and three steps back. Real change is slow. Nothing happens quickly. Do not be discouraged.

TRANSFORMATION IN RECOVERY

The second a Two gets a whiff of a loved one in need, his body is out of the chair, in motion moving toward the loved one, before his brain and consciousness can catch up. But the brave Two is deeply committed to changes that will truly allow him to touch people at depth as he marches through this sacred doorway of his own self-care. He will face his hateful inner critic, who will rise up and shout, "Taking care of yourself hurts others. They need you, and yet you turn away and toward your selfish desires. Shame on you!" The Two has permission to say to his inner critic, "Buzz off. I've paid my dues. Have a nice day."

The Two must surround himself with a few dear souls who hold his feet to the fire when he abandons himself, because he will.

Skillfully, he will retrain his patterns because he has engaged in a new experiment, and he has the knowledge and courage to withstand the horror that his inner critic is willing to dump on him. Slowly, slowly, slowly he will disengage from this mechanism, his pet robot, as he continues his commitment to this powerful edge of growth. As he does so, the intensity of the guilt and shame generated from his inner critic will continue to quiet until one day, they are merely passing mosquitoes buzzing in his ear. He can do this because, at depth, his heart is heroic and strong.

The Two must surround himself with a few dear souls who hold his feet to the fire when he abandons himself, because he will (until he doesn't). He must find people who bring him back to listening to that precious heart of his.

HELPING THE TWO

As his therapist or sponsor helping the Two, you must be the eyes he needs to spot his patterns. He will need you to point out when he too frequently over-gives, such as when he brings gifts, cards, and little things that he learns others like. You must assure him that he won't be abandoned.

As his therapist or sponsor, you will need to help create boundaries for the Two, as he has none.

When he attends AA meetings, he will notice the wounded soldiers. He will see the woman with three kids who lost her job, whose partner vanished into the wilderness of his own addiction, and he will feel her suffering. He can help her, he can ease her pain. Never mind that his own wife has left him, that he has not seen his kids in several years; here in front of him is an immediate need that he can respond to. How can he deny the palpable tugging at his heart to rescue her while totally forgetting his own needs? This is where you come in, delivering compassionate clarity. You can say, "My friend, you must leave this situation alone. You must stick with your recovery and not confuse it with a relationship. And consider this: rescue missions backfire because people really don't want to be rescued."

As his therapist or sponsor, you will need to create boundaries for the Two, as he has none. In therapy you will need to redirect his attention back to himself over and over again. The no-gifts (for the therapist) rule must be steadfastly held to. You must call out how he tries to get personal information from you to inform him how to give you the best gift. Expose his pattern gently but clearly. He compulsively wants to help whoever is in front of him, and he will listen to cues as to where they have been hurt or need attention.

The Two's boundary must begin with the mandate of his having no intimate relationships in his first year of AA. (After reviewing my past, my sponsor smiled mischievously and said, "No relationships for you for *at least* fifteen years!") Give him this clear instruction: if he feels the urge to help a damsel in distress, he must talk to you before he takes any action. Clearly and steadily mirror for him what you see. He will need to hear it more than once, so be patient but unrelenting.

As he begins to see glimpses of his pride—*I don't need help, you do*, or, *I know exactly what she needs to be happy*—while seeing himself as more loving than others, his superiority will turn to shame. With shock, he will see the times he has lied to look loving, or to please someone, or to keep someone close to him. Also painful to bear, he will see that he treats himself with disregard and hatred.

As his self-awareness grows, his ability to see more clearly the mechanism that takes his attention will sharpen. As if peeling an onion, he will notice that he continually monitors the responses of others to see if he is passed the test of being loved and wanted, or if he is being rejected. His ongoing work in recovery will be to grasp that he is constantly on trial in the eyes of his inner critic. The first glimpse of it will lay him low with shame, but with continued efforts to see his Type Two defense patterns without judging himself for it, he will begin to dismantle the marching orders that have been driving him.

Once the Two has begun recovery from his addiction, encourage him to hightail it to Al-Anon. If he is to stay sober, he must learn to identify his needs and become able to put them first and foremost. Healthy selfishness is high on his recovery agenda, as is learning what healthy nurturing of others looks like.

SUGGESTIONS FOR THE TWO

It will be incumbent upon you to provide supportive, helpful guidance to the Two as he navigates his way to health. Share the following suggestions, perhaps just one a week so as not to overwhelm him.

Begin to listen to your heart.

The Type Two develops a pride in not needing love. Having shut off and numbed himself from the love he hungers for, he begins to pride himself on not needing anything. His job in recovery is to reverse this habit and start listening to his needs and wants with the same intensity and compassion that he attunes to the hearts of others.

Try these suggestions to help him begin to listen to his heart:

- Explain that as he practices self-observing with compassion, this lightning-quick pattern of impulsively helping others will become more evident and occasionally will move in slow motion. Then a choice will appear, a gap in the hardware programming of his personality. In that moment of heart-sensitivity he might recognize that he does want something. It could be affection or acknowledgment. He may feel a passion to express his creativity. It will arrive in almost invisible form, but as he attends to these heart impressions, their strength and importance will appear.

- Let him know that slow, steady work begins by just noticing how he felt a need or desire for something, and it vanished so quickly that he hardly caught a glimpse. Without judging himself, encourage him to make a list at the end of the day of these moments. His first job is to merely observe these impressions, nothing more to be done. In time, the desire for real action will arise.

Begin to notice that resentment and anger are signs you're giving too much of yourself.

The Two has thoughts of forcefully collecting the debt others owe him if they don't notice how much he contributes to them. This "you owe me" resentment builds up, leaving him stuck in the trap of resentful giving unless he communicates openly about it.

Try these suggestions to help him notice his resentment and anger and to recognize his needs that lie beneath:

- Help him to learn to listen to his resentment. Help him hear what it sounds like in his mind-stream. Ask him, *What are your resentment thoughts? When do they commonly arise?* Have him make a list of these thoughts and what the underlying desire is that lies beneath them.
- Explain that this resentment is a sign that he wants something that's important to him, and that he has acquired a survival habit of being so indirect about his needs that no one takes him seriously.
- Remind him that healthy anger arises when he needs to defend himself from being used or disregarded. Trust it. He must learn to ask, to speak up, instead of succumbing to the idea that others haven't properly mind-read his needs. Ask him, *When did you notice your anger today?*

Notice how you indirectly ask for what you want by hinting at it.

In order to get what he wants, the Two uses strategies, such as volunteering to give his partner a massage or hugging his partner, when he actually wants a massage or a hug for himself. He reasons, *If I give her what I want* (a hug, a massage, a card, a gift), *she will surely begin to intuit that I want the same treatment.* (This thought process was explained by a panel of Twos who said, "We can see what you need. Why the heck can't you see what we need?")

Try these suggestions to help him begin to see his pattern of hinting at what he wants or wishes others would intuit:

- Explain to the Two that sensing the needs of others is

one of his super powers but that he must learn to be direct about his needs in communicating with others. Hinting doesn't work and leads directly to the feeling of being rejected, along with resentment toward the loved one.

- When you spot him engaging in this behavior, point out in the moment how he has just made an indirect request via his generous actions. This is tricky because he will feel terrible humiliation when an unconscious pattern is pointed out. Remind him that everyone has unconscious patterns, that it goes with the territory of being human. Have him practice phrases such as *I would really appreciate a hug/your help/a compliment/ acknowledgment of how my help has helped you.*

- You will need to point out this pattern to him many times because the pattern is deeply tied to his survival as a little guy when he was trying his best to avoid rejection.

Learn to endure the guilt you feel when you ask for what you want.

Guilt is the signal the Two's inner critic sends when he takes care of himself or says no to others when he needs space or time. The inner critic, committed to holding him in the role of the helpaholic, tells him he is bad or selfish when he cares for himself, which means that at any moment he could be banished forever into the loveless back alleys of his soul.

Try these suggestions to help him endure the feeling of guilt when it arises:

- Explain that he must learn to bear the guilt, and that in time, the guilt will quiet.

- Remind him that when he advocates for himself, he will be flooded with the tar-like substance of guilt. He will feel awful at first, and the guilt will feel like an indisputable fact.

- Teach him that learning to sense his body on a regular basis will build in an internal observation tower in which he can begin to experience his guilt more quickly and more objectively.

- Explain to him that when he is engulfed in guilt, reaching to a good friend for support can be very useful. He doesn't have to endure this alone. Remind him he is worthy of receiving help.

Become aware of your pride.

Thich Nhat Hahn, a Vietnamese Buddhist monk, said "Pride is the unwillingness to admit our own need and suffering." The Two often cannot sense his own need and suffering, and believes that he doesn't have emotional pain that needs attention. If he brings attention to his needs, he will feel the horrid guilt of selfishness, and if he speaks of his suffering, he fears no one will notice, and he will be deeply wounded by rejection, the very thing he is wired to avoid. It is much easier to play it safe by reaching out to help another.

Try these suggestions to help him become aware of his pride:

- Instruct him on how his pride can show up. This can be very difficult because the Two experiences humiliation when he realizes that his motives aren't always pure.

- Give him this challenge to help him recognize his pride: "For one week when you have the inner experience that you know what someone else needs or what would be good for them, resist the urge to step in or take action. Just notice the pattern and how you are unconsciously

> wired to step in as the one who knows the needs of others."

- Suggest to him that he avoid making unsolicited recommendations. Rather, encourage that he become aware of a sneaky ego pattern of knowing what is good for others, which, in the long run, pushes people away whom he wishes to be close to. Suggest that he ask first whether someone wants his help before offering it.

Learn to identify your habit of mind of ingratiation.

When the Two is stressed out and feels vulnerable to loss of love, his tendency is to go into people-pleaser mode by, for example, complimenting others as a means of creating a connection, or showering them with praise, gifts, or affirmation to keep a loving connection intact. He affirms what is good about others instead of addressing his own vulnerable feelings.

Try these suggestions to help him identify and change the habit of ingratiating himself to others:

- Instruct him that under stress or caught in his fear that he is unwanted, he is likely to over-compliment others or unwittingly magnify their successes, which has the side effect of making them feel weird because of the exaggerated positivism.
- Remind him that this is different from his intuitive capacity to actually see and name what is good and wonderful in people. The overdoing of compliments makes folks feel that there's something behind the compliments, something hidden, an ulterior motive, and that he is not sincere. Although this is not the intention, it sets him up for others mistrusting him or even mocking what appears to be his naivete.

- Let him know that you will compassionately point out this pattern when you witness it. If you can, give him living examples of clean complimenting and over-the-top ingratiating complimenting. Examples will help him.

A MESSAGE FOR THE TWO

Share this message with the Two in recovery:

Try for one week to develop your sense of humor. Each time someone asks for help, respond with, "I'll get back to you." Do not offer help. Ask yourself what it is *you* need. If someone asks for help, just for one week reply, "Sorry, I'm fasting from helping people, as I've gained pounds of over-helping on my soul, and it's slowing down my real ability to love. I promise to get back to you, but I can't help today."

Remember this: you will never lose the love of helping others, and your time spent on yourself will actually deepen your ability to give quality attention to others. As my sponsor said, "You must become an expert on putting yourself first in the realm of your recovery. Get the help you need. This effort alone with magnify your capacity to assist others."

The good news is that all of this is learnable. It may feel at times like you are rolling a heavy stone up a mountainside, but be assured that all of your efforts to become more conscious and free of your patterns will bring positive results. No effort is wasted.

CHAPTER 6

Type Three—
The Inspiring
Champion

True ambition is the profound desire to live usefully
and walk humbly under the grace of God.

—BILL WILSON, *AS BILL SEES IT*

T he Type Three, known as the achiever, the performer, the inspiring champion, is a force of inspiration, motivated to deeply express his inherent gifts brightly and fully, and to encourage through his example the capacity for others to develop and share their gifts with the world. At his best, the Three is confident, charismatic, and surprisingly humble, ever aware that the gifts he has been enabled to shine forth with are the result of the efforts of thousands of others before him upon whose shoulders he now stands. Their efforts, losses, and wins are the foundation he has launched from. Possessing a radiant and caring heart, the Three is a channel for others to shine through.

THE INTERNAL PLAYING FIELD OF THE THREE

When the Three is in addiction, his internal playing field becomes unbalanced, driving him into the unhealthy levels of his being. Instead of championing others, he gets lost in desperate need to succeed and be better than others. He becomes driven by an emptiness that he cannot fill, a despairing self-centeredness that erodes his heart wish to help himself and others shine on. This loss of contact with his heart is what he must heal to gain and keep his sobriety. The following is a brief overview of the Three's internal playing field.

Deep wound/relapse pattern: The deep wound of the Three is the feeling of being utterly worthless, a loser, possessing no value. He believes that no one wants him for who he is.

Key commandment: The Three's key commandment is to be the best; he must excel above others to feel valuable and worthy. He must put forth ceaseless effort to prove his value.

Deep wish: The Three's deep wish is to feel his value, radiance, and preciousness, to develop his talents and share them with the world. He desires to inspire others to shine.

How he sees himself: The Three sees himself as successful, confident, talented, poised, adaptable, realistic, and a cut above others.

At level 4 and below: When the Three falls into these lower levels, he falls prey to the emotional habit of vanity, in which he believes the mask of his manufactured, successful self-image. He pumps this image up to avoid feeling empty. His mental habit of deceit, in which he is constantly thinking about his self-image and how he comes across to others, engenders him to lie about what is real and true in him. He becomes a master of looking like he's got it together.

Inner critic: The Three's inner critic tells him he is okay only when he is successful and has achieved at a high level. Otherwise, he is worthless. Each victory must be followed with an even better victory. There is no time for rest. He is only as good as his last success.

At his best: When the Three is at his best he is humble, authentic, modest, grateful for those who paved the way for his success, and aware that his achievements could not exist without the help and guidance of others. Often inspired, charismatic, and super positive about achieving his goals, he inspires this in others.

THE HEALTHY THREE

The healthy Three is an inspired motivator, encouraging others with skill and faith to do their best, to see their capacities, to shine as they are capable of shining. Effortlessly and with grace, the Three supports others, championing them to celebrate the talents they have been given; he encourages them to develop and maximize their gifts and share them with the world. The Three inspires others to be the best they can be, to hide nothing—not to impress others, but to bring forth the gifts one has been given, to both revel in and experience the joy in manifesting and celebrating them.

A healthy Three—magnetic, charming, and articulate—expresses himself with heartfelt authenticity and confidence and possesses the remarkable ability to adapt to circumstances in pursuit of his goals. If one thing doesn't work, he tries another. This ingenious adaptability keeps him open and flexible, endowing him with the intuitive ability to tap into the highest ground of possibility and creativity in the present moment. Under pressure, he is poised and graceful, his inherent sense of confidence and natural competency a powerful ally. The Three believes, "I can do whatever it takes to succeed, and so can you!"

Case Study: Martin

Martin, twenty-five years sober, rose in the ranks of his state's political system. When he was healthy he could read a crowd, articulate concepts that landed positively on constituents and friends, find the positive in a difficult situation, and when necessary, graciously acknowledge defeat. He is wired with strong self-confidence, abundant energy, and a multi-talented ability to reach his goals with drive and efficiency.

At his best, his capacity to truly listen to the needs of others and to empower them to find ways to meet their needs is unmatched. Gracious and grateful to be able to help, he is humble and calls forth genuine humility in others. Right-sized himself, he invites others to occupy this common and sacred ground. He says, "When I'm present, I become a worker among other workers, and it feels great."

A writer, a speaker, and an inspiring and articulate communicator, his capacity to make sense of complicated subjects allies him with many. He has walked the razor's edge of the Three in recovery, balancing his capacity to fall into self-centeredness, compulsive attention-seeking, and self-serving acts designed to gain him approval (of which he would say, "None of this ever satisfies me or makes me happy—ever!") with his spiritual path of learning to serve the interests of the greater whole. This includes humbly asking for the guidance of his higher power, God, Goddess, the Divine, daily.

Energetic, positive, a go-getter, and motivated to be his best, Marvin's attuned heart has been the radar and guidance system for all his finest actions. His authentic, truthful, and engaging heart is what is most appealing to others and points to his primary spiritual inquiry: "Are my actions serving love or serving my ego and my image of myself? That is always the question I must ask myself, with ruthless honesty. I am ever aware of a part of me that is hardwired for self-promotion and self-seeking, and this is always slipping seamlessly into my thoughts and motivations."

Coupled with his heart practice, his gentleness and youthful spirit make him approachable and trustable. He is all he says he is, often with little fanfare or self-promotion. A humble, can-do guy (with his inner observer watching for Type Three ego activity) wired to be in action and filled with energy and ambition, he became a driving force in his political sphere. Able to see his personal flaws and robotic Type Three defense patterns (polishing his presentation in service to ego inflation) with self-effacing modesty, his need to be seen as the star, or the one who had outperformed his competitors, was rarely visible. Yes, he sought to win and rise in the ranks, and enjoyed the increased self-esteem it gained him, but he had enough presence and awareness to not play to this single note.

As he says, "Success for the promotion of my self-interests alone, to bring glory to myself, is like trying to fill a bottomless well. There is never enough money, applause, accolades, publicity. These are always fleeting moments followed by emptiness. It has taken me years to see how my self-centeredness and need for admiration constantly ruined my real happiness while sober. The problem is that I didn't see it when it was happening. Caught in my self-promoting desires, I completely overlooked my children for nearly a decade of my recovery. I was totally hypnotized by my hunger for more admiration and power. If I had these things, you couldn't hurt me. Vanity and success were my addiction—but they were never enough. It was the words of my son that stunned me.

He said, 'Dad, for most of my childhood I thought you were just this guy who was on TV. You were never here.' This utterly broke my heart and revealed the cost of my passion to promote myself."

As a result of his son's wake-up call, Martin has worked hard to establish a strong father-son bond, and his relationship with his son is the source of his deepest happiness today.

THE THREE IN ADDICTION

When he is at level 6 or 7, the best of the Three has turned to its opposite. The Three's natural modesty has turned to narcissism and self-centeredness; his genuineness and sincerity have turned to fraudulence, dishonesty, manipulation, desperation, and callousness; his abundant inspiration to champion others has morphed into unethical, self-serving actions to promote his reputation and status, often in an underhanded manner.

Unbeknownst to him, the Three suffers from a broken heart, as all the types do at these levels. His ability to truly sense what he loves to do, or how to love himself or others, has disappeared into the swamp of his vanity-driven actions. Out of touch with his value, he desperately seeks solace in the approving eyes of others, meaning he will do almost anything for admiration. He is like a hungry dog, starved for attention, and so constricted that he can't absorb any attention he does receive. When healthy, he is able to develop his talents and appreciate his successes and is less concerned with whether others approve of him or not. But at levels 6 and 7, his only source of self-worth comes fleetingly, when he extracts approval from others. Desperate for approval, his addiction has driven him to do whatever it takes to promote an image of success.

Caught in his terrible need to be seen as valuable, he no longer senses how his actions harm or denigrate others. Instead of championing others, he now competes with and undermines the success of those he is jealous of. Likewise, it is often intolerable to him to appreciate or champion the success of others. Jealousy burns through him.

He has entered the hell realm, where the survival strategies he employs to feel better send him down a slippery slide into more shame, despair, and embarrassment. He is driven to project an even more confabulated, contrived self-image of the successful one, to cloak himself in success veils, to camouflage his deepening sense of worthlessness and panic. His holy blessing will be when he no longer strives to *be* someone and rests in his innate worthiness and value. This is to come.

The healthy Three's gift of heartfelt adaptability to circumstances and people has morphed into the ability to seamlessly manipulate people with alarming skill to get what he wants. He becomes a chameleon who shape-shifts into what others value, his real nature deeply hidden in a tomb of panic. He is cut off from the very thing that guides him to what is best in him: his attuned heart. Instead of being inspired to lift others up into the light of their success, he has turned to cold, heart-dead competitiveness while capable of *acting* loving—if that is required for his deception.

Instead of inhabiting a loving and modest heart, he lives in a heart that has turned empty and vain, often driven to shameless acts of attention-gathering. If a lie about his successes will bring him attention, he will lie. If cutting down an opponent will take the wanted light of success away from his competitors, he will cut them down. Instead of experiencing deep self-worth and value, he is desperate for affirming attention, even as his inner emptiness sits in the center of his chest, a haunting ghost, wraith-like, chilly. (A remarkable documentary that captures the descent of a Type Three to these lower levels of health is *Stop at Nothing: The Lance Armstrong Story*.)

Case Study: Philip

Philip was a thirty-year-old master of disguise. On probation for his drug use and dealing, and in drug court, he appeared before the judge several times a week to report his progress and was exceptionally skilled at presenting the good face of recovery. He was doing everything required to succeed in drug court: go to daily AA meetings, work with a sponsor, attend substance abuse counseling, repair his past. He could talk the talk. After hearing him speak at AA meetings, old-timers would ask, "How long have you been sober?" He would reply three weeks, three months, and they would be shocked. "We thought you'd been sober for many years."

At his drug court completion ceremony (a one-year process) at which all the drug court folks were in attendance, including all of the probation officers and probation participants involved, Philip gave a closing speech about everything they had done for him, gratitude thick in the room. His address was so powerful that his probation officer was moved to hug him, as were several other probation officers. This never, *ever* happens.

When Philip was released from probation he moved to a different state, where he utilized his chameleonic capacity to appear other than he was. He fooled a highly regarded, street-smart female district attorney into believing he was a businessman running a business—someone other than who he was. When it came clear to him that she would never accept him as he was, he injected her with a high dose of Fentanyl as she soaked in her hot tub. He was found on the eightieth-floor ledge of her apartment building, buck naked, where he confessed his actions. "I killed her. I was so envious of her success. I killed her," he pleaded.

In the ensuing investigation, it was discovered that he had been drugging young women, taking them back to his apartment, and raping them, all while he was the star of drug court. On one occasion, instead of calling the police when one young lady was overdosing, he left her to die. As horrific as this is, it is an example of what occurs as the Type Three (or any type for that matter) loses contact with his precious heart, his ability to give and receive love, and is eaten by the jaws of blinding despair.

THE FIRST TWELVE WEEKS IN TREATMENT

When a Three arrives in recovery a curious dynamic often occurs. In groups, he can easily pick up on all the right phrases of treatment, quickly becoming treatment savvy. He can demonstrate the right intensity of emotion and can mirror—perform—what a committed individual in recovery looks like. He is instinctively able to pick up on the expectations of the counselors, and quickly reads what they want. Instantly he can put on the shine, reciting the appropriate recovery phrases and treatment insights that gain the approval of his counselors. He intuitively and skillfully becomes the sincere, recovering man.

> His turnaround begins when he sees this self-defensive behavior—his habit of seeing himself as better than the others—and the harm it does to himself.

And yet, when he returns to the residential community with other men in recovery, where he is just another client, where there is no real status to be gained, he can drop his recovery act and act superior and self-centered to the less-than-starlike clients who surround him. When his act isn't needed, he disdains others. He lives in an inflated world of self-importance and looks down on others (in AA this is "an egomaniac with an inferiority complex."). That is, he will treat others as badly as he feels, as if they have no worth or value.

His turnaround begins when he sees this self-defensive behavior—his habit of seeing himself as better than the others—and the harm it does to himself. He begins to humbly ask for help, as in, *this pattern is so quick and strong in me, I don't know how to stop it. It arises and runs through me lightning quick before I can do anything to disengage from it. Help!* This is his doorway out of the prison of his addiction and his loneliness. With ruthless honesty and compassion to self, the lock on his prison door—his vanity—will begin to loosen.

Remember, an individual who arrives in addiction recovery is living at levels 6 or 7, meaning he is unconscious and *can't see* what he is doing. He is sincerely deluded. He is overwhelmed with feelings of shame and self-hatred. To eradicate his pain, the Three reflexively imposes his suffering on other clients.

As he begins to relax and trust, at critical soul-opening moments he will radiate glimmers of authenticity and caring support toward others. You will see his soul shining, bright and beautiful, through the layers of his personality defenses. As his true radiance begins to come forth, the Three faces critical discriminations; he must learn to viscerally sense the differences in his body, emotions, and thinking center when his real authenticity is arising within him, while skillfully noticing his Type Three predilection to convincingly perform his "authenticity" to acquire approval instead of being authentic. Are his shared insights honest and truly heartfelt and bodyfelt, or are they the stuff of another mask he is wearing? This is the most difficult work because fake or performed authenticity fools him as readily as those on the receiving end of it.

He honestly may not be able to tell the difference for some time. He is so good at transforming into someone whom others applaud that he has learned to fool himself; that is, he can't see himself do it. *It does him.* The pattern runs him; he a puppet on its string. This tendency is his most challenging stumbling block, one that he must learn to observe and begin to transform throughout his recovery. As Thomas, fifteen years sober said, "Truthfully, I unconsciously, and not maliciously, begin to speak the words that will impress you, such that sometimes I can't tell whether what I've spoken is my truth or something I think you'd like to hear. I still struggle with this lightning-quick habit. It's a form of deceit, but most of the time I don't see or sense it until later. I can easily believe my own confabulations."

THE THREE'S PROTECTIVE MECHANISM IN EARLY RECOVERY

The Three aims to please others, to show them how good he can be, to attract them to his competencies and skills, to demonstrate that through his talents and achievements he is valuable, and not worthless. *Please admire me*, he prays from the deep hole in his heart. He wants himself and others to feel that he is a somebody.

He has learned to protect his wounded heart by driving toward his next success, driven to do better and better, so once his feet have hit "recovery ground," he will be off and running. In fact, at the beginning stages of his recovery, he might be vulnerable and shaken enough that he can't maintain the "successful one" mask, but once he has his bearings and has been sober and clean long enough, it will be time to get back to what he really wants: success and admiration. No sooner has he touched the real stuff of his desires than he may be out the door chasing the success he always wanted but that his addiction stopped him from attaining. All the while, the ghost of his emptiness continues to haunt him. His deeper nature will not be satisfied until he enters and rests in the realm of his sincere and humble heart.

His inability to sense his heart (and his hurt, shame, and rage), and to dodge it by pursuing the approving gaze of others, will be a fundamental relapse trigger. His addiction licks its lips and patiently waits, hidden in the folds of his suppressed and avoided suffering, a vampire waiting for his armor to crack. This addiction is very patient.

CORE RELAPSE PATTERN

The driving engine of the Three's addiction is his core fear of being a loser, of being utterly empty and without value on the inside—like the Tin Man from *The Wizard of Oz*—and that others will see this and reject him. Game over. His deepest fear is that if others know who he is on the inside, they will have nothing to do with him; he is terrified of this. At deeper and deeper levels, the Three in long-term recovery will excavate more difficult and hidden aspects of this wound, peeling the onion of his soul as he discovers deeper authenticity.

Roger explains it this way: "When I entered recovery I felt like an utter loser. I'd lost everything: my kids, my job, my relationships. I'd gone to the bottom, and I wanted with all my heart to repair my disasters. I grabbed onto AA and NA as my lifeline, which kept me sober, and although it felt good to have people support me, it wasn't enough—at least, so I thought. I knew I was biding my time and that the shame for all my losses would not be resolved until I got into action in the real world.

"In the beginning, the sorrow and humiliation were overwhelming. I surrendered to it, but as soon as I could bypass it, I did. Once I got back on my feet and was engaged again at what I considered real success, I did what I always did: I avoided or skipped over any vulnerable feelings and went into performance role, into being the successful one, shaping this persona as soon as it was in reach. Difficult emotions were speed bumps to be navigated over quickly. Not attending to what was real inside me (this would mean working the steps of Alcoholics Anonymous) led me to the new addiction of workaholism as a method to outrun feelings of shame. With abstinence from alcohol, alcohol could no longer stop my workaholism. Working the steps of Alcoholics Anonymous didn't seem practical or relevant to me.

"I've had several years of recovery at a time, but each time I go down, it's because I have lost contact with what is authentic in me. Slowing down and feeling my feelings always brings me directly in touch with the emptiness that seems to be sitting in my heart, waiting for me. It's taken me much work to finally surrender to this, feel it, and allow it space in me. This surrender has allowed my self-worth to arise through this suffering. It's been and still is my most difficult challenge, staying present to what is in my heart."

This is the gold that awaits the Three in recovery: staying present and authentic as he goes about the business of succeeding.

He continues, "This question is key for my recovery: Is what I'm doing a desperate attempt to get attention and praise, or does it serve others? Without confronting this question, I am driven to chase external things to fill my emptiness. I seem to need to relearn this lesson over and over again."

Packaging himself, marketing himself, adapting himself to what is needed to appear to be successful is a well-grooved survival habit of this type. With time and enough self-observation, the Three will sense it when it arises, and not be entranced by its siren call. This is the gold that awaits the Three in recovery: staying present and authentic as he goes about the business of succeeding.

George describes it this way: "I was trying so hard to redeem myself from past failures from drinking, driven to be better and gain more money, status, sex, that I lost all contact with my wife and my kids. Despite my wife's pleas to connect with me, I could not feel the reality of her pleas or her hurt. I thought she was being overly sensitive. When she left, I was heartbroken and devastated. It was only then, when my heart ached, that I realized I hadn't really felt my heart during seven years of recovery. Nor had I felt hers.

"The price I paid was the loss of my wife and kids, who wanted nothing to do with me. I was utterly blind and moving too fast to see the suffering I was causing them. This drove me back to AA and counseling, where I faced my grandiosity and self-importance, two dragons that had run me while sober, both defenses against feeling my emptiness and shame, and god forbid, my vanity. I didn't have an alcoholic relapse, I had an emotional relapse."

Thus, the advice of my mentor: Keep at least three men in your life who are smarter and wiser than you so that when your newly developed, slick-as-oil recovery ego is present, they can spot it for you. We all need this because this is what egos do."

As he gains time in sobriety, the Three will see his many disguises of success and how quickly they adorn him under pressure. If he can maintain compassion for what he sees, develops radical acceptance of what drives this personality machine—the fear of feeling unworthy and of disappointing others—he will have more choices and be less taken by the great dragons of vanity and deceit. He will continue to grow in his recovery, staying sober through the many difficult recovery seasons he will face on the spiritual path. Humility will be his anchor.

TRANSFORMATION IN RECOVERY

As he begins to participate in addiction treatment, the Three's natural inclination is to rise to the top of the client pack for admiration. Why? Because he is driven by the Three's mantra: I'm either the best or the worst; there is no in between. That means he must impress you by becoming what he perceives you, his counselor, values in a recovering client. He can, if necessary, shapeshift into the exact image and behavior that makes whomever he is with—his counselor, his AA sponsor, his probation officer, his wife—feels like he's *getting* it. He is experiencing insights because of *them*—skillfully and unconsciously seducing the helping listeners by flattering their counselor-capacities—when the opposite may well be true. Outwardly, he is the grateful client who appears to be rising from the destruction of his addiction, exuding humility and gratitude, when inwardly he might be inundated with emptiness, shame, and narcissistic rage.

This pattern of becoming what others admire is the Three's instinctive reaction to anxiety. It will take much time before he learns to drop the spin-doctoring of his recovery self-image. This is his nemesis, pretending he is authentic when it is only an act to get him approval. But the act will not keep him sober. Only in addressing his underlying issues will the doorway to sobriety open.

As the Three begins to drop and resist his addiction to seeking to gain the approval of others and sits with the fear of being disapproved, from the center of his being will arise compassion, self-worth, and internal support. God, Goddess, Presence, grace will arise to meet his sincere efforts to be authentic. Here, in this precious moment, he will receive what he has been so hungrily trying to get from others. As he builds the inner capacity to arrive in vulnerable authenticity, self-esteem and unconditional friendliness toward himself and others will grow.

HELPING THE THREE

Your task as one supporting the Three in recovery is to sharpen his ability to sense the difference between his authentic self and his shapeshifting mask, that is, the protective set of behaviors, words, and actions that he morphs into to impress you instead of embodying his vulnerability and authentic feelings.

You must provide the safe ground of imperfection for him, such that he realizes and begins to compassionately befriend himself and his flaws.

You must provide the safe ground of imperfection for him, such that he realizes and begins to compassionately befriend himself and his flaws. You must model this by being authentic and truly humble yourself while being ever mindful of your ego-drive to look like the I've-got-it-together counselor or sponsor.

SUGGESTIONS FOR THE THREE

It will be incumbent upon you to provide supportive, helpful guidance to the Three as he navigates his way to health. Share the following suggestions, perhaps just once a week so as not to overwhelm him.

Continue to study and question your inner critic.

The Three's inner critic has a full-time job reminding him that, in one form or another, he is a loser if he fails or falls below its standards. It will annihilate him with criticism and reprimand, all in the service of getting him to try harder, work harder, work longer, be more competitive, defeat his opponents, and above all, look successful in the eyes of valued others. He can't win at this game, he can't rest, and the game is never over. He is either the best or the worst.

Try these suggestions to help him question his inner critic:

- Instruct him to make a list of the most common inner critic messages he experiences. Then, when he notices he's in the crosshairs of his inner critic, invite him to take out a notepad and write out the attack and the time of the attack.

- Have him journal in the evening about how his inner critic messages affect him; for example, it drives him to always be working.

- Ask him to explore this question: What would happen if you didn't follow the dictates of your inner critic? Discuss his answers with him.

- Alternatively, instruct him to stop and declare in the now: *Right at this moment my inner critic is telling me I am a total failure. This makes me feel horrible!* Then take the posture of the inner critic and make a sound that expresses your suffering. *Argghhh* or *growlllll* from the belly and chest can sometimes break the spell of the attack.

Learn to observe your vanity.

Observing his vanity is difficult and painful for the recovering Three. Shame will zap him as he notices the way he inflates his self-importance in response to rejection or the need for admiration, when he feels that hit of superiority that gives him a temporary, feel-good rush of *I'm better than you!* He must learn to watch this Type Three pattern without self-judgment or blame to himself.

Try these suggestions to help him observe his vanity:

- Encourage him to slow down and witness his vanity without judging himself as bad.
- Encourage him to be lighthearted and say to himself, *Let's see what Super Me is up to today.* Instruct him to pull out his notepad when he catches himself in the act or in his particular vanity movie that elevates him above others, and write out the contents of his experience, the movie, the thoughts of *I'm better than you*, and what feelings might be hidden under this vanity movie. Explore this with him.
- In the moment of seeing he is caught in the movie, invite him to name it, such as *The Amazing Incredible Bob*, then to take a breath, find his body, and return to the present moment.
- Remind him that the less often he is caught in the movie, the more often his authenticity and ability to create healthy relationships will be available.

Notice your hard-to-see habit of promoting and packaging yourself (deceit) for others.

When under stress, the Three has the nagging habit of promoting himself, his brand, in the slickest, smoothest package and then reminding others around him just how awesome he is. He does this without even noticing it. It is a survival mechanism he learned as a little guy.

Try these suggestions to help him see his habit of promoting and packaging himself for others:

- Encourage him to notice when his ego inflates and he unwittingly begins advertising his great ability to do recovery work, drawing attention to how he has become the ideal AA member and patting himself on the back for his success. Point this out to him in real time but with compassion and nonjudgment. Truly, he can't help himself until he can. Be the eyes he needs to start seeing his patterns. Remind him that you, too, have similar patterns, that he is not alone.

- Invite him to write down when he notices this inflation pattern, to recall what he was feeling when he went into self-promotion, and what feelings lie beneath the act. Explore this with him.

- Help him to notice the results of his ego inflation: when he is hungry for attention and shapeshifting himself to appear more valuable (this is his deceit), does he push away the very people he wants in his life? Does he notice they are putting up with him, or are they actually buying his image-spinning?

- Instruct him in real time—*Bill, it's happening right now, slow down a minute*—so he begins to sense *in the moment* when he's in the Three trance. Remind him that this attention hunger is a red flag that he needs to ask for help and affirmation. Remind him that he appears to have an inner manager that instantly inflates the contents of his stories into something better. His job is to make friends with that guy. Name him *My Inner Inflater*.

Slow down. Stop action. Simply sit and be.

The problem with being a speeding bullet adrenalized in the direction of his latest goal is that he misses most everything not related to the goal, such as the people around him. He must learn to notice his pace and how it affects others and sets them up for feeling disregarded.

Try these suggestions to help him slow down, stop, and just be:

- Encourage him to take time every day to stop, sit, breathe, sense his body and his heart, and engage in just taking in the impressions of the moment.

- Suggest that he start with five minutes of quiet stillness, and when he has learned to tolerate the stillness, begin to add minutes, slowly, at his own pace. This activity alone, of facing and settling his inner striving, will begin to calm his mind and heart and his ego-achieving machine. It will give him direct insight into the mad machine of his action-energized and relentless personality. Seeing and experiencing the pattern will weaken its trance-like capacity to run him at will.

- Instruct him to stop all forward motion and check in with the people around him at regular intervals throughout the day. He can ask them, "Am I moving too fast for you? Am I blowing past your ideas? Am I being insensitive to your feelings and to your value? Please give me feedback now or when I'm caught in the mechanics of my striving to be the best."

- As he does this stopping in forward motion, challenge him to see the expressions of those around him. What emotions are emanating from their bodies, their posture, their facial expressions, their tone of voice? Can he sense this? If not, encourage him to continue with this practice until he begins to feel the presence of others.

A MESSAGE TO THE THREE

Share this message with the Three in recovery:

> If you wish to grow and succeed in recovery, you must surround yourself with individuals who can lead you to deeper and more satisfying experiences of open-heartedness and realness. You need guides to help you see how your personality habits are wired to subtly cut you off from your heart, sending you back into vanity and deceit.
>
> You might imagine that if your heart opens, it stays open. Sorry, it's not that simple. It opens, then it closes. Opens and then closes. You must keep doing the practices that help you to return to realness, where compassion and authenticity lie within you. That's how you outwit your addiction and continue moving in the direction of steady peace and happiness.
>
> As you humbly mature you begin to sense ways in which you can help others as you have been helped, not because you look good doing it or because others are praising you for your good works, but because your heart calls you to help them, with no rewards attached, no self-promotion attached.
>
> You give from the heart because it feels right and good. And you learn that this is the real satisfaction you've so desperately pursued, right at your fingertips. Since your heart is open, you can feel gratitude for the care and generosity others have extended to you, and the desire to pay this forward to others will arise. Slowly, the fast-moving trance of your personality that launches you to go into

overdrive, into performance, into shining as *the best*—will begin to weaken. Gradually you will gain eyes to see when this ego-engine has turned on (which it will over and over again—until it doesn't), and with this "seeing," you will learn to not move to its beat so frequently.

As you develop deeper compassion for yourself and the personality type habits that have driven you, you will develop the skill to notice in the moment this mechanism of your type patterns prompting you to perform. In this gentle, clear noticing, you will say to *it* something like, "My word, you are able to take over my entire soul so quickly. I want to thank you for helping me survive as a kid, but now you can rest. Sit down, ease back, and I will take over from here."

As you edge closer to what you love, to why you got sober, to the deep satisfaction of simply being here, alive, able to contribute to others, you will experience peace. As they say in the television series *Friday Night Lights*, "Full heart, clear eyes, can't lose."

CHAPTER 7

Type Four—
The Creative
Alchemist

Don't give up. What often follows endarkenment—if you
continue your inner work—is equal enlightenment.

—MICHAEL NAYLOR

The Type Four, often called the romantic, the individualist, the
creative alchemist, is endowed with a deep sensitivity to the
emotional states of others and themselves. He sees the hidden
suffering that others have attempted to bury, the pretend happiness
and conditioned, shallow joy of those around them. He is often
inspired to go to the depth of his soul, to retrieve his soul and
the souls of others, too, if they are willing. The Four thrives on
expressing emotional honesty, and when healthy, inspires others
to do the same. At his best he translates this deep journey into a
creative form through his love of beauty or artistic forms. When
addiction takes over, these gifts get drowned in intense emotional
reactivity and suffering, the inability to keep a creative focus, and
the horrid sense of being a misunderstood outsider. Substance abuse
both causes and temporarily relieves his suffering.

THE INTERNAL PLAYING FIELD OF THE FOUR

When the Four is in addiction, his internal playing field becomes unbalanced, sending him down into the unhealthy aspects of his type. The following is a brief overview of the Four's internal playing field.

Deep wound/relapse pattern: The deep wound of the Four is the fear of having no identity or personal significance, of being utterly ordinary, generic, and emotionally shallow. He feels cut off from the Divine, as though this connection has been severed.

Key Commandment: The Four is in a continual search for his authentic self and authentic self-expression. Suffering these questions, "Who am I?" and "What is the purpose of my life?" his key commandment is to make himself into an original, non-ordinary human being. Because he relies on his feelings of the moment, he rarely experiences inner stability or resolution of these questions.

Deep wish: The Four's deepest wish is to know himself, to find himself and his true significance and creative purpose. He desires to be a force of encouragement and transformation for others.

How he sees himself: The Four sees himself as someone who is emotionally sensitive, deep and honest, intuitive, passionate, creative, gentle, and able to articulate feelings. He sees himself as a unique gem whom few understand.

At level 4 and below: When the Four falls into the lower levels, he falls prey to his emotional habit of envy, in which he feels that others are happy and have a niche and he doesn't. He feels ripped off, like he didn't get the necessary instructions for living a good life. Add to this the mental habit of fantasizing, in which he retreats to his imagination to create emotional intensity, amplifying his envy by comparing his life to others. He begins to live in a fantasy self, the self he feels he should be, and then hates himself for not living up to it.

Inner critic: The Four's inner critic tells him that he is lovable and acceptable if he is unique, different, and emotionally deep, but the truth is that he is utterly insignificant, a nobody, so why try at all. Or it may encourage him to indulge in fantasy, sensuality, food, or sex as a rebellion against his soul-cracking shame and hurt.

At his best: When the Four is at his best he has transformed his personal suffering into compassion for the suffering of others and developed a deep sense of internal equanimity. At his core is a steady river of calm that, in spite of the emotional waves on its surface, remains still at his depth. He feels and senses his significance and the significance of others, and often can create a creative form that captures and heals the suffering of others.

THE HEALTHY FOUR

The healthy recovering Four is known for his ability to drop into the depths of the moment, embrace the dark and the joyful from a place of stillness and equilibrium, find humor and heart-opening compassion even in the face of horror—whatever is necessary for healthy and healing navigation of the moment. He has traveled through the swamps of his own emotional trauma and disorientation, and often is a guide for others lost in the labyrinth of their suffering. Creative and able to find an artistic expression that illuminates the soul journey, he is able to transmit tremendous hope and inspiration for those in need.

Transforming his often dark and challenging suffering into lighthearted, joy-inducing, self-deprecating humor, his ability to laugh at himself is a tremendous force of healing for others. When healthy, the Four inhabits an overflowing heart that is able to savor the beauty and uniqueness of each moment and those around him. Emotionally honest, he embodies tremendous emotional strength; he could survive and thrive in just about any difficulty thrown at him.

Case Study: Shane

Shane came into recovery twelve years ago. He was a thirty-year-old-heroin addict, alcoholic and homeless, not a penny to his name. Raised in foster homes, tossed from home to home since he was a little boy, and living on the street since age sixteen, this intelligent, creative, big-hearted Four represents the stuff of real miracles: the capacity to endure incredible, soul-killing difficulty and trauma beyond comprehension, and to arise as a deeply loving, sensitive, and kind human being. He is truly a phoenix.

Shane embodies the Four's emotional courage to persist through impossible difficulties. He has experienced first-hand the darkest of the dark, he being the rejected outsider walking the streets of Portland, hoping to cop dope or find a communal gang of drunks to get loaded with, a fringe-dweller lost in despair, sorrow, shame, and outrage. Witness to crazy moments of his father's rage then fatherless at age five, raised in an emotionally impoverished home with no strong parental forces to guide and shape him, he wandered, heartbroken and filled with rage but somehow sensing that something would someday help him.

He has worked hard to transform himself, and when healthy, he is deeply attuned to those around him, and able to sense the emotional undercurrents of unacknowledged feelings. He shoots for the core of emotional honesty and is able to articulate the depths of his feelings, can share them openly, can go where most are unable to in recovery. Because of his inner work, he is able to hold and empower others with compassion and confidence when they are lost in the throes of their personal suffering.

Deeply committed to his twelve-year-old daughter, Shane is ever aware of supporting her personal growth and creating safety for her to talk openly with him. No longer overwhelmed by the tide of his emotions, he is able to focus and follow through on his commitments, such as parenting, working, and finishing his degree.

At his best Shane is hilarious. When he talks about the inner pretzels he sometimes finds himself in, such as when he is caught in the throes of an envy attack or assumes that others are judging him as harshly as he judges himself, he articulates this in graphic Four style. His heartfelt, brutally honest storytelling captures both his suffering and gracious joyfulness at what he has seen and digested. Because of the enormous gratitude for being sober and clean today, and because of his intense labors to resurrect his life, he is deeply committed to helping others in their liberation. Intelligent and extremely self-aware, he invites others to show their flaws, warts and all.

THE FOUR IN ADDICTION

When the Four is in addiction and at level 6 or 7, he is cut off from the wonderful capacities described in Shane's case. Often shrouded in turbulent emotions, his ability to embrace and express his gifts is terribly narrowed. Instead of feeling a part of the spacious beauty that life expresses, he experiences himself as a misunderstood outsider, his precious capabilities and qualities devoured by emotional torment. Disconnected from a felt sense of his own being, his heartrending question of *Who am I?* turns into emotional rants and despair. Furious that he wasn't given the right ingredients and right chances to live happily, he is held captive by rage, envy, and self-pity.

Identified with being different from his family and culture, the Four struggles to create a unique identity. His capacity for compassion turns to narcissistic rage; his ability to sense and feel the depths of his being turns to preoccupation with each passing emotional state; his gift of understanding and articulating the suffering in others turns to compelling self-absorption. His gifts—gentleness, compassion, emotional honesty, and clarity—turn to bitter despair, emotional reactivity, hyper-sensitivity, elitism, entitlement, and hostility.

In addiction, the Four imagines a fantasy self that he wants to be—an idealized version of himself—and then mercilessly beats himself up for not attaining it as he compares himself to what he imagines he should be and falls short. He might imagine himself to be a great painter but becomes so lost in his imagination and disconnected from reality at level 6 or 7 that he fails to make the ordinary, necessary efforts needed to actually get good at painting. Then he hates himself for not living up to his fantasy self. Or, under sway of his imagination, he longs to quickly master his creative capacity, hates himself for how slow the process takes, and gives up.

This habit of fantasizing can reveal itself through the Four's dream that if he finds the right partner, the soul mate, that his life of suffering will be over. She will love him, support him, see his genius, be the mom and dad he always needed, and a great lover, too. His fantasizing makes it extremely difficult to deal with a flesh-and-blood imperfect partner who continually fails at fulfilling his infatuated dream. This habit creates terrible suffering, loneliness, and chaos for the Four who truly wants a significant relationship.

The emotional habit of envy is insidious. The Four looks over at his neighbor and imagines that his neighbor has a comfortable and happy life, doing ordinary and socially accepted things that others do, apparently having no cares in the world. Envy rips through him. He thinks, *He's happy and I'm not. I hate him for this, and I hate me for not having it.* Suffering with envy, the Four then takes a sharp turn and thinks, *Wait a second; the happiness he has is shallow and dull. I never want to be content with such ordinary, mundane pleasures. Forget that. I'll go back to my lonely apartment and write sad poetry, ponder the real horrors of suffering in the world, and be miserable. At least I'm real!* Back and forth he swings between these two poles.

Case Study: Shane

Shane explains his struggle with envy this way: "When I was first in recovery I thought that everyone else had it together and that I was the only one who really suffered. I imagined I was the weirdest outsider in the room, with a life no one could ever understand. I didn't fit anywhere, and yet a part of me liked not fitting in, liked being the one who was different and original, even though it often made me feel lonely and left out. I was angry that I'd been robbed of my childhood and gone through so much abuse and trauma.

"Sometimes I imagined myself one day being a rock star and found it very difficult to enter real life, where everyone struggled with jobs, relationships, money, kids. It was as though doing everyday life things was beneath me. Imagining myself as someone great took the edge off my low self-esteem."

THE FIRST TWELVE WEEKS IN TREATMENT

When the Four arrives at a treatment center, he seems as if he is cloaked in a thick, black veil. Mysterious, he exudes a faraway aura, and yet there is the sense that at any moment he could explode. Often he does. Hungry for emotional realness and contact while simultaneously spurning it, he wants the truth of his reality out front and seen. From his cave of mystery, he demands everyone to embrace what he has experienced: misery, disappointment, self-hatred, self-rejection, and shame. He anguishes over his losses in relationship, over his inability to anchor his unique gifts, and his unsuccessful efforts to find happiness and real purpose.

The Four in recovery is mired in a psychological struggle: safely distancing himself from others in his imagination while yearning to be with them, worried they will embarrass and shame him yet hungry in his heart for real emotional connection. He often chooses retreat—better than revealing his turbulent heart. He abandons himself and his gifts, imprisoning himself in the role of the unwanted outsider. Ultimately enraged with this position, he will respond with emotional reactivity and intensity to stimulate connection or intimacy with others. This will often be expressed as anger and discontent with staff and other clients who are not being as emotionally deep, honest, and intense as he is. If people aren't talking about their deepest, darkest feelings (which the Four assumes he knows and can sense, and on good days he can!), then they aren't being real.

When the addicted Four enters recovery and begins the journey of healing, the driving engine of his addiction is his core fear of feeling insignificant, a nobody.

Then comes the complaint and protective strategy of the unhealthy Four: these people can't truly help him because they don't know his emotional needs. They aren't able, as he is, to go to the depths of emotional truth. Hiding behind the gift of his emotional honesty, he judges and dismisses them as emotional incompetents. In a state of rageful disdain, he withdraws from them, feeling once again that he is the outsider, the only one who is real.

When the addicted Four enters recovery and begins the journey of healing, the driving engine of his addiction is his core fear of feeling insignificant, a nobody, and of being emotionally shallow, dull, ordinary, and generic, indistinguishable from anyone else. These fears will be the cornerstone of his inner work throughout his recovery. In early recovery, these feelings will feel justified because his life is in ruins. But at predictable intervals, whether he has been clean and sober six weeks or sixteen years, from his depths will arise the feeling that he is utterly insignificant, a zero. In the midst of his greatest successes these feelings will have the uncanny capability of temporarily erasing all self-confidence.

Shane describes the feeling of insignificance this way: "When I entered recovery, the feeling of shame and insignificance clung to me like tar. Walking down the street, it seemed that everyone could see my shameful life and into the depths of all my mistakes and misery. I felt utterly naked. I'd walk into an AA meeting and feel overwhelmed with self-doubt and shame, sure that everyone in the room could see my flaws. I reacted by deciding they were idiots, shallow, uncreative fools, and not worthy of my time.

"This turned to envy, where I experienced jealousy of everyone. I'd look at another recovering man and it would appear that he had a good life going on, that he was comfortable with himself. God, I wanted that. Then I'd hate myself and him. Awful stuff to go through. It sent me out onto the streets many times."

THE FOUR'S PROTECTIVE MECHANISM IN EARLY RECOVERY

The Four protects himself and his shame-filled heart ("I'm a nobody") by withdrawing into his imagination and avoiding real contact with life, which he anticipates will cause him more shame. He creates an imaginary character to live through—a fantasy self—and fantasizes himself doing incredible creative works or failing miserably. If the Four allows others to get close to him, he risks the possibility that they might say or do something that touches his feelings of deficiency and shame. Floating in the depths of his psychic waters is a ghostly tormentor who continually hisses to him, *You are insignificant and unimportant. You are insignificant and unimportant.*

His intuitive radar is hotwired to protect this sensitive and vulnerable soul-wound. It takes little to brush this hypersensitive shame-button. When he does attempt contact with others, it is often through his emotional confessions regarding his painful past. Although his emotional honesty is a tremendous gift, if he uses it too often, others struggle to hold the big emotional space needed to communicate with him.

The Four's blind spot (and self-protection habit) is that he believes he knows what emotional truth is and that everyone else in the treatment center (or AA, NA, *or the world*) is shallow and fake. He mistakenly thinks that he is the deep one. This is a compelling delusion and self-protection mechanism and can trick him into feeling people have disappointed him and let him down. He thinks, *See, it happened again. No one can understand me.* It becomes a self-fulfilling prophecy.

Although he demands that others attune to him in just the right way   and immediately—he pushes them away with his judgmental insensitivity while asserting that he is simply being honest and true to his feelings. He reasons, *How can people who don't have the courage to walk into the swamps of their personal suffering, like I do, help me? I'm justified in feeling like a victim of emotionally inept people and refusing their help. Their brand of help isn't suited to my special depth.* Mistaking his brand of emotional experience as the right or only one, he rejects or avoids everyone else, and treats them as if they were nobody, as though they were insignificant—the very feelings he wishes to avoid.

Unwittingly, the Four becomes entranced by this perspective: *What I'm looking for is deep and profound, intimate and beautiful. And I'm too deep and too intimate for you.* He mistakenly confuses honesty, depth, and intimacy with spilling and retelling the contents of his shame, his childhood suffering, his disappointment with his parents, his rage at being ripped off and misunderstood by life, or through his emotional outbursts. Little does he realize that this is a distortion of intimacy and emotional honesty, a heavy veil that obscures the real depth and significance he seeks, the passionate creative impulse he wishes to express, and the real intimacy his soul longs for.

CORE RELAPSE PATTERN

The process of deepening the Four's contact with his heart and his body, with a quiet mind, entails learning at deeper and deeper levels how his actions do not match his self-image or his imagined idealized self. The Four will confess out loud that he has discovered another level of illusion. At each discovery, if compassion ensues rather than self-hatred, he will gain a deeper sensitivity to his heart and the hearts of others. He will have a felt sense of his significance, and his innate gift to experience beauty wherever he sets his eyes will arise.

When he can, he may put into words, with exquisite precision and raw clarity, the depth and truth of his suffering. He may uncloak himself in group and let others see all the way inside his misunderstood heart, giving them front row to the inner machinations, fantasies, and the jungle of his confused emotions. Fiercely he will rip the covers off himself. Everyone in the room will grimace, guts tightening, eyes widening, leaning forward, as the Four's deep confession sweeps away the "don't talk" rule. Other men will follow suit and drop to a new depth of courageous self-expression, telling secrets they have never told, opening up the dark corners of their inner lives.

The Four will courageously sacrifice himself and his facade, inviting everyone to unmask. Gratitude will touch him when he has inspired others to express deeper self-honesty; he has given his gift. But in a few short moments, his habit of personality will return, and he will again be caught in soul-torturing angst and emotional turmoil, his emotional clarity swept up by the blinding waters of his shame and insignificance. This will be the dance of his early recovery: navigating his emotional depths with lucidity followed by disappearance into the black hole of his hurt and shame.

TRANSFORMATION IN RECOVERY

Recovery for the Four truly begins when he sees that he has erroneously imagined himself as sensitive, creative, and compassionate when his real behavior has been self-absorbed, hateful, and self-centered (levels 6 and 7 behavior). As he stays clean and sober, he will witness the countless unconscious lies he has told himself. Where he imagined he was sensitive, he sees self-absorbed, self-pitying behavior. Where he dreamed himself creative, he sees work that was never started or completed. Where he thought he was emotionally honest, he sees that he used friends to dump his feelings. Dreaming himself empathic and kind, he sees the many times he was cruel, mean-spirited, and judgmental, often in the name of emotional honesty.

As the Four sees his real behaviors revealed, remorse and humiliation will drop him to his knees.

This is the process of being stripped of one's delusions (and it will recur throughout his recovery). As the Four sees his real behaviors revealed, remorse and humiliation will drop him to his knees. It is then that he must not flee but sit with the feelings; resist attacking himself with self-hatred; and allow others to support, guide, and empower him in his walk through the fire of self-revelation. Here he must learn to rest in compassion and realize that the illusions he encounters are the result of the many moments of suffering he has accrued throughout his life. He didn't create the illusions, but he is responsible for dismantling them. This is the work of recovery and not for the faint of heart.

HELPING THE FOUR

Helping the Type Four provides many challenges for the therapist, counselor, coach, or sponsor. The Four is heavily attuned to his mood or feeling of the moment, and often takes too seriously the nuances of his changing emotional tide, at least in the beginning. He is magnetically drawn to trying to understand this fluctuating emotional world he inhabits, and it causes him great suffering and confusion. Partly because he hungers to identify who he is, he searches for this through his feelings of the moment; since his feelings are constantly changing, so is his identity of the moment.

You will witness the Four changing directions repeatedly, starting and stopping with the latest inspiration or mood swing that touches him. Your work is in helping him to "be where his feet are" and how to sort out this inner tide such that he takes practical steps in his recovery. Since the Four is subject to the force of his powerful imagination, which is potent and ever at work in his psyche, his task is to learn to translate and skillfully use this creative force instead of being used by it.

The Four's inner wish is to create a unique and creative life (in early recovery this fantasy can border on the outrageous) such that he fancies himself to be an amazing author, and because he can infuse so much feeling into this fantasy, it can register as *yes, this is who I am meant to be. This is what I should be focusing on right now. This is the real me.* That is, it registers as a temporary, felt *fact*. His feet leave the ground of reality, and because his fantasy life is so strong, imagination easily gets mixed up with the facts of his current reality.

You will need to compassionately pull him from the clouds to *now*, as in, "Right now, Christopher, you are one week sober. You are doing the important work of learning how to be sober, how to ask for help and get the help you need. Of course you are impatient, especially because you feel the suffering and heartbreaking shame of not elevating and manifesting your gifts in the world. Great patience with ordinary efforts is the doorway to the fruition of these dreams. Taking the next unglamorous small step, this is preparation for the future you wish for. But first things first, my friend. You've got to learn to walk before you can fly."

When he is caught in the tidal wave of the current high or low, your job is to be the still waters of calmness he needs.

The Four will need much encouragement around this dynamic, as his imagination machine, in concert with his inner critic, may say, *This recovery work is beneath you. You're not a failure like the rest of these dudes. You should be succeeding famously. You'll be stuck here in this insignificant life if you don't get the hell away from it.* Here, the wound of *I'm ordinary and insignificant* is used by the Four's inner critic in service of self-sabotage. Helping the Four see this pattern will help him relax and slow down.

Add to this his tendency to inflate his emotional states. You will witness him going from an inspired state—*I know it! I can be a great artist! I can feel it!*—to utter disappointment: *I'm just crap. I'm nobody. There is nothing good about me. I am a failure.* When he is caught in the tidal wave of the current high or low, your job is to be the still waters of calmness he needs. That is, be the stillness his soul craves. Teach him, through your example, how to step back from the intensity of these feelings, and remind him that these high and lows signal to him that he is feeling hurt, ashamed, unloved, so *let's talk about this.* Your grounded presence will teach him how to ground himself.

SUGGESTIONS FOR THE FOUR

It will be incumbent upon you to provide supportive, helpful guidance to the Four as he navigates his way to health. Share the following suggestions, perhaps just one a week so as not to overwhelm him.

Begin to notice how you unconsciously confirm your feelings of being a rejected outsider.

The Four looks to his environment to confirm his feelings of being flawed and insignificant. The more self-absorbed and fearful he becomes, the more he takes everything personally, as a referendum of rejection on him. He believes his feelings of insignificance, longing, and emptiness come from outside himself.

Try these suggestions to help him recognize his feelings of being a rejected outsider:

- Remind the Four that within him is a pattern that shows itself through his imagination. That is, he begins to *imagine* he is different from everyone else and that because of this difference, he is rejected by others. You must help him see that he begins to believe this fantasy (which is not based on fact) and starts to separate himself, distance himself, and act *as if* this imagined rejection is real. Thus, his very actions create what he fears.
- You must help him see how his inner critic is always whispering this story to him, trying to get him to disconnect from the help he needs.
- Challenge him to consciously be aware when he is caught in the movie *Me, Myself, I: The Great Outsider*. Have him write down the circumstances and share them with you.

Begin to notice when you avoid important activities that feel ordinary and mundane.

When faced with the methodical actions he needs to take to create more inner stability and capacity to stay sober and clean, the Four will feel that these lifesaving actions are ordinary, boring, and not tailored to his unique needs.

He will need support from a kind sponsor, a counselor, or a coach to help him stick with these ordinary, repetitious actions that can save his life.

Try these suggestions to help him notice when he avoids important activities:

- Invite the Four to begin observing the flow of his emotional feeling states.

- Instruct him to notice what he does when he is engaged in an activity and a state of feeling ordinary flows through him. What does he do? Does he stop the activity because the feeling of "ordinary" is appalling to him? Does he stay with his activity while the feeling of *this is ordinary* is still there? Remind him that his efforts to continue his work efforts while in the midst of changing feeling states is in service to his not being ruled by his feeling of the moment, which is a trap door for the Four.

- Remind him that this feeling cloud of *this is ordinary and mundane* is like a blaring signal that says, *halt what you're doing, you're going in the wrong direction, you'll be stuck in this state of ordinariness for eternity*. This may stop him from completing work he cares about, sticking with relationships that are important to him, or continuing with his recovery efforts. As my mentor said, "It's just a feeling. Don't build a damn cathedral for it!"

- Remind him that if he pays attention to his daily flow of feelings, he will notice that these unwanted feeling states visit him randomly throughout the day, and that he would be wise to see them, smile at them, and continue what he is doing.

With compassion, notice how you set yourself up for being an elitist, a mysterious, gifted outsider whom no one can reach.

The Four positions himself atop an unreachable summit (or a deep and hidden cave) as a way to compensate for feeling like he doesn't belong and is a nobody. When he is caught in the suffering of the outsider, others must pass through the narrowest of doors to reach him while he inadvertently pushes away one of his special gifts and greatest joy: his ability to connect deeply with the hearts of others. The Four must learn to walk consciously with his shame, as if it were a welcome friend that he invites inside.

Try these suggestions to help him notice how he sets himself up for failure:

- Remind the Four that this is one of the sneaky patterns of his type wherein he begins to imagine himself as entitled, as in, *I shouldn't have to work as others have to in order to succeed.*

- Remind him that although this temporarily gives him a feeling of being elevated above the ordinary efforts of others, this attitude sets him up for not working diligently through ordinary, boring, must-do efforts to bring his creations to life.

- Remind him that he must bear the suffering of and aversion to his entitlement story and continue with ordinary efforts. Encourage him to let you know when he has stopped efforts that are important to his life due to getting tangled in the entitlement of *I shouldn't have to work like everyone else. I'm better than this! This is too ordinary for me!*

Learn to observe your envy.

The Four's inner critic constantly infuses him with thoughts of envy: "Hey, look *over there* at *that person.* He has all the good stuff that seems to make him really happy."

Try these suggestions to help him learn to recognize his envy:

- Suggest that he say to himself when he notices he's caught in the storm of envy, "I'm feeling envious because

Tom has succeeded where I have not. I'm thinking that he got the support that was denied me. I'm feeding this imaginary story with my envy and jealousy right now." He can learn to catch himself in the act and simply notice how this is making him feel. Encourage him to see the story, name the trance (*How I was ripped off by life*), and then consciously drop the story, sense his body, feel his breath, and return to the moment.

- Challenge him to turn his attention toward the actual admiration that underlies his envy. In fact, admiration is at the core of envy. Invite him to remember and feel this, and to notice that admiration opens up his heart, making him more able to feel and sense his creativity.

- The concrete antidote for envy is taking direct action on what he wishes to achieve. Remind him that his practical, creative actions will quiet the flames of his envy. He could ask himself, "What might I do now to move in the direction of what I love and care for today? How can I bring out what I am gifted at instead of engorging myself on the poison of envy?"

- Have him make a daily action plan and report his efforts to you weekly.

- Encourage him in the practice of *mudita* when caught in envy. Explain to him that mudita is the capacity to delight in the happiness and good fortune of others. It is the flip side to feeling compassion for the suffering of others and is a powerful practice for transcending envy and opening one's heart to delighting in the successes of others.

Use your artistic expression as a meditation to observe your inner demons and to disidentify with them.

The Four might set an artistic goal and decide to work on his chosen art for an hour a day; then he can watch the flood of feelings and thoughts that coax him to stop engaging in his artistic efforts. He may experience waves of feelings of *I'm nobody; this is boring;* and *this isn't what I really want to do. I'll never succeed. This will take too long. No one will like my work.*

As he disciplines himself and refuses to be distracted by his changing feelings or the voice of his inner critic, he will see that these cycles of emotional and mental distraction rise and fall over and over again, and will begin to quiet as he sticks with his work. As he stays focused in his discipline, he will slowly develop an *observing witness* that can see the emotional storms and not buy into them.

Try these suggestions to help him develop his artistic expression as a form of meditation:

- Instruct him to make an aim to show up for his given creative project, such as thirty to sixty minutes in the morning he will sit at his computer to write. Ask him to notice all the thoughts and feelings that arise and meet him as he makes his effort. He must not leave the playing field of his commitment—writing, painting—even though the chant of *You're insignificant and wasting your time* may echo through him, or feelings of hopelessness might arise in his heart.

- Instruct him to notice these phenomena and then name them; for example, *there's the insignificance, there's the movie that I'll never be as good as the artist I admire, there's the feeling of hopelessness,* then stick with his creative effort. Encourage him to continue to work in the midst of the storm of feelings and thoughts.

- Remind him that this storm of thoughts and feelings will pass, and through his efforts he will develop the necessary stamina and fortitude to take healthy actions regardless of his passing moods or thoughts. Remind him that when he is swept up in a cloud of feelings or self-criticism, bringing his attention down and into his body and breath will anchor him in the moment and help him continue his efforts.

A MESSAGE TO THE FOUR

Share this message with the Four in recovery:

You of all the types are most susceptible to giving up. Don't give up. In your darkest hour, which is the darkest of the dark, there can be resurrection and joy. You won't believe this until it happens, but if you keep reaching out for help, doing what is in your hands to do, you will be the phoenix resurrected from the flames, and you will be a great gift of redemption for others. This is fact. Just don't give up—not for long, anyway.

Yes, you will go through dark passages. Just be careful of the tempting thoughts that arise like snakes in your consciousness, hissing, *You are all alone. No one suffers as bad as you. No one has been wounded as badly as you. No one is so misunderstood. It is hopeless and forever broken.*

The inner critic voice lies every time. Consider this: at this given moment, one in nine people walking the earth is a Type Four. There are millions like you, hardwired with the same psychological predispositions. Many have gotten the help they need and resurrected from the bondage of these inherited patterns. You, too, can resurrect. One day at a time. The gifts you receive will be equal to if not more than the suffering you transcend. Stick with it.

CHAPTER 8

Type Five—
The Kind Wizard

If we truly use the Enneagram to see through our beliefs
about ourselves we begin to feel more grounded
and confident, more kind and compassionate,
and more clear and discerning. Our centers are
coming online, and we are more able to live
the truths we have come to understand.

—RUSS HUDSON

The Type Five, known as the investigator, the observer, the gentle wizard, is endowed with razor-sharp objectivity, the x-ray vision to see beyond the surface of things, an incisive and laser-like passion to find the truth in reality while turning over every stone. On good days, he possesses a quirky, counterintuitive, and hilarious sense of humor (enter *The Far Side* author Gary Larson or Tim Burton, creator of *The Nightmare Before Christmas*). Able to stare the reality of impermanence eyeball to eyeball, to hold hands with death and horror (Stephen King, the horror master extraordinaire), while finding unexpected redemptive capacity in learning to quiet his electrified mind (see *Stillness Speaks* by Eckhart Tolle), he creates new niches for fellow Fives to inhabit (welcome the radical explosion of nanotechnology, computers, cyberspace, the wireless world).

At his best, the Five is deeply kind and compassionate. When addiction takes over, all these capacities turn to the opposite, and he becoming a remote alien on the planet, a nihilistic pessimist, a doomsayer and force of destruction to himself and others. His mind becomes a hallucination of horror.

THE INTERNAL PLAYING FIELD OF THE FIVE

When the Five is in addiction, his internal playing field becomes unbalanced, driving down into his unhealthy patterns. The following is a brief overview of the Five's internal playing field.

Deep wound/relapse pattern: The deep wound of the Type Five is that of feeling stupid and lost in the ignorance of the world, of having no map to navigate reality, and no niche or place in the world. He feels rejected by the world, as though he has arrived on the wrong planet. He is on his own.

Key commandment: The Five's key commandment is that he must be an expert in some area of intelligence or else he is not lovable, protected, or wanted. He must not need anything except time and room to study. He trusts nothing but his own intelligence.

Deep wish: The Five's deep wish is to feel useful and capable, to find a niche. He wishes to utilize his wisdom in service of humanity, and to inspire curiosity and intelligence in others.

How he sees himself: The Five sees himself as innovative, perceptive, observant, curious, objective, whimsical, objective, and more intelligent and quirkier than others.

At level 4 and below: When the Five is at the lower levels, he falls prey to the emotional habit of avarice, in which he avoids emotional contact with people because it drains him and scares him. Overwhelmed by his intense sensitivity, he vacates his heart and his body. Add to this his mental habit of retention, in which he tries to feel strong by accumulating, studying, and memorizing what he studies, which drives him to disengage from reality, to go into his head to live. He hides out in his analyzing mind, habitually going over what he has studied and remembered to feel strong.

Inner critic: The Five's inner critic tells him he is safe and worthwhile only when he is brilliant and can master something. As a result, he impulsively studies and accumulates more and more knowledge. He can never learn enough, however, because knowledge is not the source of his real strength.

At his best: The Five is at his best when he is generous with his knowledge and inspired to understand reality, and what is real and true about it. He seeks the truth, loves the truth, and can inspire others to do the same. He merges his capacity to love with his wisdom. He engages people and brings his gifts to the world.

THE HEALTHY FIVE

The healthy Five is known for his capacity to see through the vast maze and complexity of the moment, be it looking into the open expanse of the universe, the remarkable complexity of the cell, or navigating the dark and unseen territory of the human psyche and providing clarity and understanding. He shines a brilliant light of illumination that serves to both guide the navigation of these spaces and make sense of the vast intelligence that is reliably interfused in each speck of life.

As his best the Five is quirky and funny, realizing the absurdities individuals focus on in the face of the real majesty of life. He is engaging, connected with others, heart gentle and open, mind expansive with invention and curiosity. He is a light of courage, inspiration, and hope, shining a huge light of gratitude from the center of his being.

He joyfully gives away his wisdom and has a tender, self-effacing capacity when he talks about what he calls his weirdness and difficulty in relating to "the human beings." Aware that he fits no particular conventional role, he is at peace with this when healthy, and a welcome mat for others to be different. Here, his tenderness and kindness show through.

Case Study: Terry

Terry, a Type Five investigator extraordinaire, walks through the back door of the 8 a.m. Alcoholics Anonymous meeting, a gangly softness to his movements. With a well-navigated precision to each awkward step, he quietly moves through the ragtag Oregon crowd—a blend of all ages, genders, and backgrounds, from street drunk to scientist to lawyer—thrown together on this precious sobriety life raft. He inhabits his body ever so lightly, as if it is made of soft, transparent paper and he a puppet master guiding it along, helping it walk.

Terry doesn't have the testosterone hardwiring of Big Fred, the boisterous, hearty Eight who moves and speaks with bravado and punch and brassiness, never mincing his words (Fred's short version of the Serenity Prayer: fuck it!). Terry is not a florid emotional Four like Frank, who often shares tender and heartrending depth, real-life emotions oozing from his soul. No, Terry's energy is hard to describe—neither strongly male nor female, but somewhere between water and wind and hidden lightning.

As he approaches his seat, his gaze emits an elfin-like sense of humor and joy. He appreciates the weirdness and incongruent beauty of this gathering of serendipitously linked basement dwellers. Mixed with his offbeat joy is the curious aura of *I'm not really here, I'm posing as a quiet observer of reality*, which surrounds him like he is standing behind a thinly veiled curtain, watching the whole show. Truth is, he is examining each moment with an intense, passionate awareness. Others might catch it in his eyes, which are softly tucked back in the contours of his bony, gentle face, his piercing curiosity looking for what he calls the "illumination" behind what he observes—the prana—the life force invigorating all manifestations. In Type Five fashion he declares, with a smile as curious as a cat, that his higher power is, of course, "the Periodic Table." This, he says, is the god of his understanding.

Because he is keenly aware of the incredible miracle of his existence, Terry does not call attention to himself, does not name himself as a respected scientist, but is humbly right-sized. He quietly absorbs the pleasure of connecting with "his" people, appreciating their quirks and idiosyncrasies, cheerily sensing the invisible life force that infuses the room. All of it is taken in. Nothing is missed. Comfortable as a gnome on a barstool hanging out in the oceanic matrix of his mind, he drinks in his perceptions like the sweetest wine, quietly contemplating the unfolding possibilities.

Terry's passion is examining the process of life and death in plants and fungi at micro levels; articulating the nuances of gamma rays or black holes; "seeing" the magical network of intelligence that links earth, plant, air, water, wind, insect, animal into a living thread of life. He meditates on ever-growing storehouses of illuminated wisdom, watching stunning film clips of complex perceptions that flow across his mind screen. It's like he has an IMAX movie continually turned on inside him; it is the lens out of which he observes and engages reality, and yet he is present enough to include others in the movie. Wordlessly, he invites them into his meditation of awe, to feel the intelligent lightness and precision with which he touches the moment, and the deepening wisdom he cultivates with his perceptive acumen. His quirkiness is so sweet, people just want to hug him. And many do.

When Terry was mired in his addiction, no one hugged him. He merged with his computer screen and his electrifying imagination, and became a skilled producer of any hallucinogen that could be purchased. He is now twenty-five years sober, and when he speaks of his sobriety at an AA meeting he becomes like the wizard Gandalf in *The Lord of the Rings*, arising with his staff, striking the ground in front of the Balrog in the Mines of Moria, and proclaiming, "You shall not pass!" Tangibly, the strength and power of his commitment to sobriety penetrate the room. And then, seconds later, he has become crazy, down-home hilarious, poking fun at his absurdities. "I'm very odd, you know. Well, you can ask my wife, she will tell you!" He grins, blue eyes glimmering with joy. "I could hole up in my office for days; in fact, I love isolation. I've got to remember to come out of hiding because I could stay there forever, hypothesizing and testing my theories, studying the cosmos in microscopic detail. And before sobriety, concocting ever more powerful addictive substances! Anyhow, there's no end to how I can entertain myself with speculating and theorizing. Sometimes I get afraid to come out. You know, if a car cuts me off in traffic, I'm not sure whether I should call suicide prevention or shoot myself. As I said, I'm not that well yet."

Laughter peals through the room, and Terry's eyes widen as he continues. "Frankly, I'd much prefer to stay at home and read a book than to come to this meeting. But there's this thing called alcoholism that I must attend to. Okay, enough about me and my idiosyncrasies. Let's hear from the rest of you!" Welcome to the precious soul of the Five.

Terry is a living example of a healthy Five. He appreciates the astounding mystery and complexity of life while holding the torch of humility and compassion. Tender, whimsical, sending the steady message of *you can do this*, fighting off the urge to isolate himself (even in the meeting), and courageously letting himself be touched by the folks in the room. From time to time, tears fill his eyes as he expresses the love he feels for everyone. "I love you all," he humbly says. His heart is not dry, not lost or hidden in the internal complexities of his mind.

Now let's take a look at the journey of the Type Five.

THE FIVE IN ADDICTION

When the addicted Five is at level 6 or 7, he is stuck on one dark note: there is danger everywhere, and nothing can be trusted. (Welcome to the horrorscapes of Type Five author Stephen King. At any moment, anything can turn alien and kill you.) The Five in addiction feels incapable of dealing with anything; it all seems so pointless. His brilliant perceptiveness is lost in the vast, negative universe of cynicism and withdrawal. The Five falls prey to his worst fears of being helpless, useless, and incapable, submerged in a terrifying inner world. He thinks, *Why try? What's the point, anyway? I'm surrounded by idiots hell-bent on destroying the earth, so why get sober?* He enters addiction recovery entranced in these dark thoughts. (Is it any wonder that he is withdrawn?)

The Five arrives in addiction recovery disconnected from his inherent gifts. He has also lost contact with his ability to savor the amazing complexity of life, his innate gift of joyous curiosity now leveled to wasteful imagination and off-the-wall, fearful speculations. His niche as a true journeyer into vast and unknown territories has been stripped to his digging alone, out of sync with humanity, and lost in the sea of his secretive mind. He imagines dark conspiracies everywhere.

Disconnected from reality, from his heart and his body, he has disappeared into the far crevices of his mental world, his heart and soul like dry leaves, shriveled and juiceless. His capacities have reversed themselves—his awake, clear-minded optimism turned to nihilism; his penetrating insights turned to contentious doomsaying or insane theorizing; his innate objectivity turned to intellectual arrogance, rigidity, and eccentricity. At his worst, his visionary capacity has morphed into antagonistic pessimism and self-indulgent hatred of all living things. His life feels utterly meaningless. As one Five said, "At these levels, people become concepts, not living beings."

The Five in addiction is trapped in the ever-narrowing box of fear-filled imagination hell. He uses substances to both escape his emotional suffering and indulge and exacerbate his fear-driven, intensity-fueled mind with dark images of death and doom. Weirdly, he can become addicted to the intensity of fearful, horrific speculations. Once able to make heartfelt contact with other human beings, he has now become an alien repelled by human contact and contact with himself. Bombarded by frenzied, bizarre ideas, conspiracy theories start to take root in his soul. Everything is filled with sinister motivation.

Case Study: Terry

Terry put it this way: "I spent the five years prior to coming into recovery holed up in one room, drugging and drinking. I never went out. Hey, give me another drug-inspired psychotic state, give me more of that! I rarely ate. I was locked in, crazed, captured in my inner world. If my body wasn't on the verge of dying, I'd still be there, taking hallucinogens, drinking, and spasmodically hypothesizing on my psychotic imagery. It is pure luck that I made it out alive.

"When I came to my first AA meeting, I didn't think I had a drinking or drug problem. I just saw that you all were sober, so I kept it simple and followed the program. Thank God. I had no idea how lost in the machinations of my drug-fueled imagination I was, or that indulging in fantastical, bizarre imagery had become my pleasure-seeking escape from reality. I completely dissolved into the back chambers of my mind, where no one could touch me.

"Only when I got very sick did I notice my body dying. It was like I was watching a specimen of myself on a lab slide and thinking, *look at him, he's dying*. For fifteen years there were the voices in my head constantly instructing me to do this or that. That's how disconnected I was. If friends hadn't intervened when they did, they would have found me on the floor, a dried-up twig, frozen in place by my last hallucination."

THE FIRST TWELVE WEEKS IN TREATMENT

When the beloved Five arrives in residential treatment he immediately is confronted with his aversion to making contact with his fellow human beings. If he could receive treatment by staying isolated in his room doing group therapy via Skype, Zoom, or Facetime, or getting sober by tracking through the magnificent complexity of a *Halo 4*, he would see it as a hopeful beginning. But instead, he is thrown into a men's treatment center, forced to sit side by side with others to talk about his feelings—the last thing he wants to be doing.

> The Five, certain of being rejected, is safe and fortified in the spaceship of his mind, watching for intruders while trying to scare them away with aggressive silence or retreat.

He is not one to easily share his emotions and inner truths with others, especially strangers. If he shares too much, he fears he may vanish and disappear into the vortex of stupidity that surrounds him. Giving away trade secrets that make him vulnerable to the meanness and ignorance of others means any fool can enter his life and harm him. Unbeknownst to many, he is deeply sensitive, acutely aware, and easily hurt. His need for emotional support is only faintly registered on his radar screen.

The Five, certain of being rejected, is safe and fortified in the spaceship of his mind, watching for intruders while trying to scare them away with aggressive silence or retreat. Already self-rejecting, the Five expects rejection from others. But be certain of this: he is not as cynical and remote and anti-human as he appears, not by a long shot. If you could see him when he is feeling safe and cared for, you would see a humorous, sensitive, caring, intelligent, curious individual like Terry, who is comfortable in his own skin and more than glad to share his wisdom to improve your life.

As unavailable or intellectually superior the Five may appear, it is only a reflection of just how insubstantial and terrified he feels. He doesn't need the others in the group to confront him, scold him, judge him, coerce him, convince him, or attempt to pry him open. What he needs is an invitation to simply be so that he can settle and realize no one is going to do a full-scale assault on his soul, which would send him out the door. (I have seen many Fives hightail it after an overzealous counselor delivered poorly attuned tough love.)

Case Study: Walter

Walter is a sweet, withdrawn, lanky Five who came into treatment, a street survivor for years in Portland, Oregon. He was like a small animal tucked tightly between two rocks, scrunched down as small as he was able, his eyes peering from the darkness. Finding words was achingly painful for him, his compulsion to retreat quickly so instinctive to his survival. And yet, when he spoke, he revealed a vastly intelligent, shockingly funny, kind, and deeply perceptive human being who was certain beyond all belief that if he came out of hiding, he would be killed. Better to risk this on the street, sleeping in back alleyways. This fear jettisoned him out of rehab and into the streets over and over again, a hobo wandering, traveling light as a feather, a paperback tucked into his back pocket.

He says, "When I arrived in treatment I was people-phobic, so to attempt to speak to anyone took great effort. No one felt safe to me. I was filled with cynicism. I thought everyone was like happy sheep conforming to the latest politically correct notion. Never mind that I had been a sheep following every delusion that passed through me. I surely didn't want or need any contact with them, and I was sure they didn't want anything to do with me. But there I was, in a treatment center because I could not take care of myself.

"The delusions I fed on, which I mistook for superior intelligence and razor-sharp analytical skills, were unable to reverse my fall into addiction and utter despair. This was my first wake-up call: my analyzing mind didn't have all the answers, especially the important ones. I would relearn this lesson a thousand times. I was killing myself, and I needed help. Stuck in hopelessness, I felt that nothing mattered; everything was all bullshit. Never mind the paranoid voice in my head talking to me loudly, reinforcing this inner mess. I had no hope and was raging at the stupidity around me. My cynicism protected my vulnerability. If I didn't need you, you couldn't hurt me. My nihilism numbed out my deeper disappointment: that I didn't know how to participate in life, didn't know where I belonged, couldn't feel love, and felt like an outcast."

THE FIVE'S PROTECTIVE MECHANISM IN EARLY RECOVERY

The Five is an iconoclastic, intelligent, perceptive, sensitive soul (I'm reminded of sweet-hearted, quirky-funny, vastly intelligent Eckhart Tolle, author of *The Power of Now* and *Toward a New Earth*). Easily addicted to his intense thinking and conceptualizing capacity, he is driven to deep inquiry, seeking knowledge, clarity, and understanding. (See the Werner Herzog documentary *Encounters at the End of the World*, which beautifully demonstrates the brilliance, humor, intelligence, and elfin wisdom of a group of Type Fives living at the South Pole. trying to save humanity, and calmly realizing it's too late.)

The Five thinks about the experiences he is having instead of inhabiting and feeling them.

When the Five arrives in recovery his mental circuits are heated up and in overdrive. As one Five said, "I learned to avoid my feelings by escaping into my intense thoughts. I began to feel that who I was, *was* my intense thoughts. This became my identity, what felt like me. My heart and body seemed like they were located on a distant planet. And my thinking center was so well furnished and tantalizing, why would I want to enter drab human reality?"

The Five *thinks about* the experiences he is having instead of inhabiting and feeling them. He becomes a distant observer of reality and builds himself an inner tree fort, where he hangs out, studies his information library, and analyzes life from a distance. Having hightailed it into his analyzing mind, everything below the neck becomes alien territory. (This is called the "schizoid split.") As one Five says, "I often feel like my body is a taxicab for my head, something to transport me to my next information source. My task is to remember to feed it and give it water or else it won't work so well."

The Five's tool of protection is his probing, razor-sharp mind, which he can use to fend off others (or confuse them into stark silence) to assure that they will not reach in and touch the live wire of his helplessness, incapability, or self-rejection. He's smarter than you, more observant than you (even though he misses almost everything positive in early recovery and is emotion-blind) and feels he doesn't need you. Don't even try to sneak up on him. He sees you coming miles away. And underneath all of this, he is scared and shivering.

The Five sits at an Alcoholics Anonymous meeting as though he is wearing an invisible sign that says, "Don't talk to me. Stay away. No one is home. You are not welcome. Idiots need not apply. Contact with you could kill me. Don't try to get close to me because I know you'll reject me, drain me, and banish me to the outskirts of the cosmos. I will go there on my own, thank you. I don't need you. Needing you puts me in your crosshairs. No thank you!"

Ever aware of how small and unprotected he feels, the Five compensates for this by disengaging from his feelings and body, and heads due north into his mind, his inner library. He thinks to himself, *It feels so strange and scary to be here among these crazy people; best to simply vacate my body and my feelings so I don't feel how dreadful and afraid I really feel.* He has learned to shut off his need for people as a form of protection from suffering. He is comforted by not needing anyone or anything. Needing spells sure catastrophe. This is what he must unlearn. He is saying, "Help me, but don't let me know you're helping me because if I spot it, it will trigger my feelings of uselessness and incompetence, and I'll want to run. I'll push your help away."

You get the picture. He is suffering and in need of genuine understanding and compassion. And yet, receiving compassion intrudes on his script that he must be masterful and capable (or so says his inner critic: *I must be the independent and self-sufficient expert or else I am nothing*) before he is okay to come out and be supported. It's a delusionary trance that drives him into isolation. He is supposed to have the answers ahead of time, and yet his answers have failed him. AA members directly confront this when they say to him, "Your best thinking got you here. Better let us help you. We may sound like baboons from time to time, but we possess a rock-solid truth that can get you sober. In time you can eventually put your mind to good use, but for now, let us do a little thinking for you." Not easy words for the Five to listen to.

All this said, if the Five becomes aware of these particular tendencies, a time will come when he must choose to risk and step out, to trust another human being with his vulnerability. Give him space and time, and he will make the journey home, where, patiently waiting for him, are his deepest gifts: his perceptiveness, intelligence, curiosity, and his kind heart.

CORE RELAPSE PATTERN

Throughout his recovery from addiction, the Five will confront one overriding pattern: his habit of retreating into his analytical mind when emotions begin to touch him, when he begins to experience intimacy with another, when he begins to allow himself to have a felt sense of his body, when he dares to allow you to look inside him. Even fifteen years into recovery, as he has grown and made progress with these issues, he will be triggered to go deeper.

That's the trick of your inner critic, to wipe away awareness of your growth. He's a trickster, for certain.

His inner critic trance will arise like an evil sorceress each time, joyful to still be a part of his journey. Suddenly life, himself, and others will look like chaos, stupidity, and madness as the inner critic licks his lips and says, *Told you so. This will never end well for you.* If the Five is surrounded by wise men and women who know the complexity of the inner journey home, they will say, "Don't sweat it, dude. Chill. When your inner critic acts up, it just means you are on to something good. This too will pass as you learn more skills for navigating your patterns. No need to relapse, even though at these difficult junctures you will feel as though you've made no progress. That's the trick of your inner critic, to wipe away awareness of your growth. He's a trickster, for certain."

TRANSFORMATION IN RECOVERY

With long-term recovery, the Five will learn to intimately sense his retreat patterns: in his body as it numbs; in his heart, which goes dry in response to fear; in his mind, which starts to hyper-analyze his experience instead of being in it. He will notice his aversion to connect with people, and his tendency to withdraw. People will suddenly become objects on his observational screen, insects to examine and study and stay away from, and he himself, a disembodied investigator.

With skillful awareness, he will ask for help. He will move toward healthy people, inch by inch, instead of retreating. He won't get hooked on the stream of cynicism, hopelessness, and fear that temporarily occupies his intense stream of thoughts and impressions. He won't get taken by his addiction while retreating into his head center. He will rest in his heart and body. If not, his addiction will wrap its arms around him one more time—at five, ten, twenty years sober—masquerading as a comforting lover. Until he is *gulp* eaten by the vampire and re-engages his addictive patterns, eating compulsively, spending compulsively, drinking compulsively, reading compulsively, and isolating compulsively.

Armed with spiritual rationalizations that would make the angels squirm, the Five may not see that he has been captured again in smart-sounding justifications. The good news is that the longer he works a program of recovery, the greater resources he will have at his disposal to dismantle these patterns and to come back to the simplicity of the moment, where his capacity to connect with others and share his gifts exist—exactly what he got sober for.

HELPING THE FIVE

The Five in early recovery is often distant and secretive. He does not feel welcome and is deeply suspicious of the world he inhabits. Is he safe? Can he trust anyone? Will he be overwhelmed? His strategy is to analyze everything that he encounters and to distance himself from contact with you. Don't take it personally. Underneath the intense gaze of the Five is a sensitive soul who feels that, at any moment, too much contact with you could drain him and put him completely at your mercy. He has great doubt that you want anything to do with him. Approach him with curiosity, kindness and calmness. In his time, when he sees that it's safe, he will come out and share his many gifts. Don't think for a second that he isn't paying attention; he is.

The Five needs time and space to involve himself in recovery at his own pace.

In early recovery, the Five needs a paradigm that works for him. You can let him know how the twelve steps worked for you (or whatever system of recovery he is working with). Educate him about the dynamics of addiction, its biology, and psychology; remember, he loves knowledge. Remind him that he has the freedom to follow these sacred recovery dictates: *Take what you need and leave the rest. You have freedom to choose what works for you. This isn't a dogma machine that produces recovery robots, it's a place to discover real freedom through working your program of recovery. Find out what works for you.*

The Five doesn't need you to catalog and point out his alcohol or drug-addicted behaviors and deficiencies because he is one of the few types who, as he descends into deeper levels of crazy behaviors, can still see his actions all too vividly. Where other types shut down this perceptive ability, the Five can't (much like his cousin, the Four). Welcome him just as he is, with his cynicism and nihilism and whatever distortion works as his protective suit of armor.

The Five needs time and space to involve himself in recovery at his own pace. Pressure him and he will dig his heels in. Try to convince or coerce him and he will come up with skillful counter-arguments that will shake the roots of your faith. Give him room to challenge every assumption and belief about the twelve steps (or any system of transformation) and invite him to see if this will work for him. *Invitation is the key.*

Notice and appreciate his intelligent perception, and let him know you respect and have no war with his brilliance (even if it is slightly out of kilter at this point, or even completely off the rails). He will begin to investigate his opportunity to get sober without intellectual resistance, fueled by fear, whirring at full tilt. If your support creates room for the Five to discover for himself what truly is the antidote to his addiction, you will open the door for a real solution to arise.

Keep his options open: recovery is not a one-way street to Alcoholics Anonymous. Many get sober on Smart Recovery, Zen Recovery, a religious path, a church denomination, yoga, fitness, harm reduction, or therapy, to name a few. Everyone is different.

Drop any position you are inclined to take that suggests you know what is good for him (you don't), even though your training as an addiction therapist or recovering person might have fed you the illusion that you know what is right for others. As the twelve steps wisely suggest, be a force of attraction, not promotion. Your humble recognition that he, with the higher power of his understanding (perhaps it's the god of the Periodic Table of Elements), is the true source for discovering his path home, and will allow him to feel safe, welcomed, and respected. Your job is to point him toward his true gifts. Don't be put off by his quirks, his tendency to disappear into the folds of his mind or go into deep silence when he is afraid.

SUGGESTIONS FOR THE FIVE

It will be incumbent upon you to provide supportive, helpful guidance to the Five as he navigates his way to health. Share the following suggestions, perhaps just one a week so as not to scatter his attention and efforts.

Notice when you have fallen into the role of the expert.

As the expert, the Five teaches, conducts, shares knowledge, stays emotionally distant, and others listen. It is so easy to make this the face that he shows to the world, the one who knows stuff, who holds court, the information source. His intellectual wizardry can easily become his go-to card, his default setting for self-protection when confronted with a life situation he doesn't know how to navigate. Being brilliant and wise is not the problem; the problem is when he feels he must have intellectual mastery to feel he deserves kindness.

He must learn to notice his fear of rejection, to lean into the discomfort, to breathe and sense his body.

Try these suggestions to help him recognize when he falls into the role of the expert:

- When he discovers himself hidden behind his expertise, encourage the Five to bring his attention back to his heart. You will need to alert him to this habit as he likely will not notice when he falls into expert/teacher/ lecturer mode. Gently stop him and say, "I invite you to notice for a moment that you appear to be captured in an information fog and that you are downloading info so quickly that you don't notice my eyes have glazed over. Just notice and take this moment in. Take a breath to notice the momentum of your ideas and how they have taken you away from being present. Sense into your heart. Return to this moment. Breathe. Notice what you were feeling?"

Notice when you retreat into your mind and study humans as though they are objects under a microscope.

Faster than the Five can blink, he retreats into his head. When he begins to sense his feelings (sadness, fear, grief, anger, love), he immediately vacates his body and heart and flies to the castle of his mind, where his storehouse of knowledge brings him temporary security. He objectifies others, not sensing their feelings or behaviors with compassion.

He must learn to notice his inner critic, which arises and whispers, *If you allow yourself to sense your feelings, you will be turned into dust.*

Try these suggestions to help him recognize when he retreats into his mind and to help him feel his heart instead:

- Instruct him to keep track for one week of when his fear, hurt, shame, or anger feelings get triggered. Each time the chosen feeling gets triggered, instruct him to take a moment to sense it in his body and then log it in a small journal. Review it at the end of the day. Specifically, ask him the inner critic messages he heard or felt when he began to experience his feelings. Invite him to just notice these patterns without trying to change anything, understanding that the observation of one's patterns is what destroys their hypnotic power to entrance.
- Instruct him to share what he discovers with you, his counselor, or his coach.

Notice the ways in which you resist support.

The last thing the Five wants to experience is the feeling that he doesn't have expertise or answers, that he is incapable and judged as stupid or helpless. His personality is wired to avoid these feelings, so naturally, when he needs support and help from others, everything inside him rebels: *I should call my sponsor, but no, I think I can figure this out on my own.* What he lacks is emotional intelligence.

The Five rationalizes this resistance with thoughts of, *They can't help me. I feel stupid for needing help, so I won't ask. I am smart enough to figure this out. If I let them see my vulnerability and need, they will surely reject me. Besides, they don't really like or care about me. And most likely, I'm smarter than they are!*

Try these suggestions to help him receive your support:

- Keep bringing him back to his body and heart when he talks about emotion-filled moments in his life. Invite him to be aware of how quickly he vacates his feelings and begins to analyze them instead.
- Notice a moment when his feelings are probably being activated; for instance, his dad just died of alcoholism and he is reporting this to you as if it were a distant event. Instruct him to take a second to breathe into his body and sense his heart. Then say, "I can imagine the sorrow you must be feeling at the loss of your dad. Tell me, what are you feeling about him? I invite you to sense your heart as you speak about him, and to sense your feet on the floor. Talk a little slower and tell me about your life with your dad and the moments that touched you. See if you can stick with the vulnerable emotions that arise in you. Give them room to just be there."
- Demonstrate to him what healthy support looks like through your empathy and kindness.

Notice your rationalizations for staying separate from others.

The Five can entertain himself endlessly with his fascination of facts and knowledge. He is never bored in his mind. His compulsion is to isolate himself to acquire knowledge. Under the constant fear of feeling depleted, stupid, or powerless, and feeling unskilled at managing emotional connections with others, he builds upon what he does have: knowledge.

Try these suggestions to help him overcome these rationalizations and to begin to find his way out of this habit:

- Encourage him to take one small step toward interaction with people, to be awkward in spite of what his inner critic screams at him. *This is stupid. You should be home learning new information. There's nothing to gain by bearing with your discomfort around humans.* As he makes positive contact with people and discovers he is quite likable, he will begin to feel an internal sense of strength.

- Encourage him, for example, to approach someone at the end of an AA meeting who shared and thank them for their offering. Or he can become a greeter at a meeting, saying hello to each person as they arrive.

- Suggest that he check in with whatever group he uses for recovery and attempt to share his feelings and perceptions on a regular basis. Practice works.

- Encourage him to listen to Eckhart Tolle, a Type Five teacher who is a profound guide to developing embodied presence. (See Resources for book suggestions.)

Learn to express and feel your feelings.

When the Five shuts down his feelings long enough, when he shuts down his vulnerability to hurt, despair, and loneliness, it will soon make perfect sense to use addictive substances. When his heart shuts down, he does not experience the full joy of his curiosity, the beauty of his sensitive and loving heart, the awe and appreciation of this magnificent world and his capacity to understand it. Instead, he is mired in familiar, arid despair and scorn. His elfin humor, his great sense of childlike curiosity that delights him, that ponders the great mystery of existence, will dry and wither. Everything will lose meaning.

Try these suggestions to help him begin to express his feelings:

- Instruct him as follows: "When someone around you is expressing feelings (at a recovery meeting or counseling group), attempt to find the feeling in *your* body. Check in with your heart."
- Or this: "When someone is expressing sorrow or shame, try to imagine what it would be like to go through what they are describing. Imagine what it must be like inside them."
- And this: "When you notice you are feeling something, practice saying it out loud, in the moment: *I'm feeling scared right now, I'm feeling unprotected right now, I'm feeling useless right now.*"

Notice your intellectual aggression.

A Five will often report that when he is caught in fear, he uses intellectual aggression as a protective tool. When he is scared or feels rejected, he can eviscerate people with his intelligence, delivering the message that they are so stupid and inept that they might as well give up and shoot themselves. Caught in his patterns of fear or rejection, he can bully others with his intelligence.

Try these suggestions to help him interrupt this aggression:

- Encourage him to sense his heart when he notices himself cynically attacking others in his mind (or out loud). Ask him, *What's behind the cynical attack? Fear of rejection, of not being liked?*
- Encourage him to make regular efforts to find out how his communications are touching others. Do they feel stupid? Attacked? Inferior? Challenge him to invite trusted others to give him feedback when they feel attacked, inferior, incompetent, or stupid due to his unconscious communications.
- Help him explore the idea that when he feels rejected and not wanted, or is filled with the despair that he will never have a place in the world, he draws his intellectual guns to protect himself instead of expressing his vulnerability. Encourage him to begin to sincerely see and feel this pattern, to bring compassion to himself, and to eventually learn to resist the pattern.

A MESSAGE TO THE FIVE

Share this message with the Five in recovery:

You, dear Five, can learn to stay sober and clean. It means first admitting that you don't understand the process of recovery, have a difficult time comprehending emotional intelligence, and that support from others will not only help you but will make you feel really good in the long run. You will discover that there are many trustable human beings who are kind, considerate, and smart. When that urge to bolt and leave the playing field of recovery arises—because it will—leave only for a short while, and come back as soon as you can. Gently step into your discomfort with talking about feelings, into your insecurity with being with the crazy humans, and hang in there long enough to let the miracle land inside you. We need you, we need your gift of intelligence and creativity, and we need your kind and wise heart.

CHAPTER 9

Type Six—
The Courageous
Pathfinder

It matters not who you love, where you love,
why you love, when you love, or how you love.
It matters only that you love.

—JOHN LENNON

The Type Six, known as the loyalist, the courageous pathfinder, the trouble shooter, often embodies paradoxical qualities. At his best he is David taking on Goliath, or Michael Moore taking on corporations, gun owners, a gluttonous American medical establishment, or Samwise Gamgee carrying Frodo to the Fires of Mordor while outwitting the Balrog in the mines of Moria. The irony is that the Type Six takes on such courageous pursuits in the face of feeling terrible fear, anxiety, and hugely graphic catastrophized outcomes. Doom all around him, he steps forward into the fray. Equipped also with the capacity to endear and befriend even the bad guys and vanity-driven narcissists, he is capable of helping people become right-sized and less full of themselves, becoming, in fact, willing participants in a team effort.

THE INTERNAL PLAYING FIELD OF THE SIX

When the Six is in addiction, his internal playing field becomes unbalanced, driving him down to his negative, defensive type patterns. His capacity to unite and inspire team effort is destroyed by his anxious mistrust of self and others, and he is unable to settle and ground himself. The following is a brief overview of the Six's internal playing field.

Deep wound/relapse pattern: The deep wound the Six experiences is that of being uncertain, unprotected, and unsafe. He feels that there is nothing he can count on, within or without, and that catastrophe could arise at any moment. He lives "on guard."

Key commandment: The key commandment for the Six is that he must be absolutely sure of his next step, he must check every possible way in which things could go wrong, and he must not disappoint those who rely on him.

Deep wish: The deep wish of the Six is to experience his clarity, his inner wisdom, his unified connection with those he travels with. He wishes to feel his confidence and intuitive clarity, and to serve others as a guide and team player.

How he sees himself: The Six sees himself as responsible, reliable, determined, loyal to the bone, trustworthy, and supportive of others.

At level 4 and below: When the Six falls to level 4 and below, he falls prey to the emotional habit of anxiety, in which he feels everything could go wrong. Fear becomes his constant companion and drives him to be hypervigilant, anticipating worst-case scenarios. His mental habit is habitual worry, in which he worries if he has made the right decision, if his allies are mad at him, and if he has failed to see an unforeseen outcome. He *trusts* worry.

Inner critic: The Six's inner critic tells him he is okay if he knows what is expected of him and if he is responsible and successful in implementing these expectations.

At his best: At his best the Six is responsible, loyal to those he serves, an awesome team player, and guided by his powerful intuition, and brave and wise in the face of danger. He creates a path of safety for others.

THE HEALTHY SIX

In the company of a healthy Six, one can witness a valiant hero who embodies bravery; who has an earnest, reverent, endearing, down-to-earth sincerity; a capacity to deeply touch others with his emotional honesty; and a determined fearlessness to face and call others to truth and responsibility. He is intensely devoted to loved ones and willing to risk his safety and comfort in service of the individuals and people he is committed to. He is gifted with an exquisite intuitive sensitivity that allows him to pick up on the sometimes subtly hidden signs of trouble, such as the veiled bad intentions of others. He can see through the ego-distorted masks of difficult humans.

Add to that his generosity, kindness, and commitment to helping those in true need, to providing an equal playing field for everyone, and one is touched by the transcendent and heroic quality of his devoted, humble heart. A selfless servant (Mister Frodo!), he can lead, he can follow, and he can inspire a spirit of teamwork and fellowship in which all belong and rise to be their best. His boundless, self-deprecating humor could disarm King Kong or any wayward egotist looking to hold court over others.

Called the loyalist, the troubleshooter, the courageous pathfinder, and the watchdog, the Six is known for sensing the troublesome details of a project, intuiting what might go wrong at any moment, and often able to spot overlooked danger with pristine clarity. (Some say he can read the four corners of reality with amazing precision.). Being hypervigilant about incoming danger, he is ever aware that a mysterious lion (unpredicted catastrophe) is loose in the neighborhood, and at his best he is gracefully alert for its impending attack. Like a Jedi Knight, he feels the flow of reality and knows what comes next, and when. When less present, he is like a tremulous guard dog: on edge; pacing; feisty; certain of an unavoidable, nameless, invisible awfulness approaching. Then, his intuitive gifts vanish in the fog of suspicion, and he becomes what he fears. (Best to catch him on his good days.)

Case Study: Ronnie

When men arrive at rehab, their hearts are threadbare with hope, their souls still imprisoned in darkened bars or hypnotically trapped in time-warp scenes of horror-filled interactions with loved ones. They are empty shells, wandering ghosts without a true home. In the fog of their disorientation, they encounter Ronnie, an addiction counselor fifteen years sober and a beloved Type Six. He is so unassuming and unpretentious, so not a big deal that he is at times mistaken for one of the clients, or the janitor, or one of the aides. His message is clear: he is no different from these men straight from prison, men who are homeless or living in shelters, men wandering the streets lost and disoriented, victims of the addiction that has had its way with them. He holds an absolute and utter commitment to these men who walk through the doors of the facility.

Many new arrivals are engulfed in real, worst-case scenarios and filled with anxiety and worry. While clients are shaking and baking and disoriented in early recovery, Ronnie calms them down, checking in and alerting them to what they can expect while there, informing them of the rules, regulations, and small details that will make their stay easier. Ever alert to the men's anxiety, he goes into caseworker mode, setting them up with free clothing and needed health and dental appointments. He does this without fanfare, always projecting care and concern. Here his tender, boyish, innocent, loving heart comes online.

With all his oddness and lack of traditional male energy, Ronnie is given a free pass into the world of these wounded and rough men because of his sincerity and wish to help them. They are eyewitnesses to the way in which he navigates fear, like when he stands back, notices his own terror, and says to himself, "Okay, terror is here, but there is a job that must be done." In spite of the impending fear that something could go wrong, he engages the men, greets them, welcomes them, asserts what he knows, and they soften and disarm. His trembling courage and consistent trustworthiness—he keeps his word, doesn't lie or fabricate, tells a simple truth—catches them off guard. In effect, he teaches them, without speaking a word, how to work with their fear. Step with and through it, that's the drill.

Dancing within the flow of kaleidoscopic opposites within him—scared, courageous, humble, prideful, kind, mean, assertive, withdrawn—Ronnie radiates such simple caring, such down-home street-smartness and simple truth that the men drop their guard. *There's nothing to fear here. He's one of us.* This sometimes cranky, sometimes tremulous guy weirdly makes them feel safe and inspires them to be kind. Something in his presence engages them such that they don't feel that horrid sense of inferiority for the merciless, shameful losses they have experienced, their manhood lost in the barren tundra of their addiction.

Ronnie infuses the men with faith; they can trust him. They can count on him to help them, to tell them the truth, to not betray them. His actions communicate that he trusts them and their better selves to arise. He knows it, expects it. When they break the rules of the rehab, he doesn't reinforce what prison, probation officers, foster homes, and traumatic home environments have reinforced, that their very nature is criminal. Rather, he reminds them that it will take time to learn to pay attention to the new rules imposed on them by the rehab center, and then to incorporate these rules into their habits. He understands that they have had enough heartbreaking, soul-crushing baggage weighing their heart and soul down and that *of course* they will forget the rules. Who can remember to be hopeful when undigested suffering clogs their awareness? Men get tired and hopeless and say *fuck it* to everything. That is what suffering humans do, and worst yet, they have been taught to sabotage their own efforts because that is what has been expected of them.

Ronnie knows all of this. When someone is in rebellion mode, feeling that they have lost every right as a human being, he inquires, talks, asks how he can support them to stay on track so that they can eventually get their lives back. Gentleness works. Nonjudgment works. Treating these men with dignity works. Reminding them of their capacity for growth and change works. Reminding them that they are valued works. Ronnie gently but firmly reminds them how to navigate the sometimes intolerable circumstances they have landed in as a result of a thousand different insults to their souls, a thousand confusions acquired by life, and their addiction response to the deeply painful emergencies they have lived in.

Ronnie simply teaches what he has learned. The flow of his

genuine, soul-fostering respect for the men reaches through their protective, kill-anyone-who-approaches armor and finds the microscopic openings to their buried, innate self-confidence, awakening their true wish to heal themselves.

There are no failures under Ronnie's watch. Trying and failing repeatedly is no big deal. His often awkward actions convey that they are brothers in arms, there to serve each other, that they all walk on an even field. He lives the deeper and truer message of AA when it is working at its best: no one leads; the group serves everyone, and everyone is equal.

This is the courageous and devoted heart of the Six, the core of the Six soul. Ronnie, at his best, is an exemplar. Kind eyes when he is feeling well, steel gray eyes when facing down the dragon, a puppy-tender heart that welcomes everyone, fierce and courageous abandon and clarity when called to duty, Ronnie is a beautiful example of a recovered, heart-open man.

THE SIX IN ADDICTION

The Six who becomes addicted to substances often starts by using them innocently, to calm the whirlwind of anxiety, self-doubt, and worry he experiences, not realizing that the chemicals work from two ends. First, they shift anxiety to another sensation, maybe excitement, maybe deep numbing, or maybe a pseudo calm. For a few moments, anxiety isn't there.

The next day, the escape-state vanishes so that the moments of anxious freedom change to increased self-doubt and anxiety that sends him through the roof. If he rides that relief train too many times, it's hard to jump off. The anxiety he sought to escape has now morphed into a larger dragon of terror, along with his addiction craving. Such is the story of addiction: it starts out as a friend and turns into a dire enemy. *No one chooses this result.*

When he is at level 6 or 7, the Six in addiction feels panic and suspicion flood the waters of his emotional awareness. He enters treatment with only tiny threads of clear awareness, engulfed in the mechanical, self-defending, fear-driven patterns of his type.

Case Study: Marvin

Marvin, an Oregon farm boy, is husky and thick through the torso, wired to lift heavy bales of hay and milk cows. He arrived at rehab so thoroughly tightened by anxiety and his fear-infected imaginings that he could barely sit still in group. His suspicious eyes darted around the room, restless and searching. Everything said in group was heard wrongly through the churning fog of his worry-mangled mind.

His attention was glued to an internal movie on replay. The scenes mercilessly unfolded: He discovered six months ago that his wife of many years had been cheating on him with a neighbor. In the present throes of replay-imagination he was screaming, "How could you do that after all I've done for you, after my loyalty to you!" Never mind he had been drinking himself blind the last ten years, and barely noticed her from the alcoholic freight train that was tearing up his life.

The scenes unraveled, his mind's eye glued to them. He blew past his wife and headed to the neighbor's house—hurt churning inside him—and burst through the neighbor's front door, splitting the screen door in two. The hurt transformed into volcanic rage as he readied to pound his neighbor within an inch of his life, using a tire iron to deliver the message. It was only by a miracle that the police arrived, pried him off the neighbor, and stopped him from committing murder. Seconds away from a life sentence, his life almost destroyed, he was disarmed and jail bound.

In a whirl of cyclonal shock, Marvin detoxed in jail. Forced to sit still in a jail cell, his memories slipped through the fog of his alcoholism, revealing situation after situation in which he had hurt those he loved. He had been sleepwalking through everything important to him: his wife, his kids, himself. He had destroyed everything he cared for. The deep-felt sense that no one would support him was ice in his heart. His inner critic whispered with casual abandon, *No one wants you. You are done. Your father was right. You are hopeless. You've failed at all of your responsibilities.*

THE FIRST TWELVE WEEKS IN TREATMENT

The Six can barely sit still during first days in recovery. He feels as if he is sitting in the fire of *Are you telling me the truth? Do you know what you are talking about? How do I know you know anything?* Doubt, doubt, doubt.

The challenge for the newly recovering Six is bearing with the feelings that he can't count on anything and that everything seems ready to fall apart.

Spotting a newly recovering Six at an AA meeting is not difficult to do. The shivering quality of anxiety that courses through his nervous system is often palpable and evident. He is whirling in anxiety, suspicion, and worry, and while he looks for security, something he can trust, his inner critic reminds him, *There is not a single soul you can trust here! Are you sure you want to stay clean and sober and live in this mess, feeling uneasy all the time, fear crawling up your spine? A drink, a drug, anything would be better than this unknown territory, hanging with this ragtag group of recovering weirdos who obviously are not trustable. You could feel good right now!* Then his favorite euphoric recall scenes run through his mind-stream, where all the bad moments of his addiction are eliminated and all the good scenes are played in an endless loop of temptation.

The challenge for the newly recovering Six is bearing the feelings that he can't count on anything and that everything seems ready to fall apart. He feels possessed by the writhing anxiety on high voltage inside his chest and his inner critic incessantly talking as it inhabits his cells, bone, and skin. Assure him that things will settle down. He must starve this pattern one moment at a time, meaning that he must not escape it by substance using. He must learn to breathe, to sense his body one minute at a time. He must learn to sit through the waves of fear. More than anything, he will need compassion and a reminder that the longer he stays clean, the quieter things will get as long as he does the necessary work.

When he feels panicked and is filled with inferiority feelings, he begins to hold internal, imaginary conversations, imagining and mind-reading what others around him are saying to him. Believing his conjured, fantasized statements, he can suddenly strike out and accuse clients or friends of ill-intent, dishonesty, plotting against him, insulting him. Seconds later, having a moment of sanity and realizing he has imagined wrongly, he is filled with regret and remorse at his actions, apologizing profusely. He becomes compliant, until the wheels of his suspicion once again turn and he goes into a reactive replay at the imagined object of his betrayal.

The Six in early recovery experiences tremendous inner confusion, polarities of feeling, polarities of thought, all held in the sticky glue of pessimism: *Nothing will work. There's no one I can trust. I can never retrieve a life. It's your fault! No, it's my fault! Damn,*

I can't make up my mind! The Six in rehab can be outrageously funny, able to articulate the foibles of his doubting mind with such raw humor everyone will be in stitches, then sharply plunge into deep distrust of everyone, being oversensitive to teasing, feeling insecure and suspicious of everyone, and unable to notice a single positive attribute he possesses. Like a ping-pong ball, he bounces back and forth.

With a light heart, remind him of the inherited patterns the Type Six falls prey to when afraid: imagining the worst-case scenario and catastrophizing. Help him to intercept this pattern, to name it and observe it before the trance digs in too deep and he believes it.

Case Study: Marvin, continued

Marvin finally landed in rehab. Desperate, he was swinging on the pendulum of the Six in stress: he desperately wanted kindness yet pushed it away. He wanted to trust, he didn't trust. He raged, he begged for forgiveness. He pleaded, *please take me back*, then, *fuck you, get away from me, I don't need you!*

All of this swam through him as he sat in group. At levels 6 and 7 he could not sense when he was actually being supported and cared for by group members, friends, or counselors. A single thread of doubt often interrupted all accurate recall, and he would instantly forget that, just moments before, he was being emotionally supported by others. In a split second he would fall into a recurring trance: *No one supports me. I am abandoned. Nobody cares. It's not safe here.* Marvin was going to need a lot of tenderness, patience, and supportive learning experiences to penetrate this instant-amnesia pattern.

In the face of heartrending loss, his beautiful heart would crack open, revealing the spirit of a tender, kind boy. But seconds later, the hurt and loss would tempt him to leave the rehab and beg his wife for forgiveness. With a restraining order in place and jail the consequence of violation, he was forced to stay with his experience, with his hurt, his shame, and the men at rehab. This is the mercy of the "staying" structure, beginning with jail, then the protection order and a wife who is done with him, and finally, rehab. Merciless mercy.

Slowly, Marvin will learn to sit with his suffering, sit with the heartache, allow that vulnerable spot in his heart to open, to hold it like a small child in his arms. This *staying with it* will open him to receive and feel the love and support of others. Gradually, he will remember his value and that he is wanted and belongs.

And so, Marvin's work begins, as he courageously endures and transforms the necessary suffering of the Six's fear and mistrust. In group, he is met with tremendous compassion. Nine other guys have no trouble understanding how hurt, shocked, humiliated, and abandoned he feels to learn that his wife and neighbor have betrayed him. They understand his rages, his difficult-to-track temperament, his sudden flashes of paranoia, his broken heart, and his fierce need to blame all of it on *those two*. The men will hold space for him when he falls off his righteous horse of blame, when he realizes it was his alcoholism that betrayed and fooled him, and that he didn't have eyes to see it nor how it pushed his wife away.

A predictable cycle will ensue: shock followed by sadness followed by self-recrimination. *Why didn't I see what I was doing?* And then, self-hatred: *I am horrible and despicable! A total loser!* Then comes hopelessness. *I've destroyed everything. It's too late for me.* He will surrender and feel the suffering, his heart inching forward. Slowly, this cycle will simply wear out as he realizes the blamelessness of everyone, himself included. Kindness and forgiveness will begin to reach him. Healing will ensue. He will slowly arise out of the fog of his addiction and gain eyes to see what is real.

With practice, as Marvin learns to stop unconsciously attaching a story to his anxiety, it will begin to shift to a form of energy. Right now he unwittingly assumes that if he finds the story, reason, or cause of his anxiety, he will feel better and calm down. If only his inner critic, the dark magician pumping impressions of fear and worry and impending catastrophe through his mind-stream, would just stop doing that!

In time he will report, "I started doing meditation and stopped identifying with my mind and its attempts to explain my anxiety. I learned to bring as much of my free attention down into sensing my body as I could. This changed the level of anxiety I was feeling and gave me the ability to discover what lay underneath it: energy! In fact, I learned over time how to cultivate a quiet and still mind. What a relief."

THE SIX'S PROTECTIVE MECHANISM IN EARLY RECOVERY

The Six knows that his addictive actions have blown the doors off anything or anyone he can trust, including himself. He seriously wonders if he will ever feel supported again by anyone. Whatever certainty he had has disappeared through the window of his erratic addiction spiral. He feels he has let everyone down. His anxiety has gone full blown as his addiction has soared. At his worst, he has scared others by abandoning them, by not supporting them, by making them feel as fearful as he feels, by attacking them to unsettle their safety. He has become what he has feared in others, and he is shaking in the aftermath of his actions. How could he ever act this way?

> There is a path to healing, and first and foremost is
> the necessity of learning to develop quiet mind so
> that one can settle, be internally still, the fluctuations
> of the mind quieting like a clear, still, lake.

The Six's protective mechanism for dealing with the sense that there is no solid ground underneath him is to wrap himself around a belief, a code of behavior, a clearly defined path. *Just give me the map of what is expected.* This could be the code of AA, where the Six becomes a strict advocate of the AA rules, expectations, and philosophy. He follows it, holds on to it, as his life raft. In essence, he replaces his lost sense of inner knowing with an external form of authority. As he is obedient and dutiful, the twelve-step program becomes his missing authority. At the start, he quivers and vacillates between trying to trust again and retreating in shame for violating the very codes of loyalty and commitment he believes in.

In early recovery, the Six is torn between being compliant and following the rules, and rebelling against the rules and attacking those he seeks guidance and support from. He will test all his supporters—counselors, fellow twelve-step members, anyone who is a part of his circle of help—and push them away just to see if they will hang in. It is this rebellion and compelling impulse to self-sabotage that can undo all his efforts to be sober and clean.

There is a path to healing, and first and foremost is the necessity of learning to develop quiet mind so that one can settle, be internally still, the fluctuations of the mind quieting like a clear, still, lake. The Six will be challenged to find a technique that allows for this opening, this healing of the thinking center.

CORE RELAPSE PATTERN

The Six struggles with the *amnesia of success*. He quickly loses touch with the felt sense of successful encounters with difficulty, leaving in its place a hole of doubt. Equally palpable is the fear that he will suddenly be put in circumstances that he doesn't know how to navigate, as if suddenly lost in a strange land where no one speaks his language.

If he just prepares enough, covers all his bases, goes over all the possibilities, then he might be safe, might establish certainty and avert disaster.

It is this kind of dread that greets him each morning in early sobriety, that suddenly he will not know what to do, will not be prepared adequately, will face unpredictable, unforeseen circumstances. As a result, he may develop vigilant watchfulness for any signs of unexpected events intruding and blindsiding him. If he just prepares enough, covers all his bases, goes over all the possibilities, then he might be safe, might establish certainty and avert disaster. Nagging at him is the worry that he might have missed something, that he will be unable to divert the catastrophe he senses is lurking hidden in the next moment. He must keep working, keep preparing, do what he can in the face of feeling it is not enough. These are patterns the Six is challenged to master.

Alex, a Type Six with several years of recovery, says, "I know I'm a damn Six; I worry about everything, I second-guess everything, I don't know whose advice to take, and I don't want to take any advice from anyone. I want to be independent, but I feel like a weak little boy who is always looking for Daddy and Mommy to guide him and tell him what to do, and then I get really mad when people tell me what to do. I want to be a grown-up, but I feel like a kid.

"I'm just never sure about anything. In my head is a constant argument between warring parties, arguing about what to trust. It's awful. And every time I get sober, this is what I go through, this indecision and not knowing what to do, what not to do, who to trust, and who not to trust. Are people telling me the truth or are they purposely deceiving me? What are their motives? Man, I get so suspicious. I just can't tell. And then, in desperation, I take advice from the wrong people. I can see that now, finally."

Slowly, as Alex learns to trust his inner wisdom, as he slows his attachment to his stream of worried, self-doubting thoughts and sees this stream as an interesting sideshow he doesn't have to adhere to or attach to, his capacity for clarity and decisiveness will ensue. He will contact his inner guidance, and self-trust will follow.

TRANSFORMATION IN RECOVERY

As the Type Six begins to relax his mind, his heart, and his body, he discovers at the center of himself an intuitive something that pokes, prods, informs him of the next step to be taken. Some Sixes say they begin to feel a core of strength and intuitive wisdom arise in the quietness of their body, heart, and mind. This arising is the result of the work that the Six has done to heal his heart and the suffering he has encountered, to heal his mind of the fear-habits woven into the neural pathways of his mind, and to develop the capacity to fully relax, undefended and not on guard for unexpected danger. In this awake state, he becomes a guide to help others learn to fully relax and be here, now. Quiet mind, quiet heart, relaxed body, he teaches what he has learned.

HELPING THE SIX

As the Six recovers, he will need to question and doubt everything. He will need to know if you think he's doing okay, if he's getting better. Do you think so? Really? How can you tell? Are you just feeling sorry for him? His confidence will be in continuous flux for a good period of time. He will trust you and then he won't. Don't take this personally; he's doing the very best he can. Sometimes he will give all his trust over to you and fall into doing exactly what you suggest for him. You become his inner authority. Your job as a therapist or sponsor is to challenge him to not attach so strongly to your opinion but to begin to take baby steps toward trusting himself. But don't be surprised that just about the time you think he's fully agreed to taking one of your suggestions, he does the opposite. In fact, count on it. It's just how he's wired!

Kindly remind the Six that when he gets scared, he instinctively begins to blame others for his state of stress.

You can offer the Six this gentle observation: that in his stressed-out condition he is inclined to imagine conversations in his mind that are easy to mistake for real conversations. Encourage him to speak to this "reality" out loud; for example, "I'm having an imaginary conversation with Tom, and it feels real. I'm imagining he's saying negative things about me, and I'm believing he's actually saying this to me. It feels so real. I'm responding to him in my imagination and getting angrier and angrier. Help me sort this out!"

Teach him to get reality checks before acting. He can learn to cut the head off a delusion in the making by having a conversation with his counselor or sponsor. Teach him to understand that this pattern will manifest when he is scared or stressed. It's not his fault he has this reactive pattern, but it is his responsibility to tame it! Apologizing for his reactive outbursts will make him more conscious of the pattern, so that after enough apologies a window of awareness will open up and he won't have to ride this reactive, suspicion-horse into another imaginary battle.

Kindly remind the Six that when he gets scared, he instinctively begins to blame others for his state of stress. He must learn to observe the flood of blame thoughts and communicate it to a counselor, sponsor, or ally before he believes the thoughts and acts on them. Gently remind him that *blame does not help* and that relief does not arrive through the channel of blame.

Guide him by asking what drives these reactions. Is it anxiety? Is it the sense that the support and consistency in his life is shaky? Does he feel overwhelming fear, shame, or hurt and is projecting a catastrophe story into the future? Teach him to notice and sense the fear or hurt in the moment, allowing it to reside inside him, holding it with kindness, feeling the sensation in the body, keeping it in conscious awareness, talking before acting on the fears. This alone will help him to derail the blame train. Learning to bear fear consciously without reacting is his challenge.

In residential treatment, a go-to survival strategy for the Six is to find out what is expected of him, to learn what the rules are that, when followed, will give him a sense of stability and predictability, and settles his sense of disorientation. He will not only do his job but will notice who isn't doing theirs. His ego story, no matter how badly he is fulfilling it, is "I am responsible and wish others would be too!" He complains, "How come George isn't doing his job? I'm doing what I'm supposed to, how come he isn't? What are these rules for if no one follows them? Why aren't people more responsible like me?" Great patience, and the knowledge that he is wired this way under stress, is required of you. For a period of time he will remind you of how everyone, including the counselors, are not living up to their agreements and what is expected of them. Never mind that a trail of unconscious, over-the-edge, irresponsible actions trail him like a bounty hunter.

Your mission as a therapist is to roll with it, to not take it personally, to be steady in your receptivity to him. Be the stillness he seeks. This is the best anchor you can provide and one that he desperately needs. Even though he changes his opinion, decisions, and perspective rapidly and without warning, at least he can see that you are steady in your attention and presence with him.

As you watch him move back and forth without being thrown by it, you can, with your quiet and still presence, teach him to do the same. He will discover that in the midst of his back-and-forth internal thought-and-emotion movements, there is something steady and able to watch within him. You can teach him to begin to watch and observe himself without judgment and to use and mimic your stable and reliable presence to help him avoid being thrown off by his back-and-forth movements.

Your steadiness will begin to permeate him, touch him, touch what is at his core—his essence, his sturdy, unshakable being, a strong and steady presence. Trust this process. By being a still, grounded container of presence, you will begin to permeate his confusion with an energy that is inherent to his soul, that wants to come forward; that is, his true nature.

SUGGESTIONS FOR THE SIX

It will be incumbent upon you to provide supportive, helpful guidance to the Six as he navigates his way to health. Share the following suggestions, perhaps just one a week so as not to overwhelm him.

Make friends with your worry habit.

The Six may realize that worry runs through him unbidden, as if it has a life of its own. It is a part of his psychological hardware, a program that runs whether he wants it to or not.

Try these suggestions for helping him make friends with his worry habit:

- Work with him to give the worry pattern a name, an identity, a face, a size, a gender, and then declare out loud, "Voldemort [or Frankenstein, or Dracula] is back, running worry scenarios through my mind. Have mercy!" Seeing it and naming it can slow the trance down.
- Remind him that his mind tends to be a worry machine and that his job is to relax his attention to the flow of worry thoughts.
- Invite him to try this meditation: Sit quietly, sense your body, and follow and sense your breath. When a thought arises, label it, for example, *worried thought about my job* and then return attention to the breath. Shortly another thought will arise. Label it *thinking I'm wasting my time* and return attention to your breath. Whatever the thought, feeling, or impression, gently label it and let it go. Remind him that he will begin to have moments of quiet mind without trying and that he is learning to detach from identifying so strongly with his repetitious worried thoughts. This meditation will help him to not

be so magnetically drawn to his thoughts, to have some space and distance to notice and return to the present moment. In time, he will begin to experience quiet mind ever more frequently.

Notice your bargain with worry.

The Six unconsciously develops a belief that if he worries enough about things, he will be prepared. He must unpack this belief about worry and what drives it.

Try these suggestions to help him notice his bargain with worry:

- Ask him what he believes about worry. For instance, does he believe that if he is anxious and worried, then he will be safe and okay? Does he believe that he will end his worry by worrying? Does he believe his worry will stop bad things from happening? Does he believe that he demonstrates responsibility by engaging in worry, that it makes him a better person? (His inner critic would say so!)
- Challenge him to notice, when he is caught in a state of worry, why he thinks it's valid and good to stay worried. This will help him notice the unnecessary suffering he causes himself.
- Help him to see that his challenge is to develop a quiet mind and a willingness to let go of worrying as a way of propping up a sense of weirdly crafted, false security.

Learn to stop indulging your self-doubt.

Indulging self-doubt occurs when the Six surrenders to the back-and-forth opinions that ping-pong in his mind and prompt him to examine every possible error, leading to his continually taking the opposite side of his own internal arguments. All decisions seem equal.

Try these suggestions to help the Six learn to stop indulging in his self-doubt:

- Encourage him to develop an exercise habit that needs his full attention and gets him out of the thinking center where doubt lives. Help him to identify an exercise that he would enjoy.

- When he is engulfed in doubt, encourage him to let people support him. Suggest that he stand with his arms outstretched, parallel to the ground, for ten minutes. The physical focus it takes to accomplish this will require all of his attention, taking it out of his thinking center, the home of his worry and self-doubt. He may instead step into a cold shower for ten minutes. His worried mind will disappear in the effort to survive and not leave the shower.

Learn to trust your confidence.

The Six develops a sense of identity through his worry habits, as if saying to himself: *I worry, therefore I exist, therefore I am responsible. If I stop worrying, who will I be?*

Try these suggestions to help him anchor confidence:

- Explain that inhabiting his body wakes up a grounded sense of self-confidence along with his core intuitive capacity. Remind him that the Type Six tends to have inherited a pattern wherein he may not be able to feel and hold on to the feeling of confidence, that it may slip out of his awareness so quickly he hardly notices.

- Help him see that his inner critic may whisper, *If you feel confident, then you will surely fail. Better to be anxious and review your past or possible errors.* You'll need to work with him on this because as quick as you can blink he will be telling you about a recent victory that made him happy and confident in himself, and then will suddenly shift to how he had nothing to do with the success.

- When this happens, stop him in his tracks and say, "My doubting-Thomas friend, I just saw you vacate your success as if it didn't happen. Let's back up and have you sit in the *felt sense* of your success and the confidence you felt. Rest there, get comfortable with this because this confidence will guide you to more confidence. Remember that it is okay to feel confident."

- Encourage him to find a direct path to his body to support his body-confidence: swimming, yoga, hiking, jogging, weightlifting, body-sensing practices, tennis.

Catch yourself in the act of habitual complaining.

To the Six, complaining can feel like he is doing something. Complaining is like his habit of worrying: he unconsciously thinks complaining will create change for the better. When he is complaining, he is either supporting a sneaky sense of being a victim or feeling superior to the one he is complaining about. For instance, instead of repetitious complaining about environmental destruction, he can take a concrete action to be a part of healing the environment. He can join a group, invest time in actions to change what he is complaining about. Action, not complaint, is his mantra.

Try these suggestions to help him relax his habit of complaint:

- Remind him that he must learn to see himself complaining and resist the pull of this habit.

- Have him make a log for one week of all the times he discovers he is complaining and what the specific complaint is. This practice will be a wake-up call for him.

- Instruct him to not condemn himself for what he observes.

- Invite him to ask trusted friends to help him notice when he is habitually complaining.
- Remind him that complaining sucks his positive energy, thus disabling him from having the energy for positive action.
- Challenge him to vow to take a positive action in the area of his complaint when he finds himself complaining, to take responsibility.

A MESSAGE FOR THE SIX

Share this message with the Six in recovery:

Dear Six, you can do this! You can find support, learn to trust yourself, and learn to bring forth your wonderful gifts of serving others: connecting them to their best and heralding the underdog. The world needs you, and you deserve to be here, so keep showing up. There is much hope for you.

One day at a time, one moment at a time, trust the unfolding. Ask for help—good help—as often as needed. In the beginning, do whatever is necessary to stay sober for these twenty-four hours. Don't shoot for more than one day at a time. You can drink, drug, tomorrow, but today you will give all of your effort to stay clean. You can call whoever will help you, attend a recovery meeting online or in person, pray, read the *AA Big Book*. One day is all you are responsible for. This day is the day. You can do this. And slowly, slowly (all growth is slower that we'd wish for!), out of the fog of fear and anxiety will arise a solid inner confidence and a sense that you can trust yourself and you can trust life. Persist. Take small steps. This is learnable.

CHAPTER 10

Type Seven— The Joyful Visionary

If you want others to be happy, practice compassion. If you want to be happy, practice compassion.

—DALAI LAMA, *THE WISDOM OF COMPASSION*

The Type Seven, known as the enthusiast, the visionary bringer of hope, is blessed with an innate supply of exuberant joy and hope in all things possible. Sensing the positive potentiality of any moment or situation, his intuitive wisdom guides him directly to the visionary, the expansive, and the unexpected. He is wired with an unrelenting passion to savor and celebrate whatever is given to him, be it a joyous romp into unexplored experience or finding the precious jewel of love and hope in the darkest of hours. At his best he finds the silver lining in all things. As my dear Type Seven friend and minister, Pami, says, "Funerals are a fine place to bring humor and levity. Anything less celebrates the darkness. Death is the next adventure."

THE INTERNAL PLAYING FIELD OF THE SEVEN

When the Seven is in addiction, his internal playing field becomes unbalanced, driving him away from joy and down into hedonistic, pleasure-seeking despair. The following is a brief overview of the Seven's internal playing field.

Deep wound/relapse pattern: The deep wounding the Seven experiences is the sense of not having enough and of feeling empty, deprived, and unfulfilled. He is unable to experience happiness unless he is stimulated by something external to him.

Key commandment: The key commandment for the Seven is to keep searching for happiness out in the world, or else he will never find it. If he doesn't seek it, he will be miserable. If he slows down, he will be stuck in unhappiness. So he keeps moving.

Deep wish: The Seven deeply wishes to feel happy, to fulfill his vision, and to inspire others to do the same.

How he sees himself: The Seven sees himself as enthusiastic, joyful, spontaneous, happy, funny, and visionary.

At level 4 and below: When the Seven falls into these lower levels, he falls prey to the emotional habit of gluttony, in which nothing is enough. Nothing fully satisfies him, be it food, experience, people, or things, because he is moving at the speed of light and is unable to take in the moment. His mental habit is of anticipation, in which he tries to fill himself up with excitement by constantly thinking of his next possible activities, experiences with people, or acquisitions of things that will make him feel better, as he leaves the moment where he could actually feel content.

Inner critic: The Seven's inner critic tells him that if he isn't happy, he won't be loved. It also criticizes him for not being happy *enough*, telling him there is always something better than what he is experiencing. His inner critic wants him to always be looking for something outside himself. Over there! It's always *over there.*

At his best: At his best, the Seven is visionary, filled with gratitude for the opportunity to savor reality, generous toward others, able to savor the best, and experiences the heights and depths of joy. He is naturally enthusiastic, funny, and optimistic, fast-moving and fast-thinking, inspiring others to go beyond their limits.

THE HEALTHY SEVEN

The healthy Seven is a master of possibility and a magician at turning disaster into opportunity and healing. Infused with the passion to savor the multiplicity of positive experiences available to human beings, he is a joy-bringer and cosmic humorist, encouraging individuals to rise like a phoenix from the flames of tragedy and sorrow, and trust in the good. He both embodies a grounded sense of reality and joyously enlightens the hearts of those he touches. He also infuses them with a buoyant energy that suggests that any circumstance can be transcended or used for one's personal good.

The healthy Seven is a joyous Tigger, a radiant meteor shower of gratitude and awe, a dash of radiant splendor, a pulsing light orb from another galaxy, an emissary of great goodwill, an E.T. with limitless love and spunk. At his very best he can reinvent himself in the gap of each unfolding moment.

Case Study: Peter

Peter, a true Seven, walks into the basement of St. Jude's Church, where other members of AA are arriving, sitting, talking, being. Effervescence and exuberance radiate from his face, his thin, wiry body embracing the moment as if it were a delicious drink. Eyes lit with enthusiasm, he takes several deep breaths, absorbing the contents in the room. Wherever he casts his eyes, whatever he gazes upon, lights him up with curiosity, with improvisational possibility, with lightning-quick delight. The moment is a living entity that speaks to him, touches him, moves through him, and infuses him. His aliveness dial is set on high; like a six-year-old boy who has entered a toy store, he brims with anticipatory excitement. Simply watching him enter and walk around the room lifts others up; they feel lighter, sit easier in their chairs, as a wave of kid-like joy touches them.

Peter spills over with spontaneous generosity, the soul-stuff of goodwill erupting deep within him. He is contagious, a living conduit for the flow of generous, what-will-happen-next, ecstatic *hereness*. Others can see it in his eyes: limitless possibility streaming like a universe from his being. He's right on the edge of it, wide-eyed to the splendor and unpredictable awe and potential of the moment. Totally, completely here, drinking it in, touching it, tasting it, and glowing like a 4th of July sparkler.

As Peter saunters through the room greeting his tribe, glad-to-be-here flowing through him, he is radiant with inquisitive presence, as if discovering each of his friends for the first time. "Hey, Frank, great to see you," he delights, taking Frank in like a scoop of ice cream. "Love your scarf, Marsha! You are a flowing rainbow!" a generous welcome dancing in his eyes. "Hi, Tom, you are looking good, bro! How about those Giants!" he chimes as he swings an imaginary bat and watches the ball sail over the fence in the distance.

Every encounter is an animated, expressive exchange. And everyone is included, including the down-and-out street drunk, eyes and shoulders downcast, and carrying a huge boulder of despair the size of Kilimanjaro. Peter, taking the man's hands, looks directly into his eyes, and says, "Welcome, my friend. Glad you are here!" and means it. His clothes torn and dirty, poverty and the horror of homelessness etched deep into the sad crevices of his face, his eyes dark wells of no hope. The gnarled man replies with great effort, "Thanks, man." Eyes filled with kindness, Peter nods and squeezes the man's shoulders. There is tenderness here. Peter has walked this road, has lived it for twenty-five years. He knows street poverty in every cell of his body, and knows the desolation that awaits this man, walking the streets day after day with no home or money or family, waiting in line for food at the food pantry, the savage need to find a place to sleep at night before the cold sets in.

Peter is a healthy Type Seven, able to enter each moment with creative freshness, his kid-quirkiness arising effortlessly, his heart a well of compassion.

And then there is his amazing recovery journey. Nine years ago this precious, beautiful man, childlike, wise in such an innocent way, was living homeless on the streets of Seattle, Washington, eating out of dumpsters, sleeping under bridges, living in homeless shelters, ragged with anxiety. On the edge of death, the vampire of heroin and alcohol addiction possessed him. He, thieving, cheating, jive-and-shuck artist deceiving everyone, would help you look for the watch he just stole from you, hating you for your prosperity. He would come into AA heartbroken, light gone from his eyes, only sadness and grief left. He would stay sober for a few days and relapse again— hundreds of times.

On numerous occasions in the middle of an AA meeting, Peter would fall to the floor flailing and flopping wildly, eyes rolled back into his head, a grand mal seizure possessing him as he detoxed from alcohol. Friends say that his first year clean, he wept most of the time. Rivers of tears. Daily. Heartbroken to shreds, the memory of his wife dying in the arms of her heroin addiction a knife to his heart, he ached from the core of his being, often unable to bear it.

And yet, this shooting star of a guy got sober. One day, his soul came over the horizon, like the morning sun. He awoke. He arose. He stepped out of his soul-stunning grief and into life. And he did it in the wild fashion of the beloved Seven: in the blink of an eye, as if he were waking from the dead in a full sprint, from dark to light in a nanosecond.

Peter's intensity brings dying junkies, meth heads, coke addicts, alcoholics into the room into real time, gasping for his wisdom. No spiritual bypass here. Death, like a *Harry Potter* Dementor, hisses. One could hear a pin drop. Here, in these rooms, Peter worships at a sacred temple, and only Zen-like rigor will suffice in his quest for sobriety. From the core of his gutsy soul he declares, "No one has to drink today, or ever again. No one! Remember that!" Half rising out of his seat as he shares, a steely look illuminates him. In these moments nothing is loose and free-flowing. It is truth—the hard, take-no-prisoners, rock-solid truth he tells:

"There is simply no logical reason I am here today. I overdosed dozens of times. My heart stopped. I was taken as dead. Only on the wings of a miracle did I wake up in a hospital, still alive. And somehow sobriety took. I don't know how. It was given to me." The room is utterly still as he continues. "The key to my sobriety is discipline, one-pointed discipline. I get up each morning at four a.m. and begin my two-hour meditation practice. I start with gratitude. I say, 'Thank you, God, for my left hand, my left forearm, my left elbow, my left upper arm, my left shoulder, my right shoulder, my right upper arm, my right elbow,'" touching each body part as he speaks, rattling off this litany at a breathtaking, errorless clip. "My tongue, my teeth, my throat, my bloodstream, my eyes…my toothpaste, my food, my apartment, my deodorant, my bed, my sheets, my pillow. I then say, at least two hundred times, I love you, God."

Everyone is immersed in the pool of Peter's gratitude, appreciating the real, often taken-for-granted abundance in their lives. This is no light, life-is-easy gratitude list. This is solid granite thankfulness, etched-into-his-soul-and-retrieved-from-the-swamp-of-death gratitude. It is emblazoned on bone and in muscle, like tempered steel forged in the oven of addiction horror. It is stunning, weighty, and so very real.

For Peter, every moment is a gift. This moment of eye contact with another, this moment of smelling the coffee, feeling the warmth in the room, recognizing that he has food for breakfast and that millions are starving *right now*. This moment always is the holy moment. This moment. This moment. This moment. It is so crystal clear to Peter. *This moment I am eating pizza and millions are ravenous for food . . . I'm brushing my teeth and millions go without a toothbrush . . . I lie on my bed while so many wander homeless, no shelter or home to speak of . . . this moment.* I have yet to witness someone who so inhabits the four corners of *now* with all four cylinders burning so brightly, and with such gratitude.

Peter continues, articulating another mindboggling miracle. In his forays into dumpsters to retrieve food, lit up on drugs, hunger-starved and blinded by despair, he discovered that cardboard boxes were being thrown away by restaurants. In the midst of garbage, rotting food, stink, filthy papers, aching belly—cardboard boxes! After several months sober, something inside him stirred, and he got an urge to paint on these surfaces. Back to the dumpsters he went, collecting cardboard. Two years later, Peter is a real-time artist having no lessons; stand next to this guy, and you get that he is channeling beauty full time with every breath. His art is beautiful, hopeful, lift-your-soul art embodied in flowing, ethereal, angelic mermaids dancing in waves of celestial color. His paintings hang in shops all over downtown Seattle. His work is an expression of the mercy that saved him and the amazing Type Seven spirit that resides within him. He says, "Patricia, my deceased wife, is my muse. She is my inspiration." His eyes become shimmering pools of sadness.

Peter frequently enters the morning AA meeting with colors embedded in his hands, in his fingernails, on his clothes, on his shoes, on his face. He smiles ear to ear, sunrise bursting in his eyes. He is wired on *ready, now, here*. His body, his face, his eyes say it: I am ready to embrace this moment of beauty, ready to be touched and moved and changed, wide-open, full of gusto—bring it! Peter's spacious contact with reality is the Type Seven at his finest.

THE SEVEN IN ADDICTION

When the Seven is caught in addiction, mired in the prison of level 6 or 7, he is like an adrenaline-drugged hummingbird, darting from experience to experience, trying to fill up his horrific emptiness and despair with pleasure or any intense, over-the-top stimulation experience that can destroy his sensation of suffering, anxiety, or despair. He vibrates and moves at such a fast rate that he barely touches down, and every sensation-experience he attempts to land needs to be bigger, stronger, more intense than the sensation before, to blast him out of his numbing anxiety and bone-cracking loneliness. The truth of the matter is, his body, heart, and mind have become so shut down and hardened that nothing can touch him, nothing can reach through the anxiety-driven, chaotic intensity of his mind or his fast-racing broken heart. He has to put a torch under himself to feel anything; either he must stimulate himself or die of despair; those are the options. And he is not one to sit around for very long in despair. He will stimulate himself until he drops from exhaustion.

In addiction, the Seven's natural optimism and enthusiasm have turned to cynical, screw-you, get-out-of-my-way coldness. He is utterly empty and running as fast as he can to find something, anything, that can break through the hummingbird cage of ceaseless anxiety that has captured his attention entirely. He cannot slow down unless he drives the leaden force of heroin or alcohol into his being. Or for some, cocaine becomes the tranquilizer, not hyping him up as it does many, but slowing him down. Truth is, he will collapse from all of this and temporarily become a heavy stone that no longer flies helter skelter in the prison cage of his agonized mind and soul. A cycle ensues: manic activity followed by burnout. Back and forth. Rise. Crash. Rise. Crash. Until he gets recovery or dies in a flame of exhausting avoidance-suffering. Prison might be his saving grace.

Case Study: Bill

Bill came to rehab on the wings of a fantastical Type Seven attempt to elude the reality of his inability to feel anything. Plied to the gills with alcohol, he had lived a life of high-paced, what's-the-next-sensual-experience gusto until he could no longer feel anything inside him. Nothing could excite him. He was burned out.

Being wily and adventurous at his core and completely at a loss as to what to do with this soul-killing *boredom*—the nemesis of the Seven—he pondered with the few faculties still available to him. With a little Type Seven visioning, the answer arrived. He had never tried robbing stores before. Finally, after years, he was anticipating something new. His inner light of *this will be exciting* turned on.

Wearing a bandanna as a mask, with a plastic gun as his weapon of choice, he began entering and robbing Apple stores. Easy peasy, and what fun! He just never knew what would happen. But, short on wisdom, he hadn't considered that Portland, Maine was a small city, and after five successful robberies he was apprehended. He said later, "What a blessing. I had to go to jail, and there I got sober. I hadn't planned on this, but the outcome was such a good one. Jail saved my life."

The addicted Seven attempts to feed whatever desire arises on the screen of his consciousness quickly, adamantly, mainlining whatever possibility of pleasure and escape is within his grasp (think of Elton John in the movie *Rocketman*, for example). He behaves as if thrusting the experience like a needle into his veins, be it promiscuity, overeating, thieving, shopping, gambling, indulging in any sensual activity that might create a blip on the screen of his suffering.

This will be his behavior until grace delivers a slam dunk, dragging him down from the high wire of his excitement-driven impulses, forcing him to detox, either through ending up in jail (which saves many) or a rehab center. His ultimate fear is that if he slows down and senses what is trailing him, he will be eaten by sorrow and disappointment. He must run until he drops. With grace, drop he will, into the arms of recovery.

THE FIRST TWELVE WEEKS IN TREATMENT

The Seven arrives in recovery filled with adrenalized, fidgeting, high-strung anxiety. He is ready to burst out of his skin, brain on fire with nonstop chatter, flitting like an amphetamine-driven monkey from distracting thought to thought. He fidgets at the AA meeting, barely able to sit still, eyes darting, even after being pulverized by his drug of choice and his frantic efforts to find happiness and relief.

> ## Make no mistake, the tired body of the beaten Seven has a mind current that burns eternal.

Entrapped by the magician jailer—alcohol and other substances, wherein the playful Seven is given moments of fake-happiness experiences, the distorted comedian and prankster unleashed, he is then hammered by the dark and heavy chains of addiction grief. The flying bird now lies crushed and soul-spilled on the floor—and yet, the Seven brain is tireless and frenetic.

Make no mistake, the tired body of the beaten Seven has a mind current that burns eternal. As soon as he can muster the energy to speak, here comes a flash flood of wit, stories cross-referencing and making sense when they shouldn't, the panorama of a kaleidoscopic mind unleashed like Joseph's multicolor dream coat. Not to mention, hidden in the folds of his colorful humor is a biting, cynical, cut-you-to-the-core rage masked as humor, while the freedom and happiness he imagines is *out there*, just outside his fast-moving prison cage of high-pitched anticipations. Now, as he is stopped in his tracks, he gets glimpses that he's been pacing in the cage of his mind, while his lived life is in ruins.

In groups, the Seven is capable of moments of crystalline clarity, truth-telling, instant wisdom that is quick and inspiring, that pours through him at lightspeed, grasping many streams of understanding and articulating them into one flash of palpable wisdom. But his faster-than-lightning personality habits can streak back through the stratosphere of his psyche, and seconds after beginning to open his heart will transform him into the funniest human being alive. Able to slip-slide past any wave of grief or sadness, the genuine depth he was stepping into—gone, swoosh, disappeared.

In recovery groups, the singular difficulty that the Seven struggles with, whether in his first year sober or twentieth, is allowing himself to feel and inhabit his broken heart. It's as if he has signed a pact with himself: *I don't do sadness. I do funny. I do instigations of improbable moments. I make you laugh. I say outlandish things you would never say. I do things that would embarrass you. I keep you and myself away from hurt, sadness, or fear.*

The ultimate challenge is to help the Seven begin to detach from his mechanism of avoidance through too much humor, helping him to stay in the "room of recovery" long enough to outwit his enormous restlessness and crazy-fast mind. Others must also really, really notice that beneath the immense joy/joke-making machinery of his personality sits a soul who is lonely, whose heart is broken, who is afraid that he is anything other than funny. The therapist's or sponsor's job is to invite him to drop his persona from time to time (not give it up) so that another side of him can start to see the light of day.

Case Study: Scotty

When Scotty entered a rehab treatment facility, he was a young man who, on the spot, could contrive, create, and channel a one-man improvisational celebration of pure, unadulterated, wide-eyed, you'll-never-believe-this-coming-at-you humor. Out of nowhere, he could create a story that had rhythm, energy, intensity, and breathtaking turns. He was the funniest human being I had ever met, funny like the sweetheart of them all, Robin Williams (also a wonderful Type Seven). And the men loved him. Unanimously. In a flash, he could lift everyone's spirit from the darkest trenches. This was his gift.

And the other men, in their own way, were deeply thankful for moments of respite from their suffering. In the many dark hours at the treatment center, Scotty was a beacon of hope. In those precious moments, he was the pure force of spontaneous humor, as if all of his being was a conduit for boundless optimism and joy. There was nothing he cast his attention upon that didn't hold a nugget of outlandish, gut-busting humor. Amid these pure reveries, a real light of joy and happiness flickered in this sweet soul's dancing eyes, glowing transparencies of magic and gratitude, his face radiating deep happiness. It was as if the light of his soul, for a few moments, shapeshifted and moved through the darkness he was mired in.

Everyone at group was bathed in this happiness when Scotty was "on," when he was feeling good about himself. But later, outside of the radiance of his improvisational performance, came a dark and insidious cloud. His soul was weeping, but rarely would he let anyone see it. He would sit in my office, head in his hands, sobbing, heartbroken, a trail of devastation in his wake, outlandish pleasure hunts that had turned into self-destructive forays into dangerous sex, drug addiction, dangerous relationships, thievery, and prostituting himself. Scotty was a starving hound, forever hungry, never satisfied, desperately licking his lips on anything . . . anything . . . looking for the fix of happiness. He was agitated, impatient, insatiable, cold-hearted, a stimulation junkie.

Over weeks in treatment, Scotty's entertainment reveries dissipated. Undigested suffering would reach up into his heart chamber and close him down. Trunkloads of sorrow, grief, fear, and disappointment held him hostage. This delightful, open-hearted, so-funny-that-God-laughs young man struggled mightily with addiction, such that he would again end up smoking crack in dark alleys, or looking to trade sex for drugs or food in sodden bars, his humor turned cynical and provocative, his every breath a degradation of his pure and essential soul. Only when he landed long enough to feel his grief, to feel his broken heart, did his journey home finally begin.

THE SEVEN'S PROTECTIVE MECHANISM IN EARLY RECOVERY

The protective mechanism of the Type Seven in addiction recovery is avoiding suffering at all costs. In Alcoholics Anonymous the fourth step is taking a personal inventory. It is critical to helping individuals become conscious of what addiction does to them and those they love. A Seven may be in and out of treatment facilities for years, and although he has been instructed dozens of times that he must take inventory of his life and examine how his addiction affects him, without fail he would forget to do it. The suggestion would vanish in the wake of his current impulses. When asked why he failed to do the inventory, the Seven replies, "Well, that would make me feel bad. What good would that do me? I'm convinced it wouldn't help. I choose to focus on the positive. It makes no sense to me to focus on sadness as a way of healing. That seems utterly ridiculous."

Why does the Seven do this? Because his ego ideal, which he tries like a son of a gun to believe in and portray, is "I'm a happy, positive person." It is his mantra. Never mind that everything inside him is programmed to rigorously avoid suffering at all costs, which consequently prevents him from healing his suffering. While he thinks to himself, *I choose to look at the positive*, the rock-bottom truth prevails: he is *driven* to look at the positive. It's his *only option*, particularly in early recovery.

Notice this inner critic message, designed to keep the Seven drunk and addicted: *If you're honest and tell the truth of your suffering, you will be stuck in grief, the tar of sadness leaking into every cell of your body, for the rest of your life!* With a message like this, it doesn't take much to understand his strategy for surviving life sober: focus on the positive, be upbeat, don't complain about the past, don't dwell on the negative, be funny and entertain others, don't ask for help; keep moving, shucking, and jiving. In the words of Satchel Paige, surely a Seven, "Don't look back. Something might be gaining on you."

Howard, eight years sober, was tearing up as I described how the Seven seems to have an anti-sadness clause. He said, "I tried for so long to always be happy. That was my job. That's what got good reviews from others. Until I realized how much I stuffed my sorrow, and how it was costing me my ability to get close to others. When I finally let go, let the tears come, I thought I'd cry forever. People around me where disarmed. They actually tried to get me to stop crying. They wanted me to be the funny guy, to bring them up. I had to avoid these people for a while and give myself time to heal. Today I don't use my humor to avoid the truth of my suffering."

CORE RELAPSE PATTERN

The core fear of the Seven is that of being deprived of happiness and held captive in emotional pain. He seems to carry in his deep memory a sense of being cut off from a nurturing connection with Mom too soon, and left to fend for himself. He made a deep, instinctual vow to never be without what pleases him or brings him joy.

When the Seven senses emotional pain or any hint of deprivation, a flare goes up inside him: *avoid this.*

When the Seven senses emotional pain or any hint of deprivation, a flare goes up inside him: *avoid this.* Get too close to this early abandonment stuff and the unconscious fear will arise like a haunting ghost, his inner critic whispering, *If you let this touch you, you'll stay hooked to this emotional pain and unhappiness for the rest of your life. It will stick to you like Velcro. Once you are touched by it, it will infect you permanently. So, get your ass out of here, now. Don't linger. Get moving. Stay in motion. The sadness can't catch you if you are on the move.*

The Seven's fear of being trapped in pain and deprivation translates into a more conscious fear of being trapped by anything (person, place, or thing) that could put him in a rut or stricture, limiting his freedom. He thinks, *If I get trapped in any circumstance without a back door—if I commit myself to anything—I will become an easy target for suffering to nail me. I will be mired in darkness.* Unwittingly he commits *to being uncommitted*, triggered by the fear that he will lose the ability to be spontaneous, stripped of his choices and options, and locked into suffering. The avoidance of boredom and stagnation creates the illusion that he is moving in the right direction, but his lack of commitment creates the very suffering, the very emptiness and unhappiness, he wishes to avoid.

The Seven's growth edge is in discovering that the door to enduring happiness must be entered through his engagement with his suffering.

TRANSFORMATION IN RECOVERY

When the Type Seven begins to heal, learning to stay with and feel the suffering of his heart, he realizes how the suffering he has avoided has limited his capacity to feel deep, satisfying, heartfelt joy, that he had, in fact, been traveling on the surface of his heart. This opens the door for him to begin experiencing satisfaction, a fulfilled heart that is not grasping for anything or avoiding anything. Then he is able to abide in the present, able to feel the full range of his feelings, from sadness to fear to anger to joy to loving communion with others. Able to be still, at ease, in the moment. Life becomes an unfolding celebration. This is the true joy of the Seven coming into manifestation.

HELPING THE SEVEN

The addicted Seven has become the very opposite of his natural gifts: impatient, impulsive, a mind thinking too many things at once; a logjam of conflicting thought streams, fast synaptic impulses to go here or there. His fever-pitch movement away from his suffering has made it impossible for him to be touched by this moment, to be filled with gratitude and satisfaction in this moment. It is only by surrendering to his sorrow and bearing his impulsivity with warrior-like patience that real happiness can emerge.

When the Seven sits in a recovery meeting, an addiction group, or a counselor's office, his defense mechanisms take him away, possessing him like a flickering disco ball, splattering his attention every which way. To bear this inner activity, and to navigate it successfully, is no easy matter. More than anything, he needs to talk, needs to say out loud what is coursing through him. He needs to put a name to the continuing flood of impulses that beckon to him to go, to leave this moment. *Chase me*, they call, *or you will die*. And yet he *must . . . must . . . must* stay put. His life depends on it.

You must name these internal dynamics for the Seven because his inner psychodynamics are so fast that he gets only glimpses of them, making it difficult for him to perceive the trance he is addicted to. Encourage him to sit with all of this, spill it, talk it through, report it, until by reporting it, this tireless habit of anticipating what's next will begin to be less captivating, less hypnotizing, and he will be more able to observe what pulls his attention away. Specifically, he will get a glimpse of what lies underneath this mechanism of his fast-changing attention: fear and a heart that is starved for love; he like a hungry dog looking for a bone.

The Seven does not need to follow the dictates of a curmudgeon AA or NA superhero sponsor who declares, "Take the cotton from your ears and put it in your mouth." Better to invite him to *share or die.* For every principle spoken in recovery, there is often an equal and opposite principle. Your job is to discover the reconciling force between these two, which we can name as *balance.*

Give him space to talk, and he will quiet down naturally. Give him room to say what is occurring, and slowly he will begin to sort out what is important.

This is not to say that a word feast is what helps the Seven. Truth is, many Sevens have a difficult time with silence, and express their raging anxiety by talking. In the beginning, the Seven needs compassionate observers able to bear with his need to talk. He will not arrive at inner quiet in early recovery by being told to shut up, and in fact, this can be the worst advice to give a newcomer. Give him space to talk, and he will quiet down naturally. Give him room to say what is occurring, and slowly he will begin to sort out what is important. Listen with full attention to his adrenalized mind, help him to hold a focus in his conversation, listen with compassion and kindness, and he will sense his safety and begin to shift his conversational flow to feelings of the heart.

As Russ Hudson and Don Riso say, "Listen with all three centers." That is, be a field of receptivity and listening, be a witness for his current of Mad Hatter thinking, give him space to begin to sense his precious and anxious heart. Your presence will be infectious and supportive. And this is for certain: *listening to him without judgment will call forth his real wish to be sober and clean. Judging him will drive him away. Practice immaculate patience for his process and the Zen door to his soul will creak open.*

SUGGESTIONS FOR THE SEVEN

It will be incumbent upon you to provide supportive, helpful guidance to the Seven as he navigates his way to health. Share the following suggestions, perhaps just one a week so as not to overwhelm him.

Become aware of your emotional habit of gluttony.

Gluttony is the drive to fill up emptiness—the hungry heart of the Seven—with stuff, such as the stuff of food, material objects, sex, or whatever appears as the object of pleasure. Gluttony says *more is better.* It is often in service of the avoidance of emotional discomfort.

Try these suggestions to help him become aware of his emotional habit of gluttony:

- Help him to examine his relationship with gluttony. With great compassion, help him to examine those areas in his life where he experiences insatiableness. One hamburger wasn't enough; purchasing one shirt, one book, one pair of shoes wasn't enough; eating twice as much as needed, restlessness for more and more, like trying to fill a bottomless pit. Nothing fills it. Here you must instruct him to resist in one of these areas and begin to see what difficult state lies behind the habit.
- Remind him of this saying: *You can never get enough of what you really don't need.*
- Challenge him for one week to write down each instance of when he indulges more than is needed. Remind him to remember that pleasure is not happiness. It is not satisfaction. It is not fulfillment.

- Let him know that his job is to begin to sense his gluttony, to see it and resist taking action on it. He must slow down and be with it, to dare to see what lies underneath it.

Become aware of your impulsivity.

Impulsivity is the Seven's Achilles heel. He sees something he wants, and quick as a wink, without considering resources, right timing, or checking in with his heart or intuition, he goes for it. This can lead him to many bad choices, disappointments, and back to addiction relapse.

Try these suggestions to help him become aware of his impulsivity:

- Let him know that with just a little bit of presence or "hereness," he will begin to experience a moment of mindfulness—a gap in his impulsivity—such that his inner wisdom can guide him, replacing his habit of leaping willy-nilly toward the next better, greater, more fun, more pleasure-filled experience.
- Instruct him in this practice: "Whenever you get an impulse to try something new, change direction, or quit what you have been doing, set the intention of making no changes for a least one week. Then, before acting, check in with your counselor, sponsor, or coach to help you mindfully decide the best action." This will slowly teach him to pause and look before he leaps.

Develop disciplined focus.

Nothing will be more likely to save the Seven in recovery than his developing disciplined focus. Disciplined focus requires learning to start and finish what one has chosen to do.

Try these suggestions to help him develop disciplined focus:

- Encourage him to commit to learning to do one thing at a time, fully, completely.
- Remind him that he is inspired by beginning new adventures but that halfway into the new direction two things will occur: the first, dreaded boredom, will arise to steal the fire of his inspiration. A voice might echo in his awareness: *I'm tired of this. It isn't exciting.* Remind him that this is an illusion woven by his inner critic, who would like to keep him unfulfilled and searching endlessly. If this doesn't stop him in his tracks, the second thing will occur: his wildly visionary mind will flood his awareness with better things to do. Like waving a carrot in front of him, ideas will call him away from his chosen task. Count on these two completion-killing distractions. Challenge him to talk about these patterns when they arise, and to commit to finishing the chosen task.

Finish steps four and five.

The Seven's natural inclination is to fly spontaneously by the seat of his pants, whether flying into soulful escapades or flying into the mouth of his addiction. Since he is a fast learner with lightning-quick mental reflexes, he tends to assume that his quick intellectual comprehension of anything equates to the deep digestion of his experience. The idea of doing a step four inventory and sharing it with you, a sponsor, coach, or therapist can appear to be madness to him.

Try these suggestions to help him complete steps four and five:

- Be clear with him that he must notice his tendency to touch lightly the heavy steps, that he must finish in particular AA's steps four and five. Step four, the dungeon-dwelling inquiry: making a thorough inventory of his addictive past. Be honest with him that this means he will be standing mud deep in his mistakes, delusions, and moments of callous disregard for another and self, absorbing the moments in which he escaped responsibility and freeloaded while fleeing his broken heart. That is, he will be exploring his human response to overwhelming personal suffering. Step five, admitting his wrongs to another, will be just as scary, difficult, and painful.

- Remind him that navigating these patterns skillfully and effectively will wake up a dead-on will to stay sober. That is its purpose. Let him know that this is where the path to true and sustainable happiness starts.
- Finally, remind him that he did not choose these negative responses to pain, they developed in the darkness of his suffering; in fact, they chose him.

Become aware that your hyperkinetic communication and information processing genius can overwhelm people.

The Seven is easily excited by his next contact with a human being. *Yeah, baby, someone to vibrate with*, his psyche says. His eyes filled with ecstasy-craving, anticipatory promise, his excitability dials amping up to full volume, his toothy grin shines back at the newcomer. Once that pattern gets turned on, it's very hard to interrupt. The Seven must become aware of how his exuberant energy can overwhelm and alienate others.

Try these suggestions to help him become aware of how he overwhelms others:

- Remind the Seven that he can go unconscious with people when talking, to the point that what is so precious in him—his blazing, euphoric storytelling capacity and his joy in sharing his stories—becomes impulsive, no-holds-barred downloads.

- Let him know that his challenge is to keep contact with whomever he is speaking to, to pause, take a breath, notice that there is a real, live human being in front of him who needs real contact with him.

- Encourage him to do this practice at least once a day: When he is engaging another, check the eyes of the listener several times during the interaction (are they glazed over?) and notice their body language (are they leaning away?). Can he hear their tone of voice (bored, flat, tired of listening to you drone on)? Is he giving them ample time to share their perspective? Does he know what their perspective is, or is he preparing to talk again? He must slow down and recognize these signs.

- Challenge him to try to talk only 50 percent of the time when he is connecting with you and others. Encourage him to stay conscious of this practice and learn the deep value of listening.

A MESSAGE FOR THE SEVEN

Share this message with the Seven in recovery:

Beloved Seven, you are the maker of joy, the bringer of hope, the one who lift spirits like no other. This is your gift, your default, and where you go even when it is your turn to grieve and be cheered up. Include yourself in the equation of soul support and allow your heart to open to its suffering.

This is what empowers your capacity to bring more joy to others, and to experience something you seek more than anything: true contentment and connection with others. Learn the power of holding tender, quiet space for others.

To do this you must learn to slow down, come to a screeching halt daily, be here now in the grace of stillness, endure the squirm factor that initially can make you feel like you will burst into flames if you sit still for one second longer. Resist the temptation to soar at the slightest provocation. Develop deeper intuitive knowing through your practice of stillness meditation. Begin to trust inner stillness and inner peace, rest in it, nurture it, and a single-minded clarity will begin to settle in your consciousness. Then, the wisdom to know what to act on and what to pass on will arise and inform you. Intuitive guidance, the jewel you seek, will direct you clearly to your heart's fulfillment.

CHAPTER 11

Type Eight—
The Lion-Hearted
Protector

Without self-knowledge, without understanding the
working and functions of his machine, man cannot
be free, he cannot govern himself and
he will always remain a slave.

—GURDJIEFF, A TYPE EIGHT

The healthy Type Eight, known as the boss, the leader, the lion-hearted protector, is known for his big and powerful heart and his wish to empower those oppressed by injustice, and to be a force of inspiration for all to move through their fear or limitation, to live large, robust lives, filled with spunk and spark. *Going whole hog* is his mantra. Powerful himself, he wakes up the hidden power and potential in others. One not to mince his words, he speaks from the hip, his truthfulness searing the camouflages of those hiding in dishonesty. His presence wakes you up viscerally as you feel his pulse of life. Happy to share his gifts, he is also known for a robust and often bawdy sense of humor. He is inspired to push through the known boundaries or limitations he encounters, to joyfully step into the unknown. Not one to be held in the trance of fear, he challenges others to engage and transform their fear into strength, independence, and self reliance.

THE INTERNAL PLAYING FIELD OF THE EIGHT

When the Eight is in addiction, his internal playing field becomes unbalanced, transforming his capacity to empower others into actions that threaten, scare, or control them. The following is a brief overview of the Eight's internal playing field.

Deep wound/relapse pattern: The deep wound of the Eight is his feeling that he is unwanted, rejected, and unsafe; he compensates by raging at and fighting the world.

Key commandment: The key commandment for the Eight is that he must be in control and in charge, or others will hurt him and take advantage of him.

Deep wish: The Eight's deep wish is to be strong and in deep contact with his heart, embracing life with power and aliveness, connecting with his innocence, and being a source of empowerment to himself and others.

How he sees himself: The Eight sees himself as powerful, strong, real, alive, passionate, decisive, self-reliant, courageous, and capable.

At level 4 and below: When the Eight falls into addiction levels, he falls prey to the emotional habit of lust, in which he compensates for his broken heart by being too intense, aggressive, habitually too expansive, and by using too much physical and emotional force. Add to this his mental habit of objectification, in which he sees people as objects without feelings to be utilized and pushed around for his purposes, to do his will. He treats himself as an object.

Inner critic: The Eight's inner critic tells him that he is good and lovable when he is in charge and in control, and when he stays self-reliant at all costs. He must be the protector and boss.

At his best: At his best, the Eight is powerful, intensely real and authentic, merciful toward those oppressed, and inspired to awaken the power and capacity of others. He uses power in service of love, is robust, fearless, and very funny at times. A pioneer extraordinaire.

THE HEALTHY EIGHT

The healthy Type Eight rides the life force like a Fremen atop a Sand Worm in *Dune*, living full out in the joy of reality. His life energy is a hot, robust fuel enlivening his presence and waking up the aliveness of those he touches. He does nothing half-hearted and is impassioned to live life to the fullest, head on, no shortcuts, no bullshit allowed, inspired by what is on the edge of his known reality.

The healthy Eight, a force of truth, justice, and the protection of those disempowered, joyfully leads individuals to the cliff of their known limitations and pushes them off, his hope being to ignite their hidden potential so that they might arise and embrace life as he does. At his best, he deeply wishes to empower individuals to live bravely, full-heartedly, authentically, his fear left in the dust. He is a powerhouse, a courageous lover of human beings, a force of nature.

Case Study: Dominic

When men enter rehab they meet Dominic, a tall, broad-shouldered, kick-your-ass-swaggering, confidant-as-God, ponytailed Dominican. An addiction counselor with eighteen years clean from heroin, Dominic's fierce intensity and street-smart, bust-your-balls courage greet them like a head-high fastball on the inside corner of the plate. Instantly the men are brought to attention as if their lives hung in the balance. (Truth is, their lives do hang in the balance, and Dominic knows it.)

His I-breathe-fire presence and his penetrating, take-no-crap immediacy instantly cut through the protective shields and strategies that addicted men have learned to hide behind. Tough, often impenetrable shields forged in horrid suffering and childhood abuse, forged in the humiliation camps of American prisons, forged in so many furnaces of shame that it's amazing these men walk upright and are still breathing—these are Dominic's targets. His goal: to destroy their soul-killing armor, to give them a taste of their authentic, passionate selves and their real freedom. He is going to unhinge their defenses so potently that real strength emerges from their depths such that they remember what it feels like to be alive. That's it. Nothing else, nothing less.

This is Dominic's genius: he shatters facades with breathtaking precision. In a nose-to-nose encounter with him, for a sacred instant, the addicted man who has weight-lifted himself into a muscle-walled, pain-numbing fortress feels for the first time the real terror and hurt that slither through him like a devouring snake. Dominic can reach into the core fear of a man, touch it, squeeze it, and electrify it into awareness. He feels Dominic's presence *inside* him. That alone unhinges a man's defenses.

Somehow this ninja counselor touches the addict's soul and

wordlessly says, "You are welcome here, my brother." Men instantly experience the sanity of softening their hearts, as if he has whispered in Jedi fashion, "Your strength is in your vulnerability. Be it now." Moments of possibility arise in the thought stream of Dominic-touched men. *Maybe this crazy-wild counselor can help me. Maybe I'm not hopeless. Maybe someone sees me, gets me, and actually cares about me.*

Welcome to the world of Dominic, the fierce, healthy Eight who mercilessly wakes these men up by laser-cutting through their tough hide, severing their attachment to their iron-hard masks. Dominic, the ferocious guardian at the gate of self-respect and honor, has made the deep impact he cherishes and adores. His Type Eight compassion—fierce, hot, passionate, in your face (not gooey, soft-soaped, New Age, everything-is-nice, compassion)—sears their hearts open and invites them in, whole hog, challenging them to pay the postage in advance (as Mr. Gurdjieff would say in his book *Beelzebub's Tales to His Grandson*).

Dominic says it loud and clear: "If you men want to get sober and stay sober, you've got to develop 'testicular fortitude.' That means you rise up, you take care of your sobriety, you do what you need to do, and you help your brother in this rehab. If you disrespect your brother, if you fail to have his back, you will not succeed in recovery. You notice when your brother needs help and you give it, generously, because you make a difference, you count, and you need each other."

The fire of heroic love burns through him, igniting purpose and real hope in men who have lost their jobs, homes, families, cars—everything. In every breath, word, body movement, and facial expression he delivers the Type Eight juice: It is these men's job to stand up, claim their power, clean up their act, and meet their challenges head on.

Because of Dominic's unshakable passion and boldness, men flock to his groups to be touched by his instinctive, live wire energy, his confidence and commitment, his cocky dignity, and his no-holds-barred, irreverent, bawdy humor. Standing room only. Men hunger for his contact. He's an instigator of rough-edged compassion and truth that inspires an uncanny brotherhood among the men. He reminds these men—whose souls have been squashed as kids; who had no moms or dads; who walked the streets at age ten, no one concerned where they were, starkly alone; who were physically abused by Mom, Dad, cops, uncles, addicts, gangs; men caught up in the horror of poverty and poverty discrimination and locked into the legal system before they could barely sense what they were about—he reminds them of their innate dignity and value.

He challenges the men to embrace their honor, to drop the sabotaging behavior of thievery, belittling and bullying others, acting tough and hiding their big heart, and literally anything that disrespects another or oneself. And respect is everything, the high card. He models brave, gutsy, feisty respect and kindness. He zeros in on their Achilles heel, names it, unmasks it, challenges them with it, and parades it around the room so they see what they have been running from.

His eyes filled with steely realness and fierce compassion, he begins his groups, "What handsome and beautiful men sit before me. It is truly an honor to be in the company of such men. Let us discover what is real and true in each of you, and carry that light into the world." He looks at each one, holding their gaze. This big, bawdy, rough-neck, kick-ass guy infuses dignity into every man sitting in rapt attention, waiting for his next brassy invocation of truth, dignity, and empowerment. He will not fail them.

Side by side with his fiery incantations are tender moments. One feels his heart, his depth, often when he talks about his beloved daughter, or his Pops or Moms. The dude is old-school Dominican: family comes first!

Men love or hate Dominic; there's no halfway. He walks his talk. He knows his stuff. And his message is simple: "You can resurrect your life. You can overcome your circumstances. You have a right to be alive, to rise, to inhabit your life! And your job? Give me everything you got! Otherwise, as the saying goes, I will devour your half-heartedness. So, my brother, let's get to work."

He means it. Completely and utterly.

THE EIGHT IN ADDICTION

Under the power of addiction, the powerful Eight energy morphs into a harsh, self-destructive force. All of his attention begins to center around self-protection, being on guard and at war with life, holding power over others, defending himself when no defense is needed, and bragging and bolstering himself while threatening and demanding that others respect him and his ego plans. Pumped up with vanity and self-importance (in twelve-step terms, as a compensation for the soul suffering and soul shaming he has experienced in his depths), he has lost contact with his right size. He has moved from inhabiting a magnanimous heart to one that is hardened and rock-like. Instead of using his power to empower, protect, and strengthen others, the addicted Eight uses his power and confidence to scare people, to make them toe the line of his will, to render them weak and vulnerable, to manipulate their weakness in service of his self-protection. From a force of inspiration to a force of destruction, addiction turns him upside down.

Deeply but unconsciously sensing he has lost what he loves, he toughens himself, over-expresses his power, intimidates people, rages, and pumps up his intensity and steamrollers life. "It's my will or get the hell out of the way! If I need to hurt you, I will! If my willfulness harms you or scares you, well, too bad for you! I don't have time for weaklings and sissies! Step aside or get behind me." In essence, he inflicts the abusive treatment he received at the hands of caregivers, probation officers, prison guards. Brusque, mean-spirited, impatient, at his worst he preys on the weak, using them for sport or as pawns in his game. He must take control of everything, or he will be hurt. Life is a battlefield. Strike before he is struck. Trust no one and need no one. His motto: Never show weakness.

But reality is a bloody knife. He knows what follows when he picks up a drink or drug: repetitious scenes of anger, attack, failure, and remorse; fights with friends, loved ones, strangers; rages over not getting his way, or rants over not feeling respected or honored; fits of anger at colleagues and coworkers over their incompetence, desperate acts pointing to his suffering.

Surrender for the Eight means a humble admission of defeat, that his addiction owns and possesses him, and beats him at every turn.

He can swagger but he cannot deliver. Repeatedly he vows that things will be different, he will control his drinking. Temporarily stoked on bravado and false confidence, he will pick up a drink or drug and dissolve once again into the maelstrom of repetitious horror. At the doorway of help, the path behind him is ablaze with heart-wrenching stories that would curl your toes.

Case Study: Billy

The worst-case scenario of an Eight in addiction is Billy, a hulking forty-year-old dad who stared back at me at a detox in earth-smacking shock. "I don't know how it happened, but I was driving down the road, and somehow I swerved and killed an eleven-year-old girl. I swear I had only a couple of drinks." He paused, an icy chill slicing through the room, my heart clenching with sorrow. "I have two daughters myself," he said as his eyes pooled with tormented sadness. The specter of a five-to-ten-year jail sentence and life without his daughters squeezed him like a vice grip. I stared back into his grief-stricken eyes.

At AA meetings, Billy began to hear the broken stories of other men, men who have sat where he now sat, who have learned one primary lesson: Recovering from addiction is never a solo journey. Never. Ever. It's a team journey. (Gurdjieff's words, in *In Search of the Miraculous*, ring loud and clear here: "Doing spiritual work alone is not difficult, it is impossible.") If Billy takes on his addiction alone, he will be beaten. Addiction is a subtle, fast, and compelling force that thinks for him. His addiction had become him and possessed him, spoke through and for him, told him he was fine, that his drinking and drugging were not a problem, that the real problem was the people, places, and things that irritated him and imposed suffering upon him.

Billy needed a new strategy: surrender.

Surrender for the Eight means a humble admission of defeat, that his addiction owns and possesses him, and beats him at every turn. Surrender means letting others in recovery be the eyes he sees with, the voices he listens to, the heart he feels with, at least for now. Surrender means not fighting against this addictive force but getting wise like a fox, such that he knows how his addiction speaks to him, tempts him, taunts him, shames him, steals his attention and will, and seamlessly enters his thought and feeling stream. Billy will come to understand how the addiction possesses him and that surrender means reaching out for help and not doing recovery alone.

Surrender means that he will solve the dilemma of his addiction not through will and force, and pushing against his addiction, but through understanding, awareness, and compassionate self-observation. Surrender means he accepts that he is a human being with limited power, and that with the help of others he can get sober, can outwit his addiction, and can neutralize its force in his life.

This is the path of transformation for the Eight.

THE FIRST TWELVE WEEKS IN TREATMENT

When the Eight arrives in recovery, he arrives as a street fighter who has been slam-dunked to his knees. He's gotten up over and over again, determined to not be beaten by his addiction, determined that he can outlast it, that he can control it, that he will win. He does not surrender easily and can take self-abuse like no other. As he has lost friends, jobs, and his health, he has pushed harder, gotten more aggressive, until something finally felled him. Maybe he ended up in jail for too many assaults or OUIs, or domestic violence charges. Maybe he's cut bait on his last job due to reckless or ruthless behavior and is now without money or a work history to land a decent job.

Or, as he continued to drop down into the rat hole of addiction, perhaps he has withdrawn, finally run out of fight, bravado, or egocentric gusto, and has hidden away in a hotel room, not wanting contact with people, and drinking to end his life. Now grace has interceded, and he has arrived at a treatment center.

One way or another, the Eight has crash-landed hard. In the rubble of his fall, new perceptions grip his awareness: he cannot plow through life uncontrolled, an angry bull in a China shop driven by a rage that fuels his ego will and his sense of false power. This message rings like a huge Zen gong: *I am out of control. I cannot will myself to stop. I need help. I cannot do this alone.* Simultaneously his inner critic chants, *You are such a loser, asking for help. If you were strong you would simply control your drinking. You're a wimp, a sissy, a pussy. Prove you can drink like a man!*

When he begins to trust that he has room for his bigness, the Eight will gradually begin to show his tender side, a little bit at a time.

The Eight in residential treatment is a big force. His gift to recovery groups is his capacity to tell it like it is—blunt as birth. If you are a counselor who wants to be the big force, the top dog, or who wants nice and cooperative clients who make you feel like you're doing your job well (that is, they massage your counselor-ego), or if you are offended when someone challenges you, unveils your Achilles heel, and sees your shadow with sharp-eyed clarity, the Eight will be your nemesis, the warlord, the one you wish you could just squash. Don't try, because he's already been squashed and injured deeply and is more than willing to fight that battle again, to go toe-to-toe with you, just to register his deep protest at losing contact with his vitality and aliveness in the first place. In his opinion, he's got nothing left to lose, so let's go for it. More than anything, he needs you to see through his fiery veils into his big heart, to create room for him to embody his true strength, to assist him in wielding his passionate response to life skillfully.

When he begins to trust that he has room for his bigness, the Eight will gradually begin to show his tender side, a little bit at a time. He just needs room, a big room, for all of that. And when his protective walls weaken, be prepared for a waterfall. As grief and vulnerability open in him, his bigness takes on a new quality because, infused with his tenderness, he is more fluent and flexible, and the beauty of who he truly is shines through. This is the blessing of waiting out his firestorms.

In groups, he will need help to learn when he uses too much force and intensity in his speaking, in his posture, and in his actions. When he expands and fills the room with his presence, he will not notice it. With tenacity, kindness, and clarity, you must mirror him, help him to begin to sense how his energy can push others away or intimidate them. Courageously, amid his firestorms, you must become a still and penetrating light that reflects him to himself in real time so that he sees, senses, feels it—there I am, bigger than big, louder than loud, posturing aggression—such that a gap occurs between his instinct to protectively enlarge and his impulse to charge. Slowly, he will learn intelligent restraint, no longer a puppet on the strings of his passion, or his need to intensify himself and wield aggressive control over those around him. He'll get gut-smart, intuitively able to sense right action amid all of his instinctual passion, and then his shining heart of gold will arise.

Case Study: Shawn

Shawn is a burly, five-foot-eight, fire hydrant of a guy, muscles rippling from head to toe. For several days, he declares boldly and loudly when in groups, "This feelings stuff is entire bullshit. What good is this? How can I trust any of you when you are all faking it, all doing that fake-sweet-stuff sharing? I don't believe you, and I surely don't need it!"

Slowly, slowly, his sorrow begins to emerge. As he sees that it's safe to share, that no one will attack him when he is vulnerable, and as he witnesses the powerhouse counselor, Dominic, ferocious and tender at the same time, something breaks inside him. In a spontaneous outpouring, he speaks of times as a boy, when, at six years old, he placed himself between his towering, raging, alcoholic stepfather, and his mother, to protect her. His anger-inflamed stepfather grabbed him by his hair and drove him into the refrigerator, beat his small body blue, and threw him to the floor as his mother huddled in horror. Arising from a heap of shame, he interceded again, a fierce little guy, trying to protect his mom, and again was beaten down.

In belly-wrenching gasps, the ensuing story unfolded: he, swimming in a sea of sadness . . . through repeated scenes of violence he guided the group . . . he, failing as a protector, being forced to survive in an emotional war zone . . . and slowly but surely, he becomes that raging stepfather. "What the fuck! How could I let this happen?!" he says. The realization pierces him like a stiletto: he has become what he hated, what he vowed to never be. His rage turned toward those he swore he would protect. Tears and more tears erupt as he speaks, a fierce, unforgiving sadness pouring out of him.

Then, slowly, slowly, from the tortured well of his grief, a kid with a big, sweet heart arises in the room, his glowing blue child eyes peering back at us. He speaks and cries at the same time, expressing regret over lost opportunities, dropping his shield, grieving, and feeling deeply tender. A remorseful outpouring ensues. He has failed with everyone he has cared about. He has used the best of himself to protect himself and push everyone away, treated them like objects, thought only of his next need or pleasure or relief. Puffed himself up to hide his fear. A scared boy became a bully. His heart bleeds soul-tearing truths, nothing minimized, each brazenly real revelation dropped into the room with a chilling thud.

The group is riveted into a stunning, reverential silence by the boldness of his raw truth. From the soft, now open space of his heart come these final words: "No one wanted me. Fucking A, how can you give this kind of message to a kid!" he exclaims, the horror of his abandonment piercing everyone in the group.

The room has become a sea of tears. This Eight has opened the door of vulnerability to everyone with his courageous sharing. The effects ripple outward as the best of the men is called forth, in their big-hearted hugs, in their loving and tender glances, and in their compassionate and brotherly words. Shawn has leaped into uncharted territory, unaware that this raw sadness was waiting for him.

Matching his heroic vulnerability are the attacks of his vengeful inner critic, who now bears down on him. *You should have been strong. You failed in your duty to protect. You are a bad person.* It is here that the Eight can succumb to self-hatred. Having exposed his vulnerability—the key to dissolving his addiction—and humbly acknowledging his errors, he can easily turn his anger and rage onto himself in an act of chastisement. Because his protective patterns of hardening and protecting himself are hardwired to his soul, they will naturally begin to reassert themselves. His work is to hone the habit of open-hearted vulnerability, to trust it.

If the Eight fails to keep this door of vulnerability open, he may stay sober for a while but can unwittingly embody the hard-style, no-love-or-compassion approach that some wounded AA members succumb to. They become what is termed a "dry drunk," in which principles of the program are used against self or those they sponsor, punishment and shaming the weapons used to inspire healing from addiction. In essence, they become their inner critic and drink in the wine of negativity. It rarely works for long, and when it does, the cost is off-the-walls high. What good is it to gain sobriety and simultaneously live on the juice of judgment and criticism of self and others? What good is it to gain sobriety, yet be unable to establish loving, tender relationships with his children or partner because he can't let his guard down? (See the movie *Thank You for Sharing* to get an example of this kind of recovery, wherein the star-recovery-person functions well and is acclaimed at meetings but cannot create intimacy with his own son.)

Nevertheless, something has touched Shawn, something that was clarifying and healing. And it is by touching this inner quality of being—where true vulnerability lives—that he begins to open up to real joy, happiness, and heartfelt connection with others. In the space of this vulnerability, he must learn to land and settle, very gradually, to liberate himself from the tyrant of addiction, and his Type Eight reactive patterns that fuel it.

THE EIGHT'S PROTECTIVE MECHANISM IN EARLY RECOVERY

The Eight defends himself against being rejected or hurt by instinctively creating a protective barrier around himself, an impenetrable shell that he mistakes as power. He exudes an intense force field that unwittingly says, "Touch this force field without welcome and all hell could break loose. Your death will be close by." This push-away energy is often visually evident in his posture, his gait, his intense glance, and his dragon-fierce voice. Others get the message clearly: "You will not bully me, coerce me, or hurt me. It's not going to happen. Tread unwelcome, and I might need to bully you or hurt you." He is often addictively committed to holding this boundary while insisting that others respect him, whether he has earned it or not.

The Type Eight must learn to do what he is certain will destroy him: ask for help. So caught between the reflex of protecting himself and being the strong one and asking for help, he more easily takes on the role of protector, or defender of others in recovery, before he has gotten the real help he needs. He can lead many to sobriety while eventually losing his own.

Here's how one Eight took care of himself in early recovery: Martin, a thirty-five-year-old guy, three months into sobriety, raises his hand to speak at a men's AA meeting. He begins, as he often does, with, "I'm Martin, and this is the last place on earth I'd ever want to be, so let me be clear with all of you. You're all a bunch of pussies and assholes, and I don't like any of you. So go fuck yourself. I couldn't care less if you like me. I don't need your friendship, and I don't want it. And just get this straight: I am not following your stupid rules. Especially the ridiculous rule of no sex in the first year. Are you crazy?! That's not happening! So, are we clear?" The shock of stunned quiet permeates the room. No one moves a muscle. Then, after a deep breath, he says, "I'm Martin, and I'm a fucking drunk, and I need to be here, but I don't like it. Okay. There, I feel better."

Now five years sober, Martin laughs at himself. He's been a hard hitter from the start, tough and combative, but today he will fight for any man trying to get sober while clearly stating what he does or doesn't believe. He fiercely proclaims, "Don't let God drive you from these rooms. Don't let anyone's opinions about how to work a recovery program drive you from these rooms. I'll be the first to say that I don't believe in everything AA says, but I don't need to believe. Today I have faith. I take what I need and leave the rest. I don't know who or what God is, and I don't need to," he states, his vibrant truthfulness pulsating through everyone.

He knows he has room for growth. He says, "It's taken me quite a while to trust that it's okay for me to ask for help. But I do it for only one reason. You told me that if I didn't ask for help, if I didn't use a sponsor, I would drink. So, I do it. I don't like it, but I've gotten better at it. I do wait too long to reach out, but it's a growth curve. I show up for meetings daily. And I pray because you told me to pray to a higher power. I don't know what I'm praying to, I don't like praying, I don't believe in praying, but I know that I'm sober today because I trust what you tell me to do. And . . ." He pauses, looking around the room. "I've come to like a few of you. But don't get your hopes up!"

This trust took time. What supported him was his sponsor and fellow AA members, willing to sit with him through his storms, his raging, his don't-mess-with-me behavior, until he saw that no one was leaving him, that people could handle him, could handle his anger whether expressed healthily or not, until he settled down, landed, and became willing to be vulnerable. And then he softened, in the powerful way a Type Eight softens—like a skilled martial artist blending strength and tenderness simultaneously.

CORE RELAPSE PATTERN

The Eight's core relapse pattern is his addiction to intensity and rage and his inability to allow himself to be emotionally tender and vulnerable. At the average levels of health and below, his gut response to perceived threats is unrestrained anger and assertion, forceful and quick. When he is unaware of himself and his defensive personality patterns (that he amplifies his intensity and his use of power while unable to sense that he feels hurt or rejected), he will be prone to attacking and confronting the environment, people, groups, and more so when he feels they are attacking or threatening him in the least; often when they are not! (This is called a *sincere delusion*.)

If he stays unconscious to this internal response pattern, he will feel justified in attacking whenever he senses a threat, real or imagined. Ironically, by his aggression, he will create the betrayal by others that he fears, which he will use to further justify his aggression. This is the Eight's treadmill of repetitious and unnecessary suffering.

The core identity that runs the addicted Eight is that he is the strong one who must be formidable and always in charge.

The more unconscious he is (level 5 and below), the more he will be an attack dog simply waiting to be betrayed. He will instinctively make himself big and large and formidable, while not noticing or realizing when he has used too much power or has harmed someone by his actions. His hard-edged insensitivity will give him the illusion of being in control and invulnerable, and will set him up for rejection (a core relapse trigger) even as he simultaneously denies and deadens his need for satisfying, emotional contact with others. Ironically, this will enrage him while he remains clueless as to why he is enraged.

The core identity that runs the addicted Eight is that he is the strong one who must be formidable and always in charge. He can show no weakness. He can't feel weak. He can't feel hurt. He must harden his heart. He can't feel his need for people or his need to be nurtured. He can't soften and feel his sweetness. He must assert his independence. If he *needs* people, then he is a failure.

Welcome to the prison system of the Eight in addiction recovery. If he is ever to achieve a happy and satisfying sobriety, he will and must make a jailbreak from this heart-closed, often ruthless internal system. He must recognize the unconscious pride he has developed in maintaining this prison system, the pride he has developed in believing he has no needs, and his notion that being emotionally shut down equates with strength. Not an easy task, but certainly doable, and learnable with the help of others.

TRANSFORMATION IN RECOVERY

The Eight's journey through recovery will be a continual relearning of the precious lesson of surrender. Once sober, once both feet are back on the ground and he is no longer taken by his addiction, he will "take back his will" (as is said in recovery circles). Borrowing from a recovery analogy, while he's at a meeting of Alcoholics Anonymous, his Type Eight personality habits (and his addiction) are out in the parking lot, doing push-ups and strategizing ways to more invisibly inhabit him.

Everyone in recovery knows this stark lesson: just when the recovering addict thinks he has extricated an unwanted personality habit (these are sometimes named "personality defects," but I choose to call them "personality defenses")—presto! The habit is back and riding comfortably in the driver's seat. From somewhere in the depths of his being it reconstituted itself, and before he can say, "I'm liberated from my suffering," it's back in charge again. And—the gods be damned—it arrives in a new disguise. Welcome to lessons of real-time humility. It's very hard to get too big for his britches when his patterns have their way with him . . . once again . . . once again . . . once again.

For the Eight, the patterns of asserting himself to protect himself, of shutting down his vulnerability, are hardwired in him. His walk into the rooms of AA will give birth to his freedom from addiction, but then the long and prosperous journey begins of undoing all the ways his personality structure is configured to harden his heart, to shut down the tender capacity of his soul, to keep people at a safe distance, and to survive among others as the strong one who protects his chosen allies or intimidates his enemies. This is his *deeper* addiction, his addiction to intensity, force, and control. Slowly but surely, as a sober man, he will see how these patterns continually and relentlessly reassert through him until he realizes they have a life of their own within him, just like his substance abuse controlled him. He will experience emotional relapse over and over again until step one looks like this: *I came to believe and clearly perceive that I am powerless over my personality patterns. They are often quicker and faster than me.*

At deeper and deeper levels, during year five, ten, fifteen, twenty in recovery, he will need to relearn the deeper meaning of surrender, and how he is imprisoned by his addiction to intensity and control ("pacing the cage" of his ego, as songwriter Bruce Cockburn writes). Like peeling the skin off an onion, he will slowly but surely move toward real freedom, meaning that surrender is not a one-shot event. As he witnesses his personality in action, and as he learns to resist its dictates, gradually he will feel the heartbreak and rejection that drove him to rely on his intensity and forcefulness. Courageously, he will allow himself to feel and surrender to this. In so doing, he will deepen his capacity to feel the real strength, realness, and aliveness that he truly loves, and the capacity to connect with his spacious and big heart. Then his powerful actions will be in service of love instead of being driven by a love of power. It's a long, slow journey through the labyrinth of one's learned defenses. One can take heart that everyone moves slowly, and that baby steps are powerful.

HELPING THE EIGHT

In the first twelve weeks of recovery, the Eight will be in full-fledged defense mode, unaware that he is protecting a very delicate soft spot in the center of his heart. He will unwittingly project a palpable force field and send an intimidating message: *Do not enter my personal space unless I have given you full permission. Or better yet, make my day, and intrude. Then I can give full weight to my suppressed shame and disappointment by kicking the bejesus out of you.*

Etch this in your memory bank like a neon sign: THERE WILL BE A TEST OF WILLS.

Mired in suspicion, certain that you don't want him around, feeling rejected and not wanted from the get-go, and able to stuff this suffering into the backwater of his heart, suspicion and scorn for the weakness of others stands paramount in his mind. The idea that he needs the help of others, that he must ask for help to recover, is the living hell he has worked all his life to avoid. And yet here he is, "*at a goddamn rehab!*"

His inner critic brutalizes him: *You are a wimp. You are a sissy. Needing help—what a pussy!* It is this screaming voice of his inner critic that calls him back to a drink or drug, where real men live, where tough men navigate life and have no needs for help, love, or compassion. Any hint of this noxious, weak-kneed stuff touching him and the inner critic arises like Tolkien's Balrog in the Mines of Moria, proclaiming, *You will be killed if you let your guard down, if you make yourself vulnerable. You will be fucking destroyed. Is that what you want?* Life has taught him that he must breathe fire to protect himself.

Etch this in your memory bank like a neon sign: THERE WILL BE A TEST OF WILLS. In working with an Eight in a group, if you are unable to be honest about your limitations without becoming a withering flower, if you are unable to be challenged at the core of your being without resorting to hiding behind the smooth-as-silk, I-have-no-real-flaws, you-are-the-messed-up-client counselor mask, your goose is cooked. The Eight in group is nothing less than a dragon slayer, wired viscerally to reveal who, exactly, is telling the raw truth, including you, the counselor.

If sitting before him is a counselor who is unaware of himself and is caught unwittingly in an ego inflation story of being the compassionate counselor, here to bring compassion to suffering, inferior souls while ever-so-subtly giving the message, *I'm not messed up like the rest of you*, be forewarned. The Eight will feel this arrogance and delusion in the core of his soul, and rage will ensue. If the counselor is asleep to his personal negativity and performs counselor-kindness-and-compassion when real compassion has not been plumbed, suffered through, and earned, the Eight will instinctively unmask him. Nothing brings out the dragon fire of the Eight like false pretensions.

You may know all the compassion lines on how to be empathic, but if they do not match your real, lived, personal suffering and hard-earned, in-the-soul transformation, then you are a fraud, and the Eight will smell it five miles away—unless you possess that rare, courageous humility and inner strength that allows you to say or demonstrate, "I am limited. I cannot begin to say I understand your suffering, but I am willing to learn. Teach me." This humble admittance of your limitations and your truth, without backing down, without collapsing into a puddle of shame, without taking personal insult from the affront of the Eight and attacking, will gain his respect. The Eight is an expert in what cannot be trusted. Compassion without depth, without flesh-and-bone experience, without being earned in the fires of life wounding is not real but false and cannot be trusted. He knows this because in his soul he carries the shock marks of betrayal with this invocation powerfully echoing from his depths: *This will not happen again. Not on my watch. I will not be betrayed again. Ever!*

You will love him and you will hate him. And, if you are sturdy within yourself, you will admire him. But be forewarned: unless his self-hatred habit is softened, unless he is mirrored and shown the ways he turns against himself right on the heels of a deeply vulnerable sharing, he will undo his best efforts.

(You may want to read the book *Mother California* by Kenneth Hartman, a memoir by a Type Eight who worked through many layers of rage to finally connect with his big heart while serving a life sentence for murder. It is truly an amazing recovery.)

SUGGESTIONS FOR THE EIGHT

It will be incumbent upon you to provide supportive, helpful guidance to the Eight as he navigates his way to health. Share the following suggestions, perhaps just one a week so as not to overwhelm him.

Enlist the support of another to help you become aware of when you are too loud, too aggressive, and too forceful.

The Eight likes his intensity and the flush of power that comes with it—it's exciting and oh-so stimulating, the adrenaline rush of amped-up energy, the rush of power that deadens vulnerability and feeling of weakness, the inflated sense of self-importance. The dead bodies in his wake are sometimes the only clue that he has come off the rails.

Try these suggestions to help him become aware of when he is too loud, too aggressive, and too forceful.

- Let him know that it will take time for him to learn to observe his personality in action, so in the beginning, he must allow a trusted friend (sponsor, therapist, coach) to be a mirror for him.

- Explain that it will take many humbling moments of self-reflection to become conscious of the ways his personality habit has taken charge, to observe that he has gotten too big and inflated to communicate in a way that works.

- Help him to understand that withdrawing his identification from this adrenaline rush is big work because the rush is so blinding, fast, and intoxicating that he hardly notices he is engulfed in it.

- Instruct him to ask friends about this dynamic pattern and to alert him with a hand signal (peace sign, thumbs down, squatting to the floor) when he has turned dragon-sized. He can ask them for a signal that says, *Too loud. Too harsh. Too scary. Stifle thyself.* He must commit to stopping whatever he is doing, take a breath, and feel the intensity in his body, voice, actions.

Learn to be aware of your immediate impact on others.

When caught up in the juicy and adrenalized energy of intensity, the Eight cannot feel how he has hurt, scared, intimidated, or insulted another.

Try these suggestions to help the Eight become aware of his immediate impact on others:

- Help him learn to notice the telltale signs that he is hitting too hard, too loud, too much. He will see it in the body posture of someone he is interacting with as they shrivel away from him because he has scared them.

- Have him practice, at least once a day, consciously listening to his volume level and his tone of voice, and to become conscious of its nuances. Is his voice threatening, commanding, pushy, angry? Is he intimidating others through his physicality, pressing too close to them, coming at them? Is his chest puffed out? He must learn to notice this; his recovery counts on it.

- Have him log at the end of the day those times in which his intensity level went higher than he wished it had. Are apologies in order? Apologize immediately and with genuine humility.

Train your capacity for empathy.

When in addiction, the Eight cannot feel or sense the suffering or feelings of others; the tender spot in his heart has disappeared.

Try these suggestions to help him train his capacity for empathy:

- A powerful exercise for the Eight to develop heartfelt empathy is to learn to put himself in another's position, to realize their suffering (Gurdjieff, a magnificent Type Eight, called this "external considering").

- Have him practice visualizing and imagining what it is like to live in the skin of another, to become them in his imagination; to inhabit their body, heart, and thoughts; to become that person he dislikes, criticizes, hates, or disdains because they act weak and powerless.

- He can learn to sense their suffering, then imagine that he is *looking out at himself through their eyes*. What does he see? This active visualization of considering others, sensing what drives them and affects them, and how his presence effects them will begin to awaken his ability to feel empathy for others and to notice when he is hardening himself, hurting others, and hurting himself.

Humbly and quickly apologize when you have caused harm.

Humbly apologizing for any hurt or fear the Eight has inflicted will begin to create a wake-up call because every sincere apology builds on an internal memory that will alert him at a critical point that he is walking down a well-worn path that leads to apology. He will feel the pattern in his body, and a gap of choice will arise in him, something like, *This is a very good time to restrain whatever force of anger, aggression, or self-defense is arising in me.*

Try these suggestions to help him learn to apologize:

- Help him understand why apologizing is uncomfortable as hell to do: it's because it smacks of weakness in the eyes of his ego.

- Warn him that he will feel weak, humbled, and vulnerable when he does apologize, yet apologizing is a doorway to his peace and happiness.

- Let him know that nothing blows people away like a powerful Eight humbly apologizing for hurting, offending, or scaring them, or for being caught up in egotistical self-importance.

- Have him invite friends and coworkers to let him know when he has stunned them, ridden roughshod over them, been insensitive to their feelings, got caught in big-shot-ism, or disregarded and disrespected their approaches to problem solving.

- Encourage him to apologize quickly and to plan to do it often. He will learn to cherish the humility that arises, as it is a sign that essence is speaking through him. Apologizing will begin to give him eyes to see himself in action.

- Humbly apologize (his ego will protest loudly). Humbly apologize. Humbly apologize. And get curious. He can ask people, "How did my behavior make you feel?" This, too, will begin to give him eyes to see himself.

Learn to sit with your intensity before acting on it.

The Eight is often driven to intense action in order to avoid deadness, fear, ego diminishment, or vulnerability. He must learn to discern between seeking intensity that enlivens him and seeking intensity to avoid vulnerable feelings.

Try these suggestions to help him learn to sit with his intensity before acting on it:

- The Eight must learn restraint. Encourage him to do a meditation practice daily. Suggest that he sit quietly, noticing the rising and falling of thoughts, emotions, and the tides of his passion and intensity.
- Encourage him to learn to sit in the furnace of himself, allowing his intensity and fire to simmer, cook, clarify, settle, and purify without getting up and going into action. With time, he will notice how and when he jumps into intense action or confrontation as a means of escaping feelings of vulnerability, or as a means to express healthy inspiration.
- Point out to him in real time when you witness his adventurous spirit being called into action for life-enhancing adventures and when his defensive patterns are being activated to avoid fear, deadness, and vulnerability. Living, in-the-moment examples will give him eyes to see his patterns.

A MESSAGE FOR THE EIGHT

Share this message with the Eight in recovery:

Your deep gift is to empower others to arise and own their innate power and autonomy, to champion them to step forward into life, fully alive and lit up with passion, realness, capacity, big-heartedness, generosity, and energy. As you model and embody this in your personal action-filled, passionate life, your magnanimous heart will activate the can-do courage and personal will of those you touch. "Going whole hog," as Mr. Gurdjieff would advocate, becomes a lived mantra. Your impassioned aliveness touches a life wire, invigorating and inciting people to be resourceful, independent, able to stand on their own two feet, able to think for themselves, able to walk through whatever challenges they face. Your lion-hearted message is loud and clear: you can arise and meet your challenges, you can muster the will, courage, and wisdom to match your difficulties and claim your autonomy.

These are some of the beautiful gifts of inspiration you give to the world. Thank you!

CHAPTER 12

Type Nine—
The Gentle Mystic

Imagine what our neighborhoods would be like
if each of us offered, as a matter of course,
just one kind word to another person.

—FRED ROGERS

The healthy Nine, known as the mediator, the peacemaker, the compassionate mystic, exudes a force of gentleness, kindness, understanding, and deep acceptance of those he encounters. Like Fred Rogers, his spirit invites a loving acknowledgment of who one is, and encourages one to relax, settle, be as you are, no need to create a false edifice. His gaze, his presence say *Welcome, my friend. You belong here.* Because he has done the necessary inner work to heal his heart, to relax in his own skin, to trust in and embrace the gentle silence of quiet mind, he teaches others that there is great hope for addiction recovery, that this is learnable, and then transmits the grounded wisdom to make this happen. He teaches by examples, that like water smoothing the edges of a stone, that compassion works in the same fashion, to heal and transform the suffering one has endured into a life fully engaged.

THE INTERNAL PLAYING FIELD OF THE NINE

When the Nine is in addiction, his internal playing field becomes unbalanced and his peaceful, grounded, unifying capacity devolves into isolation, withdrawal, and nonparticipation in life. He disappears from self and others. The following is a brief overview of the Nine's internal playing field.

Deep wound/relapse pattern: The deep wound for the Nine is his feeling of having no importance; that he doesn't deserve to be seen, honored, or encouraged; and that he is nobody special. He risks all of this happening if he dares to be an individual.

Key commandment: The key commandment for the Nine is to be peaceful at all times and disturb no one unless he wishes to be banished into non-existence. He must create peace for those around him.

Deep wish: The Nine's deep wish is to feel deeply connected with himself and those around him, to trust life, to feel its warm embrace, to sense and transmit the deep peace that abides in him, to be a force of compassion in the world.

How he sees himself: The Nine sees himself as peaceful, easygoing, unaffected by life, down to earth, and able to soothe others.

At level 4 and below: When the Nine is in addiction at level 4 and below, he disengages from his feelings, goes along with the wishes of others, shuns any kind of conflict, and becomes terrifed of losing contact with his inner stability and peace. Avoiding conflict becomes his primary goal. He sinks beneath the surface of life to evade being affected by stressful circumstances. His emotional habit is sloth. He numbs himself, tunes out from his inner reality, and stops sensing what he cares about. He often feels exhausted when moving toward something he cares about. His mental habit is rumination or daydreaming. He gets addicted to the free association of his thoughts, anchors himself in a soothing, imagined, peaceful inner world, and ruminates on things that don't galvanize him to move in the direction of what he cares about. Any thoughts that pertain specifically to his own passion or yearning get lost in the sea of unimportant thoughts.

Inner critic: The Nine's inner critic tells him that he is nobody special, that he doesn't deserve to take up the time and energy of others, that his job is to simply keep things peaceful for others, to not let on that he exists and has personal passions. If he stays unnoticed, then he is good and lovable.

At his best: At his best, the Nine is able to stay centered and calm in the midst of conflict, and becomes a guide to assisting others in resolving conflict. He is attuned to the best and brightest in others while able to attend to his particular dreams and passions. He is a great force of harmony, creativity, compassion, optimism, and calm for others.

THE HEALTHY NINE

The healthy Nine is a magician, able to seep through the well-honed defenses of others with the force of an invisible and penetrating compassion. He is the force of water that wears down the hard edges of men's type-specific defense patterns. He gets inside the hearts of those he seeks to help, softens them, and lets them know they can relax and simply be as they are.

He has navigated the inner journey of a recovering man, knows the pitfalls, the disappointments, and the gentle keys that unlock the defenses of others. Easygoing, chill as one could be, he knows the inner conflicts that drive people to internal war and knows the unifying psychic waters that must be navigated to bring unity to men in conflict. Grounded in reality, he creates the safe internal psychic ground that loosens the trauma structure of the souls he helps. In his presence, the defensive layers that have protected men from hurt begin to slide off, revealing their essence.

Case Study: Marty

Marty, a lanky, six-foot-one Type Nine addiction counselor, glides across the group room, his presence seamlessly interwoven and in flow with the depth and psychological energy of the space. The men barely register his presence, he being so invisibly nimble and nonintrusive, but he is fully alive in the psychic waters of the room, extending his awareness into the vulnerable heart space of the men at rehab, touching them, feeling their energy, caring for them.

His gentle silence transmits a quieting depth that softens them and lets them know they can settle, it's safe here, safe to relax. His quiet presence takes them in, reads them without intruding or making them uncomfortable, touching their souls with such grace that nothing tightens in them or withdraws in self-defense. Sitting with a group of guys in very early recovery, all gnarled, grizzled, rough-edged, he is the landing gear for their trust-no-one rigidity and soul-scarred disappointment. It makes no difference where they have come from—the county jail, the streets, the homeless shelter, the state prison, the backwoods of Maine, the hospital ER, an STD clinic, a psychiatric hospital—all are welcome here.

Somehow this beautiful guy can hold the suffering of these men, hold it and not be broken by it, hold it with a magical nonattachment and tenderness such that it touches him but doesn't bury him. In holding their suffering with this gracious and light touch, not denying any of the heaviness or sharpness of their suffering, he teaches them by example to viscerally walk easier and lighter in the belly of their suffering. Something softens, relaxes, lets go in them. Whatever emotional chains they are bound begin to loosen. It's as though a mysterious light begins to break through their conditioned beliefs that they are losers, irretrievable drug addicts, rejected and unwanted men, failures with no hope, unredeemable men of no value.

Marty's compassion starts to penetrate these negative self-identities such that something softer, deeper, and truer starts to stir and form in them. Marty's transmission is captured in the way he speaks with earthy kindness to the men, the way he holds space and honors every man regardless of how they show up, such that the men begin to relax the death grip that their past has been strangling them in. His presence whispers, *Put your suffering down. Easy does it, my friend, let it go, breath, trust, nothing to prove here.* Like the shiatsu practitioner, he senses the psycho-spiritual meridians that are tangled in the men he works with, knows how to apply the right attention, pressure, and gentleness to these internal transmitters of emotional pain, and disarms them gently.

Marty represents the healthy Nine in recovery. What you see is what you get; he is soft spoken, right-sized, and humble. Because he has transformed his inherited emotional suffering into a mountainous stillness and kindness, he can sit exactly where these men sit, in the belly of their hurt, and peacefully abide and teach them what he has learned. It is then that men's fast-moving, hypnotizing illusions and fear impressions begin to slow . . . way . . . down . . . such that they begin to develop eyes to see their inner patterns—and without spotting their patterns, men cannot begin to heal. As they view themselves through Marty's eyes of compassion and mercy, it makes sense to extend tenderness and mercy to themselves, to relax their unrelenting self-punishment, to let love touch them.

Marty worked with another Type Nine, Rick, a burly, tormented guy mired in loss, depression, and hopelessness, nearly unable to function in any way. Rick's alcoholism had further torpedoed an already unstable interior, like mixing gasoline with fire. But Marty, with his vast stillness and enduring patience, would hang with Rick and give him simple steps; over and over he would recite them: *Rick, no hurry; here are the simple steps. Go to meetings, ask for help, get a sponsor, show up.* Rick would remember, and then he'd forget. And back on the streets he would go, a whirling dervish of chaotic agony, wandering in the despair of homelessness and alcoholic hopelessness, dead-eyed depression possessing him—and somehow, he would make it back to rehab, two legs and one arm in the grave. There Marty would be, at the doorstep, while soul-hungry vultures were sucking the last remaining blood of hope from big Rick's soul, he so very close to becoming another lifeless stone of death.

Marty would greet Rick like he had been patiently waiting for him for a hundred years. Just hanging and waiting. No big deal, just waiting. Rick, shocked numb from his last relapse, brain cooked and hard-boiled on confusion and turned into a scrambled mess, would listen to Marty with that 10 percent of him that he could still listen with, that tiny window of sanity in an otherwise torqued brain. Slowly, Marty's peace and enduring resilience would get into Rick, seep into his heart, into the thought stream of his mad thoughts, into the frozen musculature of his broken body.

Touched by Marty's healing spirit, Rick would begin again to come online, start to arise within himself, while Marty kept hanging next to him, one breath at a time, his still calmness touching the broken places in Rick, saying, "No rush, Rick, we're just watching a sunrise here. Just ease into this moment, and do one simple thing. One simple thing."

Rick, a big guy endowed with a wrestler's body, who had vanished into near-invisibility such that he inhabited a pencil-thin shell, is, seven years later, a peaceful rock of stillness and ease. He has quietly walked with Marty a thousand miles up the mountain of himself and found his soul, his sense of humor, his grateful heart, his dignity, and his strength. Damn, it was amazing to watch.

Marty, his ceaseless stillness the antidote to Rick's madness, is still humming along waiting for the next guy to help. No rush. The guy will come. He can feel it. He will be there. He is ready. No river to push here. Quiet waiting is the magnet for the next lost and broken soul. Marty is a Type Nine at his best, endowed with infinite patience.

THE NINE IN ADDICTION

When the Nine slips down the ladder of addiction, his innate capacity to be a source of kindness and support to others disappears. Lou said it this way: "When I dropped into addiction, my only wish was to be left alone so I could drink. I existed in my own private bomb shelter. The lights were off, and no one was home. I was a small flame of nothingness, utterly invisible to myself and everyone else, and that was fine with me. I was a ghost, and everything around me had a ghost-like quality, as if they had no substance, no weight to them. Everything was transparent and could be seen through. Let me drink and die alone, and don't bother me; that was my wish. I neglected everything and everyone."

The Type Nine, whose gifts of supporting others and whose unconditional positive regard for the suffering of others are the hallmarks of his humanity, slips away into the basement of his soul when addiction takes him out. Hunkered down in the inner temple of his imagination, fantasy is his primary refuge. Unlike the Eight, who becomes more explosive and volatile, the Nine grows more passive, more distant, more withdrawn, more wraith-like. It's not unusual for the Nine to be literally carried into addiction recovery by loved ones because, left to his own devices, he will die quietly (Betty Ford is a great example) but imagine he is resting. He has this dying thing mixed up with relaxing, taking a needed rest, just chilling out, while his lived life is one drink after another until he passes out, as in going, going . . . gone.

Case Study: Lou

Lou wouldn't and couldn't see any of his addiction problems and instead dropped into a drunken blur, where nothing could touch him, affect him, or get his attention. If his stoic silence didn't discourage others from helping him, if his lifeless body sitting at the gravesite of his TV didn't rivet them into hopelessness, if his dead-man-walking, I-am-a-corpse-not-a-human-being, lying-in-the-bowels-of-death didn't cut them to the bone, then his last-ditch rages would.

Lou says, "The time came when my family abandoned me, quit trying to get me into recovery, and I thought, 'Finally, I'm left alone. No more people to contend with.' One option was left: drinking until I passed out *till death*. This I did every day. My family could see my dying soul, and I did not care."

Did Lou understand what he was doing? Absolutely not. His awareness consisted of a vague, fleeting flicker of reality, fogged and blurry; everything had an indistinct, shapeshifting, undifferentiated sense to it. Reality disappeared. Occasionally, he'd feel the suffering of waking up out of a hangover but was so exhausted from his drinking, so closed down physically, emotionally, and mentally, he could barely feel it for long. So, he drank to numb out.

At one point, Lou had decided to kill himself. In the dead of winter, he went into the Maine woods on land that he owned, took a ton of booze with him, and drank with the intent to die. A week later he woke up in an AA meeting at a detox, listening to the voices of other late-stage alcoholics like himself. He remembers saying, "I'm Lou, I'm an alcoholic, and I want to get sober." He hadn't known how he got there. He learned later that two hunters found him passed out in the freezing cold and brought him to detox.

Today Lou has been sober for nine years. He reminisces, "In an alcoholic fog, death seemed like a form of sleep, a comfort to be sought. All I wanted to do was fall asleep."

THE FIRST TWELVE WEEKS IN TREATMENT

In the first weeks of recovery, the Nine's suffering will arise unedited. His defenses will be shaken. He will either crack open into reality or dive back into a familiar escape pattern: his soothing imagination. It will take a monumental effort for him to simply say out loud what he is experiencing and stay with the realizations.

Here, on this cliff of death where he dangles off the overhang, he must be seen, must be heard, cannot stay mute. Yet the inner critic voice will screech, *You are nobody special, and you better keep it that way.* When he starts to speak up and tell his truth, his inner critic will blare, *Who do you think you are? You're taking up the breathing space of others simply by being here. Shut up!* And often he will.

Marty says it this way: "When I was in early recovery and someone asked me what I was feeling, I felt like I was looking down into a deep well of foggy murkiness. I was upset, was feeling something, but the minute someone asked me about it, it would immediately become so indistinct and unclear, and fog up into a cloud of confusion, that mostly I'd say, 'I have no idea.' And I meant it. I felt a vague, formless discontent that, if rested in too long, would suddenly ascend from this fog as paralyzing anxiety. I'd immediately shut down and slip into my delusion-space where comforting dreams could settle me down."

For Marty, learning to feel the inner nuances of his feelings took a long time. His first task was to simply stay sober, keep showing up, and find someone who could guide him. He had little sense of what his feelings, wants, and needs were. He states, "I needed my counselor, my recovery friends, to teach me to identify my feelings. Often, they'd see and sense that I was sad, and they'd note it for me, bringing my attention to my voice, saying, 'You sound so sad. I hear it in your voice. Can you hear yourself as you speak?' Or bringing attention to my facial expression, they'd say, 'Your eyes are moistening. You look sad. Can you feel sadness in your face, or your throat, or your chest? What do you notice?'"

The magical inner garden of the Nine, where the weather is always good, the food so tasty, the memories always good and positive, is the escape hatch that he utilizes under stress.

He had to practice attuning to these details, sensing into them inch by inch, allowing himself to open to what was going on inside him. It was extremely difficult because he had so many buffers built in to keep his emotional experience on a thin band of experience: not too high, not too low, just a gray zone that kept him safe. He needed people to notice and teach him how to identify what was going on inside him. Slowly he learned that it is safe to feel his feelings.

The magical inner garden of the Nine, where the weather is always good, the food so tasty, the memories always good and positive, is the escape hatch that he utilizes under stress. The problem is that protecting himself by disappearing into his comforting fantasies is the exact, precise thing that calls his addiction to him. In the fog of this imagination dream, the undigested emotional suffering in the interior of his being—fear, anger, shame, vulnerability, powerlessness—can be held at bay outside of his awareness for only so long before it merges with the snake-like force of his addiction, waking it up so that suddenly, out of the blue, three years sober, the Nine finds himself drinking himself to death, not knowing how he picked up the booze in the dreary, ghost-infested alcohol aisle of Shop 'n Save. How did that happen? *I don't even remember picking up the bottle! What the heck!*

The Nine must see that he has been residing, hibernating, and building a secret garden of pleasure and comfort in his imagination, while in his lived life, real family members are hurt and have lost faith in him, and his children feel abandoned by him.

The truth is, he was mesmerized watching a euphoric recall video of his addiction life (all the good parts, that is) that had crept into his mind-stream during his emotional fog of numbness and unwittingly seduced him, saying, *Time to drink, time to shoot up, then you'll feel relaxed and at peace; then you will feel as if you are home.* As one Nine describes it, "Entering my thought stream like an old friend, erasing all memory of the terror and horror that awaits, I sipped on the euphoric recall of past drinking and drugging experiences and down I went, into the forgotten abyss of my repetitious suffering. Weirdly, it felt good to sink into annihilation, like dropping into the arms of an old friend. How can hopelessness feel good? How weird is that?" It is a song, a hypnotic movie, a videotape that is always willing to meet him, that seeks him out, that is always looking to creep unnoticed through the back door of his soul.

The Nine must see that he has been residing, hibernating, and building a secret garden of pleasure and comfort in his imagination, while in his lived life, real family members are hurt and have lost faith in him, and his children feel abandoned by him. He must see that he has avoided contact with reality by using oxycodone, painkillers, alcohol—*and his imagination*. He must see that everything has been reversed in him. His real thoughts and real suffering that brought him into addiction treatment often feel like unreal, dreamlike events that have no substance or capacity to touch him. His imaginary addiction life—where pleasurable scenes and euphoric recalled images of all his fun moments of drinking and drugging play like a nonstop reality movie in his imagination—feel real to him. (An example of this dream world addiction is depicted in the movie *Requiem for a Dream,* most especially in the role played by Ellen Burstyn. The character's imagination becomes what she experiences as real.)

He has learned to fix his attention on his imagined life, to mistake this fantasy safe zone as the real, where he is anesthetized from his life suffering until he can't avoid it. Take away the drugs that fuel the inflamed imagination retreat he has unwittingly created for himself, and he is left with no defenses other than his capacity to withdraw, to pull an invisibility cloak over himself, and simply hunker down in hiding. In that moment in early recovery, he must face into the terror that what he imagined as real was not. At this perilous point of awareness—in the cradle of emptiness in new sobriety, seeing that he has sunk into a world of illusion—recovery begins. From this tender and most vulnerable place, those around him must be his anchor of reality, his eyes to see what is real and true.

Case Study: Devin

Devin sits in group day after day, so still and quiet one would never know he was there. The second week in, it dawned on his counselor: he continually wasn't asking Devin to share, like Devin was emitting a strange force field that made him invisible. He was there on the couch, but the counselor couldn't really see him, as if he was part of the furniture. Devin's ability to emit zero life force energy was remarkable, like a Jedi Master who waves his hand and says, "Look away, counselor, I'm not here. No need to ask me any questions, move on."

His counselor called him on it. "Devin, how do you manage to avoid getting asked to share? How do you do it?" A big, sun-splitting grin crept across his face, his eyes suddenly lit up with recognition, as he emerged from his internal camouflaged bomb shelter for a brief minute. "I learned it in grade school," he said. "I just knew how to get teachers to not see me, to move past me, to pass over me as I lay quiet as a mouse. I got pretty good at it."

His counselor thought, *no kidding*. Devin skillfully emitted an atmosphere that quietly delivered the message, *Don't bother me. Don't approach me.* He could shapeshift into the client who looked like he was doing just fine. In fact, he was the master of "I'm fine." (In recovery-speak this means "I'm fucked up, insecure, neurotic, and emotional.") He had lost his family, his kids were brokenhearted over him, he didn't have a job, and he was over there on the corner of the couch looking as chill as anyone possibly could. (We say the Nine gives "good face.")

Devin's outer expression made him appear as if he were appropriately engaged, listening to others, exuding facial expressions that looked like he was paying attention (not overdoing it, of course—that would draw attention—but not totally checked out, either; right in between, where he gained no notice), adeptly not reflecting anything that might draw "counselor attention" to him. He could keep the counselor skillfully chilled out, too. Devin cultivated an enticing ambiance around him that had everyone nodding along in "spiritual bypass" mode when it came to him, all feeling hypnotically at ease with his I've-charmed-you-into-relaxing-and-overlooking-me presence. One would never know he was resting in his swamp of poisonous drug history.

Even as the vultures were passing over his near-destroyed life, he could numb into complacency. It is this sleight of hand that could eventually kill him.

What drives the Nine's passion to stay hidden behind his invisibility cloak? Fear. Utter, vulnerable, raw, I-could-die-if-I'm-seen fear.

Of course, this ability to disappear is a gift of Devin's instinctual intelligence, wherein he had learned to survive in traumatic situations as a kid and not draw dangerous attention or circumstance to himself. He could ride smooth as silk in the middle of the storm. The next thing his counselor knew, Devin had left rehab, a wave of pleasantness coating the counselor's most recent perception of him so that he didn't notice the impending signs that Devin was leaving, that he was slipping away. *He was so likable,* thought the counselor. In retrospect, like waking from a dream, it dawned on him that Devin had been gone ever since he arrived in rehab. He had hidden skillfully and seamlessly in his counselor's fast-asleep perception, and only the next day did the counselor barely notice that Devin was not in group. Where the hell did he go? Hey, did anyone see him leave?

What drives the Nine's passion to stay hidden behind his invisibility cloak? Fear. Utter, vulnerable, raw, I-could-die-if-I'm-seen fear. The Nine believes, *If I'm seen, I will be annihilated, cut off from all that I love. So, I will lie low, below the surface of my life, a stone at the bottom of the stream, life gliding over me, you not noticing me. In fact, I'm so good at hiding that **I** don't notice me, so no disturbance occurs inside or outside me.*

THE NINE'S PROTECTIVE MECHANISM IN EARLY RECOVERY

The safety of the Nine depends on his ability to avoid being affected by events and people that evoke conflict—the dreaded C word—so he retreats to his inner world, where he has collected memories that soothe him, settle him down, make him feel at ease. Having a difficult time with his wife? He has an internal repository of positive memories from those times when they were doing well. Like pulling a DVD from the archives of his mind, he can, when needed, experience the "good" wife whenever he wants to avoid his real conflicts with her. Forget the grouchy one!

The wife on the outside, in real life, might be a first-rate pain in the neck to him, but not to worry; he's hanging out with his "inner" wife, and all is well. He so loves her, and hey, what conflicts? *We're doing great! Why would you possibly want to go to couples counseling? We're good*, while his real-world wife glares at him, wanting contact with something real in him, wanting on some level to shake him awake. His real wife sometimes feels more imaginary to him than the one he has constructed in his imagination.

The Nine faces this challenge: After suffering many losses due to the habit of disappearing under stress and avoiding conflict at all cost, he will face relapse. It is only a matter of time before real life cracks into his inner sanctum and his undigested suffering needs relief.

His pattern may be that he sits at recovery meetings never complaining, reacting, or sharing his particular truth, and people think he's doing fine and doesn't need help. Underlying all of this is a fundamental childhood message that rules his quiescent behavior: *It's not okay to be seen or to stand out. You don't matter. Your presence doesn't matter.* With this message etched deeply into the Nine's psyche, the idea of asking for help is dangerous. Better to appear at peace with those around him.

The Nine in early recovery experiences deep anxiety. His comfortable world has dissolved, and he is racing as fast as he can to establish a new sense of inner stability, to feel as though he's got things back in place, all the while projecting the image of being at ease. Yet here he is at AA or NA meetings, or in a support group surrounded by grumpy, unpredictable, recovering strangers who speak out, sometimes blunt as birth, sometimes crude and rough and threatening, mostly edgy and not peaceful. The Nine must learn to navigate this dangerous chaos, to rise and be seen in this hornet's nest of unpredictability. He must learn to notice that while his body is at an Alcoholics Anonymous meeting, he is often with his family in his imagination, or chewing on comfortable thoughts such as *wouldn't it be nice to drink* as a diversion to feeling his anxiety. Over and over again he must bring himself back into the meeting, here and now, leaning into his real suffering, finding a way to tell the truth of his soul, dropping his invisibility cloak.

He must face his strongest escape route: his attempt to unify with those he loves via his imagination, holding up the hope that he can return to his dissolved life instead of actually doing the recovery work. The twelve steps, getting a sponsor or coach, letting himself be seen, working with a therapist, uncovering internal dead bodies of suffering—this is the work he must do. Not imagine; do.

CORE RELAPSE PATTERN

The Nine in recovery has a clear core relapse pattern: he can disappear even as he is sitting right in front of everyone. One Nine said it this way: "As I sit in a recovery group, it appears as if I'm listening. But I'm often off in my imagination, constructing a cozy Hobbit hole and stockpiling it with all the stuff that makes me feel good."

This is what the Nine does so well. He remembers the positive times with friends, lovers, and family, taking in only the positive impressions of the past like a wonderful visual drink and deleting negative memories that try to reach him. He habitually returns to the illusion that all is well, doing his best to avoid the horrific feeling that, at any moment, this imagined peace can come undone, a tidal wave of disorder swamping him. In this safe bubble everything is fine with his family and kids, nothing has been lost, there are no fights, his drinking hasn't harmed anyone, and there is no crazy behavior that he can remember.

The baseline sleeping pill of the Nine is that he easily forgets what is critical to his growth and development.

He can edit all of the suffering that has brought him into recovery without even thinking about it. It is this escape habit that must be destroyed if he is to get sober and remain sober. If he doesn't, then one day, as soft as the quiet wind, the Nine has disappeared from meetings, leaving the playing field of recovery. The gentle presence gently left. He was hardly noticed. Where did he go? What happened? Later investigation will reveal that he *forgot* to show up for his counselor's meeting. He made a list of recovery meetings that he was going to attend, but he forgot about them. He doesn't know why. He was going to see his sponsor today, but he spaced it out. He completely forgot what happens when he drinks. It's as though the knowledge that would scare the shit out of him regarding his drinking got deleted from his memory tracks.

This sleepy forgetfulness is typical of the Nine in early recovery and can reemerge in later recovery. The baseline sleeping pill of the Nine is that he easily forgets what is critical to his growth and development. He flows with the stream of things, hides, or gets lost in the waves of the moment where he is not detectable to himself or others. It is then that his partner abandons him (in his imagination he thought all was well), friends tire of him, his connections with others lose vitality because he can't show up as a fully feeling individual in the matrix of his own life. His spouse and friends want to shake him to see if he's home or if he has any juice, spine, aliveness, fire, or individual perspective, as in, *Dude, do you ever get angry? Does anything move you?*

Once he begins to slip into complacency and stops doing inner work, the Nine's type patterns will sneakily resurrect.

At year five, ten, fifteen of his recovery, when personal losses occur, when his unconscious strategy to avoid being disturbed actually causes the disturbance the Nine wished to avoid—disruption and abandonment—his addiction slips quietly into his soul-stream and takes over. Or, after initially breaking through the chains of drug addiction, slipping in the back door comes a replacement addiction: overeating, shopping, indulging in video games. He unwittingly finds new comfort systems that become his protective shield for avoiding any further contact with his real and felt sense of himself. (We know this happens with all the types; they stop one addiction and pick up another, almost instantly.)

One spiritually seasoned Nine puts it this way: "Like all the types, I began my recovery by finally allowing myself to feel both my internal and external disturbances. I learned I can handle this. I felt an initial aliveness that was liberating. Then I found a new and improved automatic pilot, a new pattern of survival, that allowed my newly awakened *real* awareness to slip beneath the waves."

Every new awakening, stretching the Nine into new openness and vulnerability and humility—which feels so good—can be followed by a new, slippery ego version of *I'm sound asleep again and wearing a healthier-looking mask*. Unconsciously, the Nine can step away from a newfound aliveness while imagining he is still open and present. (All the types do this, which is why the person in recovery needs sponsors or mentors to remind him when his ego has slipped back into central position. It's human. Know that this is what happens in recovery.)

The Nine's well-honed survival habits don't disappear because he has had a few months or years of opening his heart. His ego pattern is itching to sneak in through the back door of his awareness. When he is in a challenging period of recovery, the Nine can unknowingly hide behind a new form of showing good "recovery face"—all is peaceful and calm within him even as he falls back into an age-old survival invisibility. This fundamental principle applies: *You grow, or you go.* Once he begins to slip into complacency and stops doing inner work, the Nine's type patterns will sneakily resurrect.

TRANSFORMATION IN RECOVERY

I watch Dominic, the majestic Type Eight counselor, work with Frankie-the-Flower, a Nine in recovery. Dominic's gift is to give a client a name that exposes their weakness and strength and then use it to point to their growth edge. He sees that Frankie is terrified, that his backbone is shaky if not nonexistent. Dominic, being a protector of the weak, does what he does. He loves a guy out of hiding. He helps them grow a backbone.

One day in group, his back to Frankie, Dominic said, "Now let me tell you guys about Frankie-the-Flower from New Yawk," his twang sliding through his words. "I saw him with his kids yesterday, and I noticed how much he loves them, how much he revered them, how passionately he cares about them. Oh my god, his eyes lit up like the New York sun. And his kids, the look in their eyes—they adore him. They couldn't take their eyes off him. Frankie over there looks so quiet, but don't you buy that crap for one second. He cares for his kids from the belly of his soul. Here he's got fire; not wimpy fire, but sizzle, passion, guts. He just doesn't show it. His passion, if you notice closely, is found in his gentleness. Hey, everyone needs to cultivate gentleness and kindness. And this is muscular, dudes, muscular gentleness and kindness," Dominic said, his eyes hot with conviction. "And when he gets over his fear, he will touch all of you. His kindness will melt you down into a kinder version of yourself."

Dominic turned to Frankie-the-Flower and held him in the gravity of his attention. Frankie was in tears. Dominic, who had named Frankie's inner world, had seen him, had felt deep inside

Frankie's soul and touched the chords of Frankie's real and caring heart.

He continued: "I can only imagine after the kids left from the visit, the heartbreak that cut through him, that almost knocked him breathless. I saw this. He was sitting over in the corner with his head down, chest sunken, both grieving and raging at himself. See, Frankie is deeply sensitive, and he cares passionately about the people in his life, so much so that he can't find words yet to convey his love and caring for them, and he's way more alive than you might notice. But we've got to notice him and help him find words to call out these feelings so that he begins to name what is beautiful within him—so that he can realize his gifts. When he gets really quiet, when he's disappeared before your very eyes, when he is so quiet that he dissolves into the couch, you know that some intense stuff is going on, so we got to help him notice this, and coax him out. Right, Frankie?"

Because of Dominic's magnanimous words, Frankie now had a felt connection with a very real part of his soul that mattered to him. He had been handed a precious jewel: the compelling reason for getting sober and walking through all the inconceivable, god-awful discomfort of early recovery. Dominic's words had touched the very fabric of his heart, the "real" in him, and the real in him felt good. Frankie was developing the eyes to sense and feel himself.

Dominic, his eyes teary, too (it is an honor to see a powerful man, filled with the granite of courage, be so vulnerable), said, "Okay, enough of this soft crap. Next thing you know, you'll have me doing yoga and eating vegetables, and this ain't happening soon. That's it, dudes!" He turned to Frankie. "Just remember this, Frankie-the-Flower from New York, whose soul is as soft and lovely as a flower, I have your back. We have your back. You can come forward and be seen. We want you to shine your light here. It is time for you!"

Frankie, blown away by how he had been touched, said meekly, "Thank you," and bowed his head in humble thanks. This is called loving a guy into reality. Over the next several weeks, Frankie started talking in group, telling his truth, arising, and the others discovered that he had an unexpected, belly-splitting sense of humor. Dominic continued to turn the fire of truth up in him little by little, saying, "Come forward, my brother, you belong here."

It is in these holy moments that the power of love is evident. This, above all else, is what calls men to sobriety: sheer love and kindness for the suffering of the others, naming it, seeing it, and calling it forth. Powerful.

HELPING THE NINE

Where working with the Eight focuses on restraining his overuse of intensity, working with Nine focuses on waking up his intensity, turning up his life-light, calling him out of hiding, and empowering him. The core message of the Nine's inner critic warns him that if he is not peaceful, or the people around him are not at peace—meaning, if he can't fix the upsets and conflicts of others—then he is not lovable.

The Nine needs space and room to move. Trust in his process, understanding that stepping into life and taking steps to assert or nurture himself feels as alien as learning Russian.

It is important for the therapist or counselor to understand the Nine's recovery needs. The first is simply this: pressuring him to change only locks the Nine into resistance ("change will destroy all my peaceful connections with those I love, so back the fuck off"). The magic trick of the Nine is to pretend he is going along with your good intentions and thoughtful advice so that you'll get off his back while he digs his heels in, in protest: "Hell no, I won't go." Encouraging and inviting the Nine out of hiding works far more effectively than applying pressure, which means that there is an element of patience that you must be comfortable with to help him. You have to get it out of your head that you know how quickly the Nine should be moving. You don't.

The Nine moves as slow as molasses to stay invisible, where he is safe. Then, when you're not looking, he will burst forth and fly by you in the jettisoned flow of his personal transformation. The ultimate question is, can you be patient enough to trust his chosen speed? Can you stay away from that well-intended AA recovery habit of saying things like, "This is an action program, and you're not taking any action! Speed this ship up or you will relapse." The Nine will yawn, externally agree, and then hide out. Take the pressure off him, and he will get curious about coming forward.

The Nine needs space and room to move. Trust in his process, understanding that stepping into life and taking steps to assert or nurture himself feels as alien as learning Russian. He is hardwired to accommodate you and then accommodate you some more. Buried down deep is a wish to have a life. Your job as a counselor or sponsor is to notice this, notice the signs of his meaningful preferences, point to them without expectation, to simply reflect, as in, "I feel your wish to get connected with your kids." Notice it and notice again because as his real passion arises on his screen of perception, it will disappear as quickly as if it were never there in the first place. You can say, "I notice that when you talk about your dreams or hopes, you quickly change the subject and bring attention back to others in the room. What's it like to talk about what you want? What were you feeling when you were talking about a dream to be a teacher? Where did you experience that in your body?"

Mirror him, feel and name for him what he appears to be feeling. "I noticed that when you spoke, I could feel anger. Did you feel it? I often experience it in my belly. Where did you notice it in your body?" A Nine may report that when he feels anger, he dissociates from it so quickly that he doesn't notice he was even experiencing it. You could reflect, "I just noticed your anger. Where did it vanish to?" Be patient when he replies, "I don't know. I don't know where my feelings vanish." Keep gently and patiently noticing. When he finally gets it, when he drops into the sensations of his feelings, watch for a revolution in his awareness.

SUGGESTIONS FOR THE NINE

It will be incumbent upon you to provide supportive, helpful guidance to the Nine as he navigates his way to health. Share the following suggestions, perhaps just one a week so as not to overwhelm him.

Transform your habit of habitually accommodating the wishes of others.

The Nine frequently says yes when he means no. He says yes when he doesn't know what he wants. He agrees instinctively and smiles as if he agrees, even if he wants something else. He fails to notice the wrenching feeling of self-abandonment in the pit of his stomach, with volcanic rage simmering deeper still.

Try these suggestions to help him weaken his habit of accommodating the wishes of others:

- Encourage him, when he is offered a choice, to practice saying, "I don't know. I'll need to think about it. I'll get back to you." For the fun of it, he could also practice saying, "Hell no. That's the last damn thing I want to do. I don't know what I want, but I do know what I don't want." Ask him to see what fun he can have with this.

- Encourage him to sense the difference between going along with the wishes of others because he actually doesn't have a preference or because he is afraid of conflict.

- Challenge him to make a list of the conflicts he avoids and to make an intention to engage at least one of them this week.

- Help him to speak his truth by giving him "option" sentences he can try on. Have him try this when asked what he wants: "When you ask me what I want to do, I get anxious really fast because I don't know, and then automatically go along with what I think you want. I need work it simply saying, *I don't know. Give me some time to think about this. I'll get back to you.*"

Have trusted friends alert you to the signs that indicate you are angry, sad, or fearful.

The Nine has developed protective patterns that edit out his anger, his right and need to have a voice, and any emotional responses that draw attention to him. He can speak angrily and not feel it. Occasionally, he can erupt like Mount Vesuvius, but that, too, will slip back into the vault of *what the heck was that?* He needs his friends to help him out of hiding, people who teach him about the particular camouflage he is unknowingly hidden in.

Try these suggestions to help him ask for support in recognizing his feelings:

- Encourage him to ask trusted friends to help him recognize his feelings. He needs a friend who lets him know when his body is showing signs of rage. You could reflect to him, "Do you notice that you are growling like a cornered animal? Do you notice your fists are clenched and your face is tense and hard? Can you sense this in your body? When you speak, listen to your angry tone of voice." Or you might say to him, "If I'd experienced what you experienced, I would be deeply sad (or angry or fearful). I wonder if you can find this feeling inside of yourself?"
- Give him examples from your life in which feelings were evoked and how you worked to stay connected to them, so that he has a role model to study.

Become aware of your sloth or disengagement from what you care about.

The Nine's personality machine often registers sloth as tiredness. He finally gets excited about something, and then he feels as if someone pulled the plug on his energy. Time for a nap. Time to withdraw. Time to forget the excitement he just felt.

Try these suggestions to help him become aware of his sloth:

- Explain that he must learn to observe his pattern of getting excited followed by a strangely soothing loss of energy or a mesmerizing loss of clarity about what he wanted. Poof! Gone!
- Challenge him to write down any moments when he feels inspired about a goal or activity as soon as he experiences them. Then have him review his list at the end of the day. Does he still feel energized by his goal or activity, or has it slipped away into a hidden bunker in his soul?

- Challenge him to choose one of these inspired ideas and to take a concrete action on the chosen goal whether he feels like it or not. This could be writing an essay, journaling, meditating, or starting an exercise program. Remind him that he might, by his actions, resurrect his inspiration should it dissolve.
- Instruct him to begin working with noticing and collecting his dreams, wishes, and inspirations and against the forgetting mechanism of his type.
- Have him check in with you each evening with the results of his labors.

Become aware of how you express your anger passive-aggressively.

The Nine silently does things that irritate the hell out of people and yet can't understand why they are furious with him. *I'm so peaceful; what is their problem?* His spouse asks him to please pick up after himself and he says, sure, hon, I got it. And then, day after day, when confronted about the ever-growing mound of his clothes on the floor, with the kindest of hearts and biggest puppy dog eyes, he says, "I am so sorry. I'll get to those straight away!" And he doesn't.

Try these suggestions to help him recognize his passive-aggressive anger:

- Remind him of his Type Nine pattern to show anger indirectly. Give him examples of how this might show up in his life: expressing anger at his wife by forgetting important dates, or being consistently late, or by agreeing to actions that he fails to follow through on.
- Help him begin to sense whether these are passive-aggressive actions designed to upset him partner while he looks peaceful and chill.

- Ask him to talk about moments when others have expressed outrage at him for things he failed to follow through with. Is there anger at the root of his behavior? What is the anger he needs to express directly?
- Challenge him to ask him loved ones when they notice his passive-aggressive patterns.

Learn to sense your body.

The Nine is wired to have his attention stolen by his inner fantasy world and his ruminating thoughts—dilly-dallying on stupid stuff (as one Nine noted), losing connection with his dreams and aspirations, spacing out and forgetting his commitments.

Try these suggestions to help him learn to sense his body:

- Ask him to notice sensations that arise of their own volition as he inhabits his body.
- Recommend that he make it a practice to sense his body for at least ten minutes each morning, going through each limb, hand, foot, trunk, face, mouth, jaw, eyes, just bringing the focus of his attention to his body. Learning to inhabit his body through sensing practice will set up an observation tower internally where he can begin to sense directly when he checks out into Type Nine dreamland. He will learn to *feel this.*

Begin to notice the voice of your inner critic.

The Nine's inner critic whispers several messages through the thought waves of his mind. *You're nobody special and shouldn't take up much space. Your opinion doesn't matter. You are lovable when you bring peace to everyone. It's your job to settle everyone down.*

Try these suggestions to help him disengage the inner critic:

- Instruct him to consciously attempt to go in the opposite direction of the inner critic's instruction when he hears its message. That is, take up space, talk louder, express your opinion, let everyone know your preferences, don't go invisible. Assert, assert, assert. If he hears the message *You're responsible for everyone being peaceful*, say out loud, *Not my monkeys, not my parade.* Or, *nice try, critic; have a nice day. I cannot control or change anyone, thank you very much.*

- Instruct him to relax his habit of trying to reach in to calm the emotional waters of others.

- Remind him he can be chill inside himself, that this is where his strength and inner work lie. Invite him to try to allow others to be upset and responsible for calming themselves down.

A MESSAGE FOR THE NINE

Share this message with the Nine in recovery:

Beloved Nine, you are on a journey of discovery. Note these wise words of A. H. Almaas:

"Your conflicts, all the difficult things, the problematic situations in your life are not chance or haphazard. They are actually yours. They are specifically yours, designed specifically for you by a part of you that loves you more than anything else. The part of you that loves you more than anything else has created roadblocks to lead you to yourself. . . . It will go to extreme measures to wake you up, it will make you suffer greatly if you don't listen."[1]

That said, you are ready to rock 'n' roll your way down the aisle of recovery. Yes, there will be bumps, but they will be good bumps

---

1. A. H. Almaas, *Diamond Heart Book One.*

that provide growth experiences. And besides, although you are playing the most difficult game in town, you can rest assured that it is the one game truly worth playing.

As one recovering man said of the benefits, "You can't even begin to imagine the gifts that will come from your labors because you've never thought of them or perceived them. So, hang on through the dark times, because every journey of endarkenment is followed by equal enlightenment. Be of good cheer. Although the end is near, so also is the resurrection. The best is yet to come." This is all so very true in my experience. There is great hope for you. Commit to the work with everything you can, and your path will unfold.

CHAPTER 13

The Dynamics of Relapse

Unconditional kindness is the one thing that can penetrate the defenses, confusion, and sufferings of the addicted individual.

MICHAEL NAYLOR

An individual who has successfully been in recovery and sobriety for many years will likely have made many changes to his life. He may have reestablished his career, recovered his family, renewed friendships, and repaired a lot of the damage that was done during his active addiction. Unfortunately, this also has the potential to lull him into a false belief that he is free from the addiction or that he can now control it. (See the appendix for a list of some of the patterns, pitfalls, and misunderstandings that contribute to an individual's relapse into his substance abuse patterns and the protective patterns of his Enneagram type.)

Relapse is often just around the corner, no matter how long the sobriety. However, keep in mind that millions have recovered from addiction and live fruitful and positive lives. They have navigated all the stages of recovery in a variety of ways, which lends itself to the wisdom that there is no one way to get sober or maintain sobriety. We learn every day of new and creative ways individuals have used to support their transformation.

The man who has relapsed after a period of clean time might say, "I didn't see it coming. In retrospect, I see that I stopped talking to people, stopped expressing what was going on inside me, became resentful and unhappy, and blamed everyone for my suffering and difficulties." In other words, he returned to his addictive behaviors.

Old habits established at levels 6 and 7 have the capacity to reappear when an individual stops taking healthy actions to stay awake. The negative feelings one experiences at level 6 can actually feel safer and more familiar, while moving up the levels to higher states of well-being can initially feel frightening and disorienting. This phenomenon cannot be emphasized enough. One would think that feeling better would be easy, but it goes against the grain of personality habits. It takes time to rest in feeling good and feeling that one deserves it.

This tendency to be gravitationally pulled back into one's familiar world is as predictable as the rising sun. After some time, sober and clean, making strong efforts to restore one's life to sanity by making amends to those one has hurt, and working hard to be honest and in integrity with oneself and others, the recovering individual unwittingly can stop doing the very practices that allowed him to stop substance use and begin to feel better. ("Okay, I'm fixed now! No need to continue my practices. I've done the work I need to," or, "That's enough of feeling good. I want to go back to 'normal.'")

He stops attending twelve-step meetings (or whatever group has helped him), stops working on himself in counseling; stops talking about difficult emotional issues; stops meditation, yoga, or connecting deeply with others; and stops engaging in the spiritual practices that have expanded his awareness and aliveness. In so doing, his center of gravity drops down to level 6 and the persuasive voice of his addiction is there to meet him. *Greetings from the abyss!* Before someone can yell, "Your hair is on fire!" he is back into his addiction. As is often said in AA, "You're either moving in the direction of your growth or heading back to your addiction." That's the rule, and there is no way around it.

Differently, an individual might stay close to AA and yet not address the issues that his personality type and its fixations create or cover up. He has problems communicating with his wife and kids but doesn't seek specific help for it. He may think, hey, *I worked hard to get sober, that's enough! Maybe this problem will pass on its own. I've grown enough.* He has difficulty with intimacy in friendships, but he doesn't take on the issue because he thinks AA (or whatever he has used to get sober) should magically fix it, or because he can't tolerate the feelings of vulnerability that arise when he faces his undigested emotional issues; that is, these feelings rattle the doors of his Enneagram personality patterns with all its fears. Unbeknownst to him, this vulnerability is a door through which he can experience deeper and continued happiness.

Alternatively, he may not listen to his heart's desire to grow, expand, and seek adventures that have real meaning for him (and move him up the levels of health), and fails to pay attention to his boredom or the absence of his passion. He begins to feel dissatisfied and thinks he needs to go to more AA meetings, or sponsor more people, or redo the twelve steps. But he is at a new pivotal point that his recovery has prepared him for: his intimacy and relationship issues, taking action on his true inspirations, and his desire to live more fully.

For many individuals, the call is to move beyond AA (but with AA as a foundation, or whatever path has brought him sobriety) into deeper realms of spiritual growth and awareness, where even more amazing adventures await. There are far too many who fail to step forward through these doors and begin to rust emotionally and psychologically. In time, the individual relapses. One day, in an emotional fog, he picks up his drug of choice and is gone.

Avoiding the issues that need to be addressed is a form of disconnecting from oneself and reality, a form of numbing that sends an individual back down to levels 5, 6, or 7, setting the stage for addiction relapse. Understanding the Enneagram-type numbing patterns becomes critical for both the therapist and the client. If a man stays numb and bored long enough, resisting his soul's calling to grow and expand, his addiction will come online quickly. This same individual, hibernating in states of boredom, numbness, safe and deadening routines, or emotional stagnation, will fall back into the swamp of his addiction when a catastrophe arrives. And it does—he loses someone he loves, or a job, or something he values. Suddenly, shocked and overwhelmed, he finds that addiction is at the ready.

Another pattern occurs: A recovering man five, ten, fifteen, or twenty years sober suddenly begins to feel a nagging, mysterious emptiness in his life. On the surface, everything is going well: he has a good job, a family, and friends. Out of what feels like nowhere he begins to feel an unfamiliar loneliness and meaninglessness. In response, he doubles his recovery work, but nothing touches it. Weeks, months, even years roll by as everything continues to lose its meaning. He begins to feel emptiness intruding upon everything. He has no language for it. (If he understood the Enneagram, he would be prepared for this phenomena, that is, the more one grows and expands and moves up the Levels of Health, the more light is thrown onto deeper suffering he has not healed.) He is ashamed. He feels he is failing in his recovery. He no longer tells friends about his situation, as they suggest he's not working a good recovery program, but he knows he is. He begins to despair. He thinks he's done something terribly wrong to feel this way. His self-confidence weakens. Out of the fog of this confusion, his addiction curls up around him like a cozy friend, and he relapses.

As a result of his healthy efforts to be sober, he has unknowingly invited the arising of undigested suffering from his past: deep rage, shame, hurt, or terror from his childhood. Insufficiently aware and unprepared for the navigation of these inevitable patterns, he is often shocked and struggles to understand the disorienting feelings.

The nature of the soul is to heal and expand itself, and with each new expansion the individual experiences more joy, openness, tenderness, compassion, and confidence. Whatever emotional knot of suffering blocks the way to further growth and expansion then arises for healing. Once again, the individual is challenged to confront and heal the deep wound patterns of his type. Many in recovery don't know about this dance of growth followed by a deep dive into new undigested trauma, going back and forth until one has truly reconnected fully with oneself.

With the intrusion of new and difficult emotional states or feelings, the individual often feels temporarily disoriented. This new emotional, psychological material is unfamiliar and unknown and unnamed. He might feel that he shouldn't be feeling this way, not after all these years of work in recovery and groups! In fact, this newfound suffering and difficulty are exactly what is needed for a successful journey to more freedom and expansiveness. He can either suppress and dodge this mysterious doorway by numbing himself and closing down or engage it and get the help that he needs. If he numbs or avoids the feelings, he will drop back down the levels, inviting his addiction to slide its way back into his being. In a state of defensive numbing, his addiction *will* take him.

Unexpected crisis (loss of job, divorce) also stimulates buried feelings from childhood that were never expressed and grieved (the abandonment of a father or mother, for example). These emergencies are more likely attended to by getting therapeutic help, but if not attended to, and overwhelmed by the sudden suffering, his instinctual type patterns will come on board to block or disassociate from the painful feelings, all of which drive him into the lower levels of awareness (6 or 7), where he is no longer in contact with reality and forgets what substance use does to him. Everything is made undeniably worse.

These are some common relapse addiction patterns that recovering individuals will encounter on their journey toward more freedom. The good news is that they are all foreseen and can be prepared for. Once an individual has unwittingly fallen to levels 5, 6, or 7 due to unexpected or confusing suffering, the defense mechanisms common to his type block his capacity to sense what is real and hinder his ability to resurrect himself. Which is why it is said, "Stay close to people who know you. When you go unconscious, they will be the first to notice. You will be the last."

A WORD ON DEPRESSION

Depression has the effect of activating and *intensifying* an individual's deepest type fears and defensive patterns because depression stimulates despair and hopelessness. Depression is real.

There are some who, no matter how much inner work and healing they do to change their emotional patterns, no matter how much love and kindness they receive, still cannot avoid their depression. In this case, an individual is experiencing a biochemical imbalance in the brain and must use antidepressants to alleviate his depression. Without the correct antidepressants, no matter how hard he works he will eventually relapse. A human being can only stand to feel awful for so long, especially when he is making efforts to heal himself. He must not feel defeated if antidepressants bring him relief; it is a blessing. He must utilize the blessing because without it, all of his efforts will feel like they are in vain.

A FINAL NOTE

Recovery has been achieved by millions of people on the planet. Vast networks of support are available via twelve-step groups, Christian groups, Buddhist groups, Sober and Smart Recovery Groups, Men's groups, and more. Each man is responsible for finding his way, and the therapist or sponsor must be careful to not assume that what worked for one man will work for others. Dogmatic belief in only one way to recovery pushes many away from getting the help they need.

Remember that some individuals will fall many times at the hands of their addiction. Work with them to not be discouraged. Many people finally get sobriety after numerous attempts.

The order for recovery is this:

1. Don't give up.
2. Get up one more time than you've been taken down, and you will get sobriety.

Keep this book close at hand so you can reference it regularly before, during, and after meetings with your clients. The road to recovery is never-ending, but by applying the unique information herein, you will be helping your clients with specific action steps to deepen their mental, physical, emotional, and spiritual health, and offering them a roadmap to lifelong recovery.

Your position and role as a therapist, sponsor, or counselor is incalculably invaluable to your clients' recovery. By learning the nuances of the Enneagram personality types and how they play into the addiction recovery of each individual, you are increasing your skill and ability to offer unique, customized, client-specific support to each and every person who is traveling the road from addiction to sobriety and health.

Remember, no one chooses to be addicted. It is a response to overwhelming suffering and heart break. The addiction chooses the suffering person.

Pitfalls of Maintaining Recovery

Review the following list of recovery pitfalls with a client, and have him identify the ones that are most important to him at this time. Discuss what his awareness of these relapse dynamics is. For the most part, his job is to be aware: Is this happening? If so, what are the causes of these responses? Are they a problem? What actions are needed to protect his sobriety?

Using this inquiry and the items he has addressed invites an opportunity for him to tell the truth of his experience. Maybe he finds AA dogmatic and too religious. *Let's find a group that you feel attuned to.* Maybe he's been hurt or shamed by someone in recovery. *Let's talk about ways to work with your hurt feelings.* Maybe one of the listed issues trips him up. *Let's explore it and problem solve.* Perhaps he truly feels that the following inquiries have no value for him. *Not a problem. He's in charge of his recovery and his life.* Your goal is to remain an objective, nonjudging force of understanding for him, and to truly realize that you do not possess the knowledge or plan for his evolving life. He must discover this on his own. Your trust of his judgment will invite him to return to you when he is in need.

These are the pitfalls that lead to relapse:

- He stops using the practices and support system that got him sober and clean, and helped him get healthier.

- His core Enneagram wound or trance pattern slips back into the driver's seat.

- He fails to surround and align himself with people who care for him and his transformation, and who inspire and challenge him to stay on course.

- He stops talking about what is real and true inside him.

- His patterns slowly reassert and cover his newly open heart, causing him to lose contact with the clarity that brought him into recovery.

- He is unaware of the power of his addiction identity and how it talks, whispers, threatens, and lies.

- He has a hidden belief that he is not wanted or cared for. Deep down, he believes that he is unforgivable and that he deserves to continue to suffer for the suffering he has caused others.

- He places all his hope for alleviating his suffering in work, finding a relationship, or being successful in the world instead of working on himself with equivalent efforts.

- He picks up other addictions to help him avoid feelings of emptiness, shame, anger, and sadness.

- He stops taking the next growth action, thinking he has done enough growth.

- He feels vulnerable and unsure when he is moving in the direction of growth and into new and unknown territory.

- He returns to familiar friends, family, and neighborhood and slowly but surely returns to perceiving reality through his old, conditioned impressions.

- He experiences survivor's guilt, wondering how he can liberated if family and friends still suffer with addiction.

- He thinks that he doesn't need to continue his transformation work because he feels so good.

- He is not aware that growth is a process of four steps forward, three steps back.

- He doesn't give back by helping others with his gifts.

- He doesn't realize that feeling good is something he will need to develop tolerance for.

- He doesn't realize that he will need to develop great compassion for seeing his Enneagram patterns replay inside of him hundreds of times before the type patterns weaken.

- He feels like he is allowed only so much help, so when he a new crisis arrives, he doesn't ask for the needed help.

- He doesn't realize that spiritual growth is like peeling an onion, or, as Riso-Hudson say, excavating the true self at deeper and deeper levels. He will slowly need to navigate his emotional suffering.

- He doesn't consciously anticipate what his addiction triggering looks and feels like, so he doesn't make a plan of action to respond when an emergency arises.

- He doesn't have an emergency medical kit, that is, trusted friends who give him eyes to see himself.

- He doesn't make amends when he needs to.

- He doesn't practice good self-care, such as eating well, meditating, exercising, and getting enough sleep.

- He experiences addiction amnesia, forgetting the incredible suffering his substance use has caused himself and others.

- He begins to have euphoric recall, becoming enchanted on imagining past drug experiences and idealizing the good times.

- He fails to realize that undigested suffering or trauma will be triggered and will need real attention.

- He stays rigid in one system of growth and fails to notice that a particular spiritual path or practice is no longer working for him.

- His will to continue his practices weakens.

- He fails to realize that the further along on his spiritual path he is, the more subtle and insidious his patterns will become for a period of time.

Resources

The resources here are offered as additional sources of information.

BOOKS

On the Enneagram

Daniels, David, and Price, Virginia. *The Essential Enneagram: The Definitive Personality Test and Self-Discovery*. New York, NY: HarperOne, 2009.

Gurdjieff, G. I. *Meetings with Remarkable Men: All and Everything, 2nd Series*. London: Penguin Group, 1991.

Hudson, Russ. *The Enneagram: Nine Gateways to Presence*. Read by the author. Sounds True, 2021. Audiobook.

Ouspensky. P.D. *In Search of the Miraculous*. London: Paul H. Crompton Ltd, 2004.

Riso, Don Richard. *Personality Types: Using the Enneagram for Self-Discovery*. New York, NY: Houghton Mifflin, 1996.

Riso, Don Richard, and Russ Hudson. *The Wisdom of the Enneagram: The Complete Guide to Psychological and Spiritual Growth for the Nine Personality Types*. New York, NY: Bantam, 1999.

Rohr, Richard. *The Enneagram: A Christian Perspective*. Crossroad Publishing, New York, NY, 2001.

Riso, Don Richard, and Russ Hudson. *Understanding the Enneagram: The Practical Guide to the Enneagram*. New York: Houghton Mifflin, 1990.

On Recovery

Brand, Russell. *Recovery: Freedom from Our Addictions*. New York, NY: Henry Holt, 2017.

Burroughs, Augustin. *Dry: A Memoir*. New York, NY: Picador, 2003.

Jamison, Leslie. *The Recovering: Intoxication and Its Aftermath*. New York, NY: Little, Brown and Company, 2018.

Mate, Gabor. *In the Realm of the Hungry Ghost*. North Atlantic Books, Berkeley, CA: 2010.

Prentiss, Chris. *The Alcoholism & Addiction Cure: Addiction Ends Here*. Los Angeles, CA: Power Press, 2007.

Rohr, Richard. *Breathing Under Water: Spirituality and the Twelve Steps*. Franciscan Media, 2021.

Sheff, David. *Beautiful Boy: A Father's Journey Through His Son's Addiction*. New York: Houghlin Mifflin, 2018.

Wilson, Bill. *Alcoholics Anonymous Big Book*. New York, NY: Alcoholics Anonymous World Services, Inc., 2001.

Wilson, Bill. *As Bill Sees It: The A. A. Way of Life*. New York, NY: Alcoholics Anonymous World Services, Inc., 1967.

Wilson, Bill. *The Twelve Steps and Twelve Traditions*. New York, NY: Alcoholics Anonymous World Services, Inc., 1981.

On Mindfulness and Healing

Anderson, Bob. *Stretching* (40th anniversary ed.). Bolinas, CA: Shelter Publications, 2020.

Brown, Brene. *The Gifts of Imperfection: Let Go of Who You Think You're Supposed to Be and Embrace Who You Are*. City Center, MN: Hazelden Publishing, 2010.

Cameron, Julia. *Walking in This World: The Practical Art of Creativity*. New York, NY: Tarcher, 2002.

Carson, Richard D. *Taming Your Gremlin: A Surprisingly Simple Method for Getting Out of Your Own Way*. New York, NY: HarperCollins, 2003.

Chödrön, Pema. *How to Meditate: A Practical Guide to Making Friends with Your Mind*. Boulder, CO: Sounds True, 2008.

Chödrön, Pema. *Welcoming the Unwelcome: Wholehearted Living in a Brokenhearted World*. Boulder, CO: Shambhala Publications, 2020.

Crowley, Chris, and Lodge, Henry. *Younger Next Year: The Exercise Program*. New York, NY: Workman Publishing, 2016.

Goldberg, Natalie. *Writing Down the Bones: Freeing the Writer Within*. Boulder, CO: Shambhala, 2010.

Hyman, Mark. *Food: What the Heck Should I Eat?* New York: Little, Brown Spark, 2018.

Lama, Dalai, and Tutu, Desmond. *The Book of Joy: Lasting Happiness in a Changing World*. New York, NY: Avery, 2016.

Lyme, Alan, and Powell David J., and Andrew, Stephen. *Game Plan: A Man's Guide to Achieving Emotional Fitness*. Las Vegas, NV: Central Recovery Press, 2012.

Rohr, Richard. *On the Threshold of Transformation: Daily Meditations for Men*. Chicago, IL: Loyola Press, 2010.

Suzuki, Shunryu. *Zen Mind, Beginner's Mind: Informal Talks on Zen Meditation and Practice*. London: Shambhala, 2006.

Tan, Chade-Meng. *Joy on Demand: Choose Healthy Habitual Happiness*. New York, NY: HarperCollins, 2022.

Tolle, Eckhart. *Practicing the Power of Now: Essential Teachings, Meditations, and Exercises from the Power of Now*. Novato, CA: New World Library, 2001.

Tolle, Eckhart. *Stillness Speaks*. Novato, CA: New World Library, 2003.

WEBSITES

For more information on the Enneagram and addiction, please visit the author's website, *The Maine Enneagram Center for Transformation & Well Being*, at https://enneagrammaine.com/.

For interviews with the author and clients of various Enneagram types, please visit his YouTube channel at https://www.youtube.com/channel/UCx_qYTt7r4vE4qUp27zAdXg.

For Enneagram courses and events, please visit Russ Hudson's website at https://russhudson.com/.

For the Enneagram type test (RHETI), see https://www.enneagraminstitute.com/rheti.

For the Daily Enneathought, Type descriptions, or Enneagram Institute workshop listings, see https://www.enneagraminstitute.com/.

For information on the International Enneagram Association, of which Michael is a Professional Member, see https://www.internationalenneagram.org/.

For information on men's spiritual work, see https://illuman.org/.

For deep emotional transformation, see the Hoffman Institute at https://www.hoffmaninstitute.org/.

MOVIES ON ADDICTION

The following is a list of excellent movies that involve addiction.

- 6 Balloons
- A Star Is Born
- Beautiful Boy
- Ben Is Back
- Bill W.
- Candy
- Clean and Sober
- Crash
- Crazy Heart
- Dopesick
- Flight
- Four Good Days

- Hillbilly Elegy
- My Name is Bill W.
- Requiem for a Dream
- Rocketman
- Smashed
- Thanks for Sharing
- The Glass Castle
- The Wisdom of Trauma
- Traffic
- Walk the Line
- When a Man Loves a Woman

About the Author

MICHAEL NAYLOR, M.Ed., is a licensed addiction counselor (LADC) and certified addiction clinical supervisor (CCS) with forty years of experience in the addiction field, with focused attention on men's recovery and transformation. He is the CEO of The Maine Enneagram Center for Transformation and Change and teaches workshops and coaches in the United States and internationally. He has trained extensively as an Enneagram teacher through the Riso-Hudson certification, authorized teacher, and Enneagram Institute faculty process and is an International Enneagram Association (IEA) Professional and annual presenter at IEA conferences. He also is a trained professional coach (CPCC) certified through Co Active Training Institute (CTI). He hosts a YouTube channel called *Maine Enneagram Interviews* in which he conducts in-depth interviews with all the types.

For more information or to contact Michael, visit https://enneagrammaine.com.